Matthew Arnold

AND

American Culture

JOHN HENRY RALEIGH

Matthew Arnold

AND

American Culture

UNIVERSITY OF CALIFORNIA PRESS

BERKELEY AND LOS ANGELES

1961

UNIVERSITY OF CALIFORNIA PRESS
Berkeley and Los Angeles, California
CAMBRIDGE UNIVERSITY PRESS
London, England

*Originally published in 1957 as Volume 17
of the University of California
Publications: English Studies*

Second printing, 1961
(First Paper-bound Trade Edition)

Printed in the United States of America

FOR JO

Upon the glazen shelves kept watch
Matthew and Waldo, guardians of the faith,
The army of unalterable law.

T. S. ELIOT

L'humanisme, ce n'est pas dire «Ce que j'ai
fait, aucun animal ne l'aurait fait», c'est dire:
«J'ai refusé ce que voulait en moi la bête, et
je suis devenue homme sans le secours des
dieux».

ANDRÉ MALRAUX

PREFACE

IN THIS STUDY of Arnold's influence in America I have arbitrarily but necessarily imposed a chronological end point at about 1950. Post-1950 critical statements by two subjects of the book—T. S. Eliot and Lionel Trilling—have therefore been excluded from consideration. This exclusion may well have the effect of oversimplifying the thought and opinion of both men, and, if this is so, I apologize both to them and to the reader.

It is a pleasure to give thanks to those who helped along the way. My first thanks must go to Professor Willard Thorp, who suggested the subject to me in the first place and who guided, encouraged, and criticized the first painful efforts. Professor James D. Hart read the manuscript at two different stages and offered detailed and valuable suggestions and criticisms. My thanks go as well to Professors Carlos Baker, Josephine Miles, Gordon McKenzie, Roy Harvey Pearce, Mark Schorer, Wayne Shumaker, and the Board of Editors of this series.

The Interlibrary Loan Service at the University of California has been efficient, thorough, and good-humored, as has been my editor at the University of California Press, Miss Helen Travis.

A "University Faculty Summer Fellowship" at the University of California allowed me a free summer in which to write this book.

For quotations from copyrighted material I have been granted permission by the following: Rinehart & Company, Inc., for *The Life and Letters of Stuart P. Sherman,* by Jacob Zeitlin and Homer Woodbridge; The Viking Press for Lionel Trilling's *The Liberal Imagination;* Charles Scribner's Sons for W. C. Brownell's *Democratic Distinction in America;* and Harcourt, Brace & Company, Inc., for T. S. Eliot's *Collected Poems 1909– 1935.* The three-line quotation on the leaf preceding the Preface is from the poem "Cousin Nancy," from *Collected Poems*

There is a final debt, named in the dedication, which I cannot fully assess, much less properly acknowledge.

JOHN HENRY RALEIGH

CONTENTS

Introduction 1

Part One: Groundswell

I. Henry James 17

II. Arnold in America: 1865–1895 47

III. William Brownell 88

Part Two: Ebb

IV. Arnold in America: 1895–1930 129

V. Stuart P. Sherman 158

Part Three: Resurgence

VI. T. S. Eliot 193

VII. Lionel Trilling 220

VIII. Matthew Arnold and American Culture 246

Notes 269

Index 297

INTRODUCTION

Matthew Arnold's writings, literary, social, religious, and cultural, have enjoyed and still continue to enjoy an extensive vogue in the United States. From 1865 to 1950, from Henry James to Lionel Trilling, they have made converts and disciples. No other foreign critic, and perhaps few native ones, have acquired such a reputation and exercised such a palpable influence on American culture, and Arnold would seem to be in modern criticism almost what Shakespeare was in the drama, a classic example of the man and the moment in proper and successful conjunction. What criticism needed at his time he provided. What it still needs he provides.

At first glance the period during which Arnold made his initial impress—post-Civil War America—would not seem to be auspicious at all, especially for the work of an English critic. American culture had just recently produced its own prophet, Emerson, its own poet, Whitman, its own novelist, Hawthorne, and its own humorist, Mark Twain, all of whom were unmistakably *sui generis*—these in addition to such peculiarly American talents as Thoreau and Melville. The United States had even begun in a sense to patronize the Old World by sending back to it a highly cultivated literary ambassador, Henry James. Whitman, indeed, gained his first fame and first serious consideration in England itself; and young Matthew Arnold, among others, sat at the feet of Emerson. And, in spite of the fact that England herself was enjoying her great and weighty Victorian age, with its Dickenses, George Eliots, Tennysons, and Brownings, and was continually sending her emissaries to the province across the sea—Dickens himself, Thackeray, the Trollopes, Froude, Arnold, and others—still it would not appear that the younger country was a complete cultural dependency and was greatly in need of advice from the parent.

Moreover the outraged feelings of Northern Americans over England's position—or the position of its upper classes—during the Civil War was by no means forgotten at the conclusion of the conflict. And the professional patriots were not the only ones to feel a lingering rancor towards England. Even such an admirer of the European and English heritage as James Russell Lowell could hardly bring himself to forgive England for her pro-Southern sympathies; he wrote to Leslie Stephen in 1866: "I confess I have had an almost invincible repugnance to writing again to England. I share with the great body of my countrymen in a bitterness (half resentment and half regret) which I cannot yet get over." In 1869 he wrote despairingly to E. L. Godkin of the possibility of a war between the two nations: "My heart aches with apprehension as I sit here in my solitude and brood over the present aspect of things between the two countries. We are crowding England into a fight which would be a horrible calamity for both . . ."[2] But the Civil War, too, with its blood and agony and toil, was thought to have had a baptismal function and to have raised American culture to a wiser and sadder maturity. The United States had suffered the ultimate tragedy of drenching the maternal soil with fraternal blood and could therefore no longer be considered immature. As Lowell put it: "A man's education seems more complete who has smelt hostile powder from a less aesthetic distance than Goethe."[3]

At the same time, the West in its entirety had finally opened up after the Civil War; and it seemed that the center of gravity of American culture would finally shift, as it had always been promising to do, away from the Atlantic Coast with its ties to Europe and towards the beckoning heartland with its virgin promises. As far back as 1844 Emerson had remarked that in America technology was playing an equivocal role. It was binding the country together and extending its limits, but, especially with the increased speed and efficiency of ships, it was also binding the Atlantic states closer to Europe. Counteracting this, however, was the fortunately opening West:

> Luckily for us, now that steam has narrowed the Atlantic to a strait, the nervous, rocky West is intruding a new and continental element into the national mind, and we shall yet have an American genius. How much better when the whole land is a garden, and the people have grown up in the bowers of paradise.[4]

In "Democratic Vistas," that great post-Civil War survey of prospects, Whitman, who was in some respects Emerson's disciple, proclaimed: "In a few years the dominion-heart of America will be far inland, toward the West."[5]

Added to all these post-Civil War factors which encouraged either antagonism or indifference to English culture were the immemorial and continuing antagonisms against the Old World in general. Lowell said, in "On a Certain Condescension in Foreigners": "... every foreigner is persuaded that, by doing this country the favor of coming to it, he has laid every native thereof under an obligation, pecuniary or other ...,"[6] and "For some reason or other, the European has rarely been able to see America except in caricature."[7]

Literary criticism itself was still ambiguous precisely because of the pressure exerted by the English. As John Burroughs said, an American reviewer's opinion of a poet was never clear-cut and objective, but was always influenced, pro or con, by what the English thought. If the English critics, for example, happened to like a poet, this liking could have any one of three contradictory effects upon the American critic: "... if he is favorably inclined toward the poet it strengthens and confirms his good opinion; if not, it dazes and bewilders him, or else irritates and embitters him."[8] To illustrate the embitterment, Burroughs drew the following picture of Theodore Watts, an English critic who had given Whitman himself a negative appraisal: "... dirty thick-witted cockney blackguard. A cur is never more a cur than when he lifts up his leg over the carcass of a dead lion."⁹ And even if a foreign influence were allowed, it was usually specified that it should not be English—"our English Grandmama," as Poe put it.

This was the atmosphere into which Arnold intruded his critical writings, and there can be no doubt that some of Arnold's popularity resulted from the fact that he was so captious about the English themselves; many an American critic agreed, with deep satisfaction, that the English were indeed narrow, heavy, and provincial, as Arnold charged. At the same time, many of the adherents of Arnold were precisely those who were given to the purest Anglophilia and were least expressive of the more vital parts of the national consciousness: the early *Dial* of Chicago, which would not accept Whitman; professional New Englanders; bringers of gentility to the Middle West; ladies' clubs in the provinces of the South. The attitude of extreme Europe-worship manifested by these groups was, in its way, as unbalanced as the ferocious nationalism of professional Westerners and the purblind anti-intellectualism of the "Know-Nothings."

And yet there persisted, in spite of all, a deep-seated and genuine feeling for England and its great past and an almost ineradicable feeling of kinship, strongly knit by language, culture, and common interests. This feeling could emerge in the least expected of places, in the utterances of Whitman and Mark Twain, for example. Whitman said to Sidney H. Morse in 1887: "... we, you know, believe in old England's glory. It far enough exceeds her shame."¹⁰ And Mark Twain, after visiting Westminster Abbey at night, wrote:

As we turned toward the door the moonlight was beaming in at the windows, and it gave to the sacred place such an air of restfulness and peace that Westminster was no longer a grisly museum of moldering vanities, but her better and worthier self—the deathless mentor of a great nation, the guide and encourager of right ambitions, the preserver of just fame, and the home and refuge for the nation's best and bravest when their work is done.[11]

For decades, the greatest American critics, in spite of their desire for an indigenous literature, had been insisting on the need of listening to and heeding foreign critics and for gaining sustenance from foreign culture. Poe wrote in 1836: "...nothing but the most egregious national vanity would assign us a place...upon a level with the elder and riper climes of Europe..."[12] For Americans, he thought, are in danger of "liking a stupid book the better, because, sure enough, its stupidity is American."[13] As for nationality in literature, "...as if any true literature *could be* 'national'...—as if the world at large were not the only proper stage for the literary *histrio*."[14] Nevertheless, Poe finally counseled patience and warned against despair, telling his countrymen that it was ridiculous for them to think that because they were not Homers in the beginning, they should all be Benthams to the end.[15] Lowell, in 1867, ridiculing these same extravagant hopes and fears, described Americans as thinking that if the minuscule Avon had engendered Shakespeare, then the "mighty womb" of the Mississippi must perforce produce a literary titan.[16] But this hope too was ridiculous:

The themes of poetry have been pretty much the same from the first; and if a man should ever be born among us with a great imagination, and the gift of the right word,—for it is these, and not sublime spaces, that make a poet—he will be original rather in spite of democracy than in consequence of it, and will owe his inspiration as much to the accumulations of the Old World as to the promises of the New.[17]

For it would only be side by side with European literature that American literature would prove itself: "...our culture is, as for a long time it must be, European; for we shall be little better than apes and parrots till we are forced to measure our muscle with the trained and practised champions of that elder civilization."[18] Even Emerson, for all his proclamations urging complete independence and a rejection of Europe, would admit that in certain spheres the restraints of the older culture were needed, and he said, in "Social Aims": "Much ill-natured criticism has been directed on American manners. I do not think it is to be resented. Rather, if we are wise, we shall listen and mend."[19] Mark Twain, half in jest and half in earnest, in a "speech" planned for but not delivered to a group of Americans in London on July 4, 1872, remarked, on noting that the English now import the American sewing machine (without claiming to have invented it), the sleeping car, and sherry cobbler: "It has taken nearly a hundred years to bring the English and Americans into kindly and mutually appreciative relations, but I believe it has been accomplished at last."[20] Whitman himself was as much a cosmopolitan as a nationalist and, generally speaking, deprecated only the English influence and then only aspects of it, for he was a great admirer of both Carlyle and Tennyson. All mankind was a brotherhood anyway:

...the commonhood, brotherhood, democratization, or whatever it may be called....the cause of the common bulk of the people is the same in all countries—not only in the British islands, but on the continent of Europe and allwheres...we are all embarked together like fellows in a ship, bound for good or bad. What wrecks one wrecks all. What reaches the port for one reaches the port for all....I hope I have in "Leaves of Grass" expressed it...[21]

Behind all these expressions of the international or cosmopolitan impulse was the feeling, growing stronger as the nineteenth century wore on, that technology, willy-nilly, was binding the world closer and closer together and that the old American dream of an independent sanctuary in the West and an independent literature was fast becoming a hopeless fiction. As Lowell put it in 1867:

Literature tends continually more and more to become a vast commonwealth, with no dividing lines of nationality.... Journalism, translation, criticism, and facility of intercourse tend continually to make the thought and turn of expression in cultivated men identical all over the world.[22]

The possibility of Arnold's being well received was immeasurably enhanced by the fact that so much of what he had to say—and he always thought of the United States as constituting an audience as well as England—had been anticipated or hinted at by American critics and prophets themselves, notably Poe, Emerson, and Lowell. With Emerson—when we remember Arnold's acknowledged early discipleship—this is not at all surprising. Each of these critics was, of course, unique, as was Arnold, but, scattered throughout their writings, one can find many of the sentiments that Arnold was later to express in his fashion.

Poe, of course, with his antimoralistic bias, his Coleridgean love of metaphysics, and his necrophilia, not to mention the disasters of his personal life, was a direct antithesis to Arnold, and yet there were at least two things that he insisted upon that are direct anticipations of what Arnold was to say later. First, and relating to the theory of criticism, Poe insisted, as Arnold did later, that literary criticism was not history or philosophy or psychology, but was simply the "seeing the thing as in itself it really is," or "criticism." As Poe put it: "Criticism is *not,* we think, an essay, nor a sermon, nor an oration, nor a chapter in history, nor a philosophical speculation, nor a prose-poem, nor an art novel, nor a dialogue. In fact, it *can be* nothing in the world but—a criticism."[23] Poe exerted no great influence on his own age or those succeeding, but when Arnold later stressed the same thing, the necessity that criticism be simply criticism, he was to be regarded as a purifier.

In matters of the critical practice of the day Poe denigrated the two great English voices of his time, Macaulay and Carlyle, who were precisely the two critics that Arnold thought had captured the British public and from whom this public must be weaned. One of his own aims was just this. Poe professed amazement that Emerson should defer to Carlyle: "I have not the slightest faith in Carlyle. In ten years—possibly in five— he will be remembered only as a butt for sarcasm."[24] And of Macaulay, whom Arnold was to warn against by saying that one should not confuse the mastery of logic and rhetoric with perception of the truth, Poe said practically the same thing: "We must not fall into the error of fancying that he is *perfect* merely because he excels (in point of style) all his British contemporaries."[25]

But it is Emerson and Arnold, bound by mutual admiration and influence, who, in spite of their manifest differences, reveal the most resemblances; and it would not be too much to say that some of the things, by no means all, that Arnold was to say were effective because he had learned them from Emerson himself, who had first preached them at Americans.

First of all, Emerson diagnosed the nineteenth century, just as Arnold was to do, as a time of criticism, introspection, solitude, and of the torment of unbelief—in short, the world of "Dover Beach." In a retrospective account of New England written in 1871, Emerson said that it was an age of "splits" and "cracks," when men grew to be reflective and intellectual and inclined to solitude. Literature itself had turned critical: "The most remarkable literary work of the age has for its hero and subject precisely this introversion: I mean the poem of Faust."[26] Authority and antiquity, the two cornerstones of traditional stability, were being called into question, and experimentalism in all things had taken their place.[27] At the same time, mankind was suffering from a new disease, the torment of uncertainty and unbelief;[28] and one of the reasons for this decay of belief was, in Emerson's eyes as well as Arnold's, that religion had become excessively anthropomorphic, too much concerned with exaggeration about the *"person"* of Jesus.[29]

Nevertheless, it was good that religion had finally become morals (a concept which was to be, in fact, Arnold's view of religion), and the demise of dogma was an unqualified good. In Emerson's view, theology was but the rhetoric of morals, and he rejoiced in the fact that the mind of the age had advanced from theology to morals.[30] "Our religion has got as far as Unitarianism. But all the forms grow pale."[31] Emerson held, as did Arnold, that morality was at the base of everything, and that, without religion ("the iron belt") it was all that man had to guide his life: "We are thrown back on rectitude forever and ever, only rectitude,—to mend one; that is all we can do."[32] Morality is finally at the base of everything, personal or public; and the moral sentiment is the backbone of both culture and character.[33] Moreover, morality was for Emerson, no matter what the state of religion, innate, and the idea of right existed primordially in the human mind.[34] Arnold makes the same claim in his notion of the "power not ourselves that makes for righteousness."

Emerson's view of nature, with all its complexity and its tendency to apotheosize and to equate the natural and the human or to find correspondences between them, was yet marked by a fear of nature's impersonality and indifference, the two characteristics that Arnold, despite his love of nature's physical beauties, was to stress. In 1863 Emerson recorded in his journal Arnold's sentiments on the subject: " *'Beauty,'* Matthew Arnold said, 'Nature would be a terror, were it not so full of beauty.' "[35] Or, as Emerson himself said in his "Politics": "Nature is not democratic, nor limited-monarchical, but despotic."[36]

Although an ardent democrat, Emerson yet had the distrust of the untutored masses that Arnold had, and he warned: "Leave this hypocritical prating about the masses. Masses are rude, lame, unmade, pernicious . . . and need not to be flattered, but to be schooled. . . . I wish . . . to . . . draw individuals out of them. . . . Masses! the calamity is the masses."[37] Society must still have an aristocracy, an aristocracy of talent, to lead it: "Every human society wants to be officered by a best class, who shall be masters instructed in all the great arts of life; shall be wise, temperate, brave, public men, adorned with dignity and accomplishments."[38] Arnold was to say that everything had to come finally from the "remnant"; similarly, Emerson insisted: "Literary history and all history is a record of the power of minorities, and of minorities of one."[39] For Emerson there was inherent in society a "primitive aristocracy," distinguished not by its superiority in dress but by its powers of expression and action.[40] Furthermore, the existence of such a class was not injurious, so long as it was dependent for its superiority only on merit.[41] Arnold was to make much of the "grand style" and attribute it to a good aristocracy, which, since it must necessarily and justly disappear, would yet take something desirable out of human life and would leave only, in its place, a gross plutocracy; so too Emerson said: "I know the feeling of the most ingenuous and excellent youth in America. . . . We have a rich men's aristocracy, plenty of bribes for those who like them; but a grand style of culture . . . does not exist, and there is no substitute."[42]

For culture is all-important, and, as Arnold was to preach its efficacy as an antidote against anarchy and as a modifier of power, in *Culture and Anarchy,* Emerson said in *The American Scholar* that ambitious men could only be turned away from the exclusive pursuit of money and power "by the gradual domestication of the idea of culture."[43] And the duty of the real man of culture was a public one, as it was with Arnold's man of culture. He should, said Emerson, cheer and raise his fellow men, accept poverty and solitude, and keep up the standards. For the dissemination of culture, then, Emerson said, as was Arnold to say, that the state itself must take the ultimate responsibility: "Yes, government must educate the poor man."⁴

Finally, behind both Emerson and Arnold was a deep feeling for the two great poets of Romanticism, Wordsworth and Goethe, for the secular religiosity and love of nature of the one and the intellectual power and self-control of the other; and in an article in *The Dial* called "Thoughts on Modern Literature" Emerson acknowledged his debt to both, as Arnold was to do later and at length and repeatedly.

Thus, in spite of the radical differences between the two critics and the many points on which they would explicitly disagree— on the proper relation of Europe to America, on transcendental philosophy, on the problem of evil, on the question of individualism—there yet remains a great commonality of interests. Emerson, in his analysis of the qualities of the nineteenth century, in his prophecy that morals must replace religion, in his insistence that the moral sense was inherent, and in his warnings that nature was despotic, that a natural aristocracy of individuals must replace the "grand style" of the departed aristocracy, that the "remnant" was the source of all that was good, and that culture was at the basis of character, was the antidote for power, and must be diffused throughout all of society, was both Arnold's teacher and Arnold's preparatory force in America.

To a much lesser degree, Lowell also, contemporaneously with Arnold, and, unlike Emerson, antagonistic to Arnold, made some of the points that Arnold was to make. One of Arnold's chief strictures upon English culture, and, by inference, American culture, was that it lacked a "centre," a steadying intellectual core of opinion such as French culture possessed, which acted as a centralizing force upon the intellectual life of the nation as a whole. Lowell, in his diagnosis of American culture, found just this fault in the United States, and he said in an introduction to the collected works of Poe in 1857: "The situation of American literature is anomalous. It has no centre, or, if it have, it is like that of the sphere of Hermes. It is divided into many systems, each revolving round its several sun..."[45] Later, in 1867, Lowell remarked: "It is the misfortune of American biography that it must needs be more or less provincial, and that, contrary to what might have been predicted, this quality in it predominates in proportion as the country grows larger.... Our very history wants unity..."[46]

After having visited the United States in 1883–1884, Arnold was to conclude that American culture, whatever its successes, was still not "interesting," and for this judgment he was censured by many American reviewers. Lowell had said the same thing, however, in 1867, even using the same word: "We are great, we are rich, we are all kinds of good things; but did it never occur to you that somehow we are not interesting, except as a phenomenon?"[47] Above all, Lowell lamented the weaknesses of American criticism. In a letter to C. F. Briggs in 1845, he said:

But I have never yet ... seen any criticism on my *poetry* ... that went beneath the surface and saw the spiritual.... Criticism nowadays deals wholly with externals. It looks upon every literary effort as a claim set up for a certain amount of praise, and answers every such claim accordingly.[48]

And many years later, in 1887, in "Our Literature," Lowell gave a brief history of American culture stressing all of the factors that had prevented the emergence of a genuine literature, which, it would seem, he still thought had not appeared. The conditions of America were, he said, entirely novel, with a reading class small and scattered, men of letters few and isolated, no intellectual "centre" or "capital," and a people largely and of necessity materialistic; "Criticism there was none," and what there was was "half provincial self-conceit, half patriotic resolve to find swans in birds of quite another species."[40]

It was this general feeling that American culture lacked a criticism that was to speed Arnold's reputation and influence. There have been few literary generations in American history— the last two are notable exceptions—that have not lamented the absence of either a literature or a criticism or both, but in the nineteenth century the laments were especially heartfelt and, perhaps, uttered with some justice. Not only did there seem to be no general tradition, but even the great individual figures, such as Poe or Emerson or Lowell, seemed to offer neither precedents nor principles. All the earlier Arnoldians— James, Brownell, and Sherman—expressed the feeling that not only had they no "centre" from which to work, but that their greatest predecessors in the field of criticism in America were either flawed or incomplete. Thus they, and a host of lesser littérateurs, turned to Arnold, who seemed to offer a complete criticism of literature and life and a set of principles for dealing with both.

PART ONE

GROUNDSWELL

CHAPTER I

HENRY JAMES

WHEN YOUNG HENRY JAMES, untried but aspiring, appeared upon the literary scene of America in 1864, as a critic for the *North American Review,* and looked about for the tradition that he thought so indispensable a part of the writer's equipment, he could find, he thought, none. Reverencing art for its aesthetic values, he found himself in a world of criticism which was either narrowly ethical or loosely sociological. Reverencing tradition, he could find no tradition to build upon in American culture. In *Hawthorne,* James lamented the fact that, compared to any European county, America was a poor place for the writer. He contrasted barren America to the "denser, richer, warmer European spectacle,"[1] and went on to enumerate, in a famous apostrophe, all the historic items that America lacked. And these lacks were fatal, for "the flower of art blooms only where the soil is deep, . . . it takes a great deal of history to produce a little literature, . . . it takes a complex social machinery to set a writer in motion."[2]

If there was no general tradition to build on, neither was any help to be had from the literary activity of the day. Poe's contention, made in the 1830's, that American criticism was simultaneously and contradictorily engaged in puffery of Americans, puffery of Europeans, puffery of New Englanders, and, withal, given over to the "cant of the general," had still not been controverted in the 'sixties. And in 1884, James could still say: "Superior criticism, in the United States, is at present not written . . ."[3]

Of sages and prophets in the 'sixties, James could have had his choice, perhaps, of Poe himself, of Emerson, or of his friend and mentor, James Russell Lowell; but each of these critics was, in James's eyes, unsatisfactory, and in later years he was to document his disapproval. In *Hawthorne,* James characterized Poe's criticism as "the most complete and exquisite specimen of *provincialism* ever prepared for the edification of men";[4] and in an essay on Baudelaire he declared: "...it seems to us that to take [Poe] with more than a certain degree of seriousness is to lack seriousness one's self. An enthusiasm for Poe is the mark of a decidedly primitive stage of reflection."[5]

James did admire Emerson's moral force and power: "With Emerson it is ever the special capacity for moral experience—always that and only that."[6] But even in his capacity as moralist Emerson was limited by the provincial society in which he lived. The plain, God-fearing, practical society of Concord was, according to James, not fertile enough in variations; it gave no complications, no real disorders or sense of evil. It was characterized, in sum, by "a ripe unconsciousness of evil." Although James contested Arnold's pronouncement that Emerson was not primarily a literary man, still he himself disapproved of Emerson's placing secondary importance on books: "...there is a latent incompleteness in his whole literary side."[7] And in his own writing Emerson displayed neither form nor style. Thus in a large sense he was not well-rounded: "...there were certain chords in Emerson that did not vibrate at all."[8]

James was a personal friend of Lowell's and admired him greatly but does not in any sense seem to have regarded himself as a disciple. Writing an obituary of Lowell in 1891, James said that since the two had been good friends, he lacked the detachment to judge Lowell properly. And although he could say of Lowell, "There are places where he seems in magical communication with the richest sources of English prose,"[9] still James indicated a certain degree of reservation about Lowell's critical powers by prophesying that although the poetry would live, he could not tell (and it did not matter) whether the essays would.

James's ultimate detachment is perhaps best indicated by the observation: "From what quarter his [Lowell's] disciples in the United States will draw their sustenance it is too soon to say: the question will be better answered when we have the disciples more clearly in our eye."[10]

Behind all these adverse judgments on James's part lay the ever-recurrent, root charge that American society was provincial and produced unbalanced men of letters: provincial Poe, with his specious logic, his erratic learning, his "slashing" reviews; innocent Emerson, blandly smiling over the abysses of evil which lurk at the heart of the human situation.

I

In 1865, just after James had begun his official literary career by reviewing for Godkin's *Nation* and Norton's and Lowell's *North American*, Ticknor and Fields published Matthew Arnold's *Essays in Criticism*,[11] and James was given the book to review for the *North American*. Arnold was by no means a stranger to him, for he had long known the poetry. But he seems to have been acquainted with the prose as well, which had been appearing in English magazines, for he wrote in a review published in July, 1865: "Mr. Arnold's *Essays in Criticism* came to American readers with a reputation already made;—the reputation of a charming style, a great deal of excellent feeling..."[12] Beyond this, James has recorded that Arnold was his constant companion during just this period. In *Notes of a Son and Brother* James lovingly described the summer of 1865, its friendships and its serenity, "such right conditions for the play of young intelligence and young friendship, the reading of Matthew Arnold and Browning..."[13]

The review itself consists mostly of praise, with some qualification. For example, he calls Arnold's reasoning questionable (although he was later to change his mind on this stricture).

He also says of Arnold's style that, although he is attracted to it, its resources are limited. (In 1884 he was to call Arnold one of the two or three best prose writers in English.) But the laudation far outweighs these cavils. Just the fact that the subjects of the essays are purely literary is, says James, a strong recommendation, for he, like Arnold, regrets the fact that such collections are so few in Anglo-Saxondom. Arnold's writing expresses great sensibility and great good nature; he is, to sum up, "sympathetic."

Arnold's contentions in his first two essays about the superiority of French criticism and literary standards had aroused considerable opposition in England, but James agreed emphatically with Arnold: "Nothing could have better proved the justice of Mr. Arnold's remarks upon the provincial character of the English critical method than the reception which [the *Essays*] provoked."[14] James further admired Arnold's intelligent amiability in dispute and the fact that he was always civil. In an argument, nevertheless, Arnold had the courage of his convictions.

Young James had very decided views on the qualities which the ideal critic should possess, and Arnold had at least two of the great powers—"the science and the logic." At this time James thought, and stated with some reluctance, that the rational powers were most important for the critic. "The best critic is probably he who leaves his feelings out of account, and relies upon reason for success."[15] But even so, James admired the sensibility of Arnold. "Hundreds of other critics have stronger heads; few, in England at least, have more delicate perceptions."[16]

James mentions the celebrated paean to Oxford as an example of this "sentimental" or "romantic" strain in Arnold, "...romance being the deadly enemy of the commonplace; the commonplace being the fast ally of Philistinism, and Philistinism the heaviest drag upon the march of civilization."[17] Although admitting that perhaps Arnold is too fond of reiterating Goethe's eulogy of Schiller, namely that Schiller's greatest virtue was to have left so far behind that bane of mankind, the common, James thinks that for the general public this idea cannot be too often repeated. He even defends Arnold's immortal reiteration about "Wragg—poor thing," on the grounds that it is the critic's duty to take care of such nothings as these: "Great truths take care of themselves; ... the critic deals in contributions to truth."[18]

James adds more examples of the nicety of Arnold's feelings, citing particularly Arnold's comments on "distinction" in the essays on Maurice and Eugénie de Guérin; his remarks about Coleridge in the essay on Joubert; the "felicity" of his translation from Maurice de Guérin's *Centaur;* and finally the whole body of quotations with which he furnishes his second essay in order to prove the necessity for the establishment in England of an authority like the French Academy.

Turning to Arnold's actual theories of criticism, James gives a brief and straightforward exposition of the now familiar Arnoldian doctrines: "disinterestedness," "the best that has been known and thought in the world," and disdain for the purely practical and material. Once more James defends Arnold against the attacks of the "Philistine" press. To the contrary: "It [Arnold's critique] reaches us too. The facts collected by Mr. Arnold on this point have long wanted a voice."[19]

James also admires the flexibility of Arnold's critical program:

But the great beauty of the critical movement advocated by Mr. Arnold is that in either direction its range of action is unlimited. It deals with plain facts as well as with the most exalted fancies; but it deals with them only for the sake of the truth which is in them, and not for your sake, reader, and that of *your* party. It takes *high ground* which is the ground of theory.[20]

He agrees with Arnold that the sole function of criticism is to make the truth known, not to apply it practically. Arnold's condemnation of the English preoccupation with the practical is turned by James upon America: "Here is no lack of votaries of the practical, of experimentalists, of empirics. The tendencies of our civilization are certainly not such as to foster a preponderance of morbid speculation."[21]

James concludes his estimate by selecting the three chief virtues of Arnold's critical approach. The merit of any individual essay in the collection is that it has a well-defined subject and sticks to that subject. The merit of the book as a whole lies in the fact that its author takes "high ground."[22] "The manner of his Essays is a model of what criticism should be." Finally James says: "Mr. Arnold's supreme virtue is that he speaks of all things seriously, or, in other words, that he is not offensively clever."[23]

It hardly needs saying that at this point James was an "Arnoldian," and there is abundant personal testimony to that fact. In *William Wetmore Story and His Friends* James tells how the prospect, some years later, of meeting Arnold for the first time, "in prose and verse, the idol of my previous years," made him "fairly stagger with a sense of privilege."[24]

Behind the specific judgments on Arnold is the implicit feeling, on James's part, that Arnold is light and bright, "sweetness and light," if you will, that he is sensitive, flexible, intelligent, and, in a word, "civilized." James best expresses this feeling through the fine haze of nostalgia of *The Middle Years,* when he tells of meeting Frederic Harrison at tea. On this occasion he was seated

... opposite to Frederic Harrison, eminent to me at the moment as one of the subjects of Matthew Arnold's early fine banter, one of his too confidently roaring "young lions" of the periodical press. Has any gilding ray since that happy season rested here and there with the sovereign charm of interest, of drollery, of felicity and infelicity taken on by scattered selected objects in that writer's bright critical dawn?—an element in which we had the sense of sitting gratefully bathed, so that we fairly took out our young minds and dabbled and soaked them in it as we were to do again in no other.[25]

Specifically, Arnold was to influence James deeply in two ways: in the area of general ideas, as the exemplar of culture and the cosmopolitan commentator; and in actual critical method, as the flexible, "perceptive" critic.

II

Good books often seem providential, in that they formulate for us our own thoughts. In Emerson's words, "there is no pure originality. All minds quote ... The originals are not original. There is imitation, models, and suggestions, to the very arch-angels, if we know their history."[26] And, in the realm of idea and attitude, Arnold was for James a kind of archetypal angel, for in Arnold he was to find a persuasive and explicit statement for many of his own latent convictions: the necessity for cosmopolitanism in literature and life; the usable richness of the European cultural tradition; the imitable excellencies of French culture (but always remembering that the French worshiped the "Goddess Lubricity"); the woeful inadequacy of many Anglo-American standards; and, finally, the fact that art must be *both* aesthetically appealing and morally sound.

James was by nature and upbringing a citizen of the world. "Father's Ideas," as the sons called them, made it inevitable. The many travels to and from and over the Continent, the constant immersion in, but never commitment to, various religions, ideas, and settings, encouraged even a certain rootlessness, especially in Henry junior, but it also finally developed in him, with many qualifications and with no sense of absoluteness, a commitment to Europe. It should be remembered, as it so often is not, that no one was more aware than James himself of the irony involved in an American's reverence for Europe. "An

American of course," he said in *English Hours,* "with his fondness for antiquity, his relish for picturesqueness, his 'emotional' attitude at historic shrines, takes Oxford much more seriously than its sometimes unwilling familiars can be expected to do."[27] Nevertheless, irony to the contrary notwithstanding, for James the historic longing was there from the start. Even before the age of twelve (although it must be noted that the observation was made in reminiscence) and while he was still living in New York, James could react to Bryant's Art Gallery thus, "and I have not forgotten how, conscious that it was fresh from Europe—'fresh' was beautiful in the connection!—I felt that my yearning should all have gone out to it."[28]

The actual thing was to prove even more irresistible. Of his first visit to France he remarked: "Had I ever till then known what a charm *was?*—a large, a local, a social charm, leaving out that of a few individuals."[29]

Europe spoke to him of two things: art and history. In Paris:

Such a stretch of perspective, such an intensity of tone as it offered in those days; where every low-browed vitrine waylaid us and we moved in a world of which the dark message, expressed in we couldn't have said what sinister way too, might have been "Art, art, art, don't you see? Learn, little gaping pilgrims, what *that* is!"[30]

French streets called up an image of antiquity and a phrase of Arnold's: "And there was always a place of particular arrest in the vista brief and blank, but inclusively blank, blank *after* ancient, settled, more and more subsiding things, blank almost, in short, with all Matthew Arnold's 'ennui of the Middle ages'..."[31]

Besides being the voice for the European tradition, Arnold also appealed to James as the apostle of "high seriousness." When Arnold said of the function of criticism (in the *Essays in Criticism*): "Its business is ... simply to know the best that is known and thought in the world, and by in its turn making this known, to create a current of true and fresh ideas," he found a ready convert in the young book reviewer who was later to be accused of substituting art for life. And of course "the best that is known and thought" was the general Western heritage; and therefore a devotion to literature, far from being a dilettantish diversion, was immediate, central, and all-important. It was, indeed, close to the base of character itself, as James remarked in a memoir of Charles Eliot Norton:

...a strong character reinforced by a great culture, a culture great in the given traditions, obeys an inevitable law in simply standing out. Charles Eliot Norton stood out, in the air of the place and time...with a greater salience, granting his background, I should say, than I have ever known a human figure stand out with from any: an effect involved of course in the nature of background as well as in that of figure.[32]

The converse of this respect for literary cultivation, in both James and Arnold, was a repugnance to vulgarity in any form. The burden of Arnold's protest against the Philistine was that he was "vulgarized." For James too, the word "vulgar" expressed the extremest distaste. In 1869 he wrote to his mother from Florence his views on traveling Americans, repeating Arnold's critique of the middle class:

There is but one word to use in regard to them—vulgar, vulgar, vulgar...What I have pointed at as our vices are the elements of the modern man with *culture* quite left out. It's the absolute and incredible lack of culture that strikes you in common, traveling Americans.[33]

Although Arnold, with some pleasure, battled the Philistine throughout his career, James, by and large, stayed out of the arena. But he finally suffered his unfortunate contact on a fatal night in January, 1895, at the lugubrious performance of *Guy Domville,* of which he wrote to his brother William: "The thing fills me with horror for the abysmal vulgarity and brutality of the theatre and its regular public . . ."[84]

And when Arnold, in "A Word About America," said that Americans were merely Englishmen on the other side of the water with the Barbarians (aristocracy) quite left out and the Populace (the lower classes) nearly left out, and with the Philistine predominating; that the American experience was apathetic to the powers of beauty, intellect, and social life; that Americans in general were ill-bred, their schools inadequate, and their manners atrocious; that Murdstone, the bitter Philistine, and Quinion, the rowdy Philistine, held complete sway—James found the argument unanswerable. As Arnold records in his letters: "At any rate, Henry James, the novelist, being asked by Knowles to write a reply to it ["A Word About America"], said after reading it that he could not reply to it, it was so true, and carried him so along with it."[85]

The antidote to all this "vulgarity" and lack of culture was, for both men, a knowledge of the French. Here once more Arnold reinforced an existing predilection in the young American, who from earliest youth was an admirer of George Sand, Merimée, and Balzac. *Essays in Criticism* had not only espoused French ideas in general but was concerned, in the main, with French literary figures. As James said in his review: "It [Arnold's spirit] exhibits frankly, and without detriment to its national character, a decided French influence."[86]

Both men admired George Sand extremely, and the strength of their enthusiasm is indicated by the fact that, while both possessed a strong ethical bent in their attitude toward life and literature, and toward French life and literature particularly, neither ever lost his enthusiasm for George Sand, no matter how extravagant her personal affairs had been. In his two essays on George Sand, Arnold refrained from comment on her personal life, although, as may be seen in his strictures on Shelley, he was by no means reluctant to condemn private peccadillos. James, more sophisticated in this respect perhaps than Arnold but equally devoted to the cause of personal rectitude, also refused to stigmatize George Sand for her private life, although he did not hesitate to condemn others, such as Maupassant. He regretted only that her love affair in Italy with Alfred de Musset became a national "cause célèbre," for this was a "colossal indecency." But toward most other French writers, and in general attitude toward French culture, James and Arnold shared an equivocal and peculiarly Anglo-American point of view, simultaneously admiring the French for their aesthetic craft and seriousness and for their high level of general culture and distrusting them for what was considered their immorality or amorality.

Arnold's admiration for French culture was so perfervid that he was accused by some of his fellow countrymen of being "un-English." In his *Essays in Criticism* he asserted: "In England there needs a miracle of genius like Shakespeare's to produce balance of mind, and a miracle of intellectual delicacy like Dr. Newman to produce urbanity of style." Arnold claimed that this balance of mind and urbanity of style were common in France, because in that country there was an organized body of critical taste to which all authors must appeal, whereas in England and America they appealed only to the tastes of a "promiscuous multitude."

Yet, in spite of his love of things French and in spite of the fact that he thought the dull Saxon must be leavened with aery Celtic spirit, Arnold remained, in the last analysis, a "Teuton" at heart. As Frederic Faverty, the student of Arnold's ethnography, says:

But a consideration of his work as a whole shows that he placed his deepest trust in the "serious Germanic races." Theirs were the sterling virtues, theirs the solid, if also unhappily the stolid, qualities which the world must fall back on at last. It is because he knows them to be strong that he speaks chiefly of their weaknesses. By pointing out their defects, he will enable them to become stronger still.[37]

And the French "lightness" of character led of course—for Arnold, as he said several times, was in actuality a Philistine himself—to immorality. To a French correspondent, M. Fontanes, Arnold wrote in August, 1873: "Selon Ste.-Beuve, Proudhon disait que 'la France était tournée toute entière vers la fornication.' "[38]

Such plain speaking as this was not permissible in English; instead, the charge became euphemized into a pronouncement, in "Numbers," that the French worshiped the "great Goddess Lubricity,"[39] and that worship of that goddess would cause the ultimate ruin of France. The Gallic element had finally produced "l'homme moyen sensuel," and contemporary French literature, catering to this element, was unsound.

James's total and final estimate of French culture was not so sharply phrased as was Arnold's, but it was essentially similar. In spite of his strong ethical bias, James was too much the writer himself to condemn a literature for its choice of subject matter alone, even though the decision came hard for him. In 1868 he reviewed for *The Nation* a novel by Ernest Feydeau which, like so many French novels, was concerned with adultery in advanced circles. James's comment upon it expresses the problem of the critic who is concerned with both aesthetic and ethical values.

One may say that the great mass of readers are superficial, that it is only here and there that they possess sufficient moral vigour to react against the subtle drowsiness of conscience which accompanies the perusal of the works to which we allude [French novels], and one is therefore led to write them down.[40]

This is the Anglo-American moralist speaking. James then went on to remark: "But one ends by feeling the pulse of his own conscience, and, finding it steady, concludes that, on the whole, in the interest of art it is good policy to prohibit nothing which makes a claim to artistic merit."[41] However, like Arnold, James finally threatened the French with God's wrath:

But [this review has many *but's*] we cannot help believing that, in the great city where they have reached the extravagant pitch registered by M. Feydeau, a reaction is destined to come, either in peace or in violence. Meanwhile, in other great cities where things are fortunately not quite so bad, we can very well afford to let Parisian chroniclers pile up documents for future antiquarians...[42]

In 1875 James went to Paris with the intention of making it his permanent home, but, after less than a year's residence, he gave it up in disgust. While in Paris he was personally acquainted with France's great literary circle, consisting of Flaubert, Turgenev, Zola, the Goncourts, Daudet, and Maupassant, but even before his visit he had become convinced that the very air they breathed was unclean: "Novel and drama alike betray an incredibly superficial perception of the moral side of life. It is not only that adultery is their only theme, but that the treatment of it is so monstrously vicious and arid."[43]

The same attitude toward the French recurs again and again in *French Poets and Novelists,* in which James, like Arnold, considers himself a kind of moral watchdog, and says of Baudelaire:

People of a large taste prefer rich works to poor ones and they are not inclined to assent to the assumption that the process is the whole work...He [Baudelaire] tried to make fine verses on ignoble subjects, and in our own opinion he signally failed.[44]

Finally James could stand Paris no longer. He described his feelings to his brother William in 1876:

...my last layers of resistance to a long-encroaching weariness and satiety with the French mind and its utterance has fallen from me like a garment. I have done with 'em forever, and am turning English all over ... I have got nothing important out of Paris nor am likely to.[45]

Yet like Arnold he remained a devotee of French intelligence and integrity in art. He admired the French for their preoccupation with the artistic life and their "high seriousness." He admired their critics, such men as Scherer and Sainte-Beuve. In a letter to Howells, in 1908, apropos of his own Prefaces, James said, and he was thinking of the French: "They are, in general, a sort of plea for Criticism, for Discrimination, for Appreciation, on other than infantile lines—as against the so almost universal Anglo-Saxon absence of these things ..."[46] Of French literature in general James had written to Howells from Paris in 1884, after he had regained some of the perspective he had lost in 1876:

I have been seeing something of Daudet, Goncourt, and Zola; and there is nothing more interesting to me now than the effort and experiment of this little group, with its truly infernal intelligence of art, form, manner—its intense artistic life. They do the only kind of work, today, that I respect; and in spite of their atrocious pessimism and their handling of unclean things, they are at least serious and honest. The floods of tepid soap and water under the name of novels that are being vomited forth in England, seem to me, by contrast, to do little honour to our race.[47]

This equivocal attitude which both James and Arnold have toward the French stems from their deepest concern, namely that art should be both aesthetically satisfying and morally sound. Both condemned the simple-minded morality of the official nineteenth-century English and American culture, but they were equally vehement in utter distrust of its antithesis, "Art for art's sake." As Jerome Buckley says in *The Victorian Temper,* a "moral aesthetic" was at the heart of Victorian theory and practice of art, and Arnold was its prime spokesman: "Perhaps more insistently than any other critic, Matthew Arnold demanded for his time a subject matter sound in moral values and a style designed quietly to convey larger truths than private feeling could intuit."[48]

Arnold phrased his double preoccupation with beauty and truth in *Essays in Criticism* in the well-known summation:

... poetry interprets in two ways; it interprets by expressing with magical felicity the physiognomy and movement of the outward world, and it interprets by expressing, with inspired conviction, the ideas and laws of the inward world of man's moral spiritual nature. In other words poetry is interpretative both by having natural magic in it, and by having moral profundity.

James expressed similar views in *French Poets and Novelists:*

To deny the relevance of subject matter and the importance of moral quality of a work of art strikes us as, in two words, very childish ... The crudity of sentiment of the two advocates of "art for art" is often a striking example of the fact that a great deal of what is called culture may fail to dissipate a well-seated provincialism of spirit. They talk of morality as Miss Edgeworth's infantine heroes and heroines talk of "physic"—they allude to its being put into and kept out of one's appreciation of the same, as if it were a coloured fluid kept in a big-labelled bottle in some mysterious intellectual closet. It is in reality simply a part of the essential richness of inspiration ...[49]

Art, then, is inextricably Beauty and Truth, Inner and Outer, Private and Public; and James not only accepted Arnold's dictum that "poetry is a criticism of life," but expanded it to include his own area of writing: "Literature in general is a criticism of life—prose is a criticism of life."[50]

III

In matters of practical criticism, Arnold was to pull James away from his youthful dogmatism and concern with "principles" and "reasons" to a reliance on pure sensibility and perception.[51] On this we have James's own testimony. In *A Small Boy and*

Others he recorded his youthful delight at seeing a dramatic performance of *Uncle Tom's Cabin*. His delight, however, was nothing so juvenile as that of enjoying the play for itself; it consisted, rather, of an ironic detachment, which observed critically the reactions of the sensibilities:

> ... the point exactly was that we attended this spectacle just in order *not* to be beguiled, just in order to enjoy with ironic detachment, and at the very most, to be amused ourselves at our sensibility should it prove to have been trapped and caught. To have become thus aware of our collective attitude constituted for one small spectator at least a great initiation; he got his first glimpse of that possibility of a "free play of mind" over a subject which was to throw him with force at a later stage of culture, when subjects had considerably multiplied, into the critical arms of Matthew Arnold.[52]

But he was "thrown" into the arms of Arnold only gradually and over a period of years. In his early reviewing days James was rather rigid and dogmatic. He condemned out of hand and very severely, for example, novels by Trollope and George Eliot, both of whom he was to praise later in life.[53] His most crucial reversal, however, was on Sainte-Beuve, for in tracing out this particular change of attitude we can see James in a direct switch from rigidity to flexibility, from reliance on general principles to reliance on individual perceptions.

In an early review of a book by Edmond Scherer, whom he admired and who, along with Arnold, was a potent influence upon him, James paused to contrast Sainte-Beuve with Goethe:

> There is small criticism and there is great criticism. But great criticism seems to us to touch more or less nearly on pure philosophy. Pure criticism must be of the small kind. Goethe is a great critic; M. Sainte-Beuve is a small one. Goethe has laid down general principles; M. Sainte-Beuve has laid down particular principles; and, above all, he has observed facts and stated results. Goethe frequently starts from an idea; M. Sainte-Beuve starts from a fact; Goethe from a general rule, M. Sainte-Beuve from a particular instance.[54]

It was precisely this suggestion of a lack of philosophy and reasoning, the danger of a too freewheeling sensibility, that led young James to make one of his few adverse comments on Arnold, whose "judgment," not builded upon the rock of reason and principle, was "questionable."

By 1880, in a review of Sainte-Beuve's correspondence, James was praising the French critic for almost the same qualities for which he had once damned him. Now, Sainte-Beuve has a mind "so rich and fine and flexible that this personal accent, which sounds everywhere in his writings, acquired a superior savor and an exquisite rarity":[55]

This is the Sainte-Beuve of my predilection—I may almost say of my faith—the Sainte-Beuve whose judgments had no element of vulgarity, but were always serious, comprehensive, touched with life. I see no element of narrowness or obstinancy ... I only see the perceptive mind, the intelligence.[56]

When writing the preface to *Portrait of a Lady,* many years later, James could warn a hypothetical young novelist that "... criticism based upon perception ... is too little of this world."[57]

The later autobiographical works have as one of their recurrent themes the necessity for freedom of impression and for the exercise of unlimited curiosity in critical appreciation. In *A Small Boy and Others,* after remarking that he was thrown into the arms of Arnold, James continues: "... this was a brave beginning for a consciousness that was to be nothing if not mixed and a curiosity that was to be nothing if not restless."[58]

Here James used the word "curiosity" as a synonym for flexibility. In *Culture and Anarchy* Arnold had remarked that the word "curiosity," though it carried a bad connotation in the Anglo-Saxon world, bore a good one in the Continental countries; and had maintained that real criticism is just the exercise of this faculty. So too for James, unlimited curiosity became the greatest virtue of the novelist, and he refers to this trait as his "vice" in the preface to *What Maisie Knew,* where he mentions "the author's irrepressible and insatiable, his extravagant and immoral interest" in life and people.[59] As always with James, the supreme values of art were the supreme values of life, and the highest praise which he could bestow upon an individual was to characterize him or her as possessing a detached and free curiosity about life. He described his adored cousin Mary Temple as having a "sublimely forewarned curiosity" in her attitude toward everything.[60] He characterized his younger brother Bob similarly: "...the same intelligence that was so sharp and sad, so extraordinarily free and fine and detached in fact, as play of mind, play of independent talk and of pen..."[61] Here, embedded in James's individual style, are the key phrases of Arnold's critical vocabulary: "intelligence . . . free . . . detached" and "play of mind."

James's mature criticism, which was shaped by an original mind and which was geared to subjects, such as the art of the novel, far removed from the extensive socio-politico-religious interests of Arnold, cannot, of course, be called "Arnoldian." In the matter of reliance on perceptions, James was to go far beyond his original tutor, into the late labyrinthine manner which could find more implications in one perception than most mortals glean in a lifetime of experience. James himself probably best described his mature criticism: "I like ambiguities and detest great glares; preferring for my critical no less than my pedestrian progress the cool and the shade to the sun and dust of the way."[62]

In going beyond Arnold, James ultimately was led, through him, to the critic he had most belittled in his early reviewing days, Sainte-Beuve. Arnold himself had always admired the

French critic, had met and corresponded with him, and in some sense regarded the older man as his mentor. In his obituary of Sainte-Beuve, Arnold said: "We who write these lines knew him long and owed him much."[63] For James, too, Sainte-Beuve became the most subtle and intelligent of critics. By 1884 James was praising Arnold for his resemblance to the French critic, saying that Arnold "... reminds the particular outsider who writes these lines ... just the least bit of the great Sainte-Beuve ... I venture to express, I may confess that the measure of my enjoyment of a critic is the degree to which he resembles Sainte-Beuve."[64] But he makes some significant reservations, perhaps in memory of great influence that Arnold had had upon him as the ideologist of European-American consciousness:

I do not in the least mean by this that Mr. Arnold is an imitator, that he is a reflection, pale or intense, of another genius. He has a genius, a quality, all his own, and he has in some respects a largeness of horizon which Sainte-Beuve never reached. The horizon of Sainte-Beuve was French, and we know what infinite blue distances the French see there; but that of Matthew Arnold, as I have hinted, is European, more than European, insomuch as it includes America.[65]

James was so quintessentially self-conscious, so prolific, and so long-lived that he managed, in some way or another, to document most of the things about himself that, with other writers, usually have to be inferred. And in 1884, while Arnold was touring America and almost twenty years after James had first read *Essays in Criticism,* James wrote for *The English Illustrated Magazine* an essay, already referred to, entitled "Matthew Arnold," in which he tried to sum up his debt and the debt of his generation to the great critic who was now reaching the end of his career. In some ways the essay is ritualistic and formally celebrative, faintly smelling of the charnel house and written in the tone of "Let-us-now-praise-famous-men," as if Arnold had already passed on to the ultimate respectability and could therefore be praised unstintedly. In deprecation of his elaborate tribute James wrote privately of it to Thomas Sargeant Perry, who himself regarded Arnold, Scherer, and the German Julian Schmidt as the three greatest living critics.[66] In the letter to Perry, who had not liked Arnold on his tour of America, James exhibited some of that amiable but far-reaching contempt that so many bright and successful pupils eventually feel for their former teachers:

> I am very sorry you didn't like poor dear old Mat. I like him—love him rather—as I do my old portfolio, my old shoe-horn: with an affection that is proof against anything that he may say or do today, & proof also against taking him too seriously. And after all, Zola *is* lubric. Vide, for my sentiments on Mat., a charming article in MacMillans' new (illustrated) Magazine for January next, in which I have expressed nothing but tenderness & in a manner absolutely fulsome.[67]

As between public praise and private patronage, which has in it some of the shame that we all feel after we have praised unreservedly, we should perhaps pursue, in interpretation, a middle way. Nevertheless, since the article is general in nature and attempts to trace out the influence that Arnold had upon the English-speaking world, it can be regarded as a fairly accurate and objective estimate, whatever were James's private sentiments at the time. James began his estimate by recalling how fresh and desirable Arnold's voice had sounded when it was first heard twenty years ago. If the freshness seemed to have faded, it was only because Arnold's ideas and phrases had become part of the common stock of all educated minds. He had come upon the critical scene when much work needed to be done, and his success left little to be desired.[68]

Of the general effect of Arnold's work James said:

> The effect of Mr. Arnold's writings is of course difficult to gauge; but it seems evident that the thoughts and judgments of Englishmen

about a good many matters have been quickened and colored by them. All criticism is better, lighter, more sympathetic, more informed, in consequence of certain things he has said, ... he has added to the interest of life, to the charm of knowledge ...[69]

James then mentioned the number of "expressive phrases" to which Arnold has given currency. The constant reiteration of "sweetness and light," said James, has increased the civility and facility with which ideas are exchanged.[70]

Concerning Arnold's combats with their mutual enemy the Philistine, James continued:

Above all the atmosphere has gained in clearness in the great middle region in which Philistinism is supposed to abide. Our author has hung it about—the grey confusion—with a multitude of little colored lanterns, which not only have a charming, a really festive effect, but which also help the earnest explorer to find his way.[71]

Most important of all, Arnold has succeeded in his mission as the self-appointed apostle of culture:

The much abused name of culture rings rather false in our ears, and the fear of seeming priggish checks it as it rises to our lips. The name matters little, however, for the idea is excellent, and the thing is still better. I shall not go so far as to say of Mr. Arnold that he invented it; but he made it more definite than it had been before—he vivified and lighted it up ...

... It is Mr. Arnold, therefore, that we think of when we figure to ourselves the best knowledge of what is being done in the world, the best appreciation of literature and life. It is in America especially that he will have the responsibility of appearing as the cultivated man—it is in this capacity that he will have been attentively listened to.[72]

During the nearly twenty years, then, between his first reading of and his mature judgment upon Arnold, James seems to have been confirmed in his enthusiasm. His few youthful objections were reversed or forgotten. The prose style that in 1865 was "limited" in resources is now one of the best two or three in the language. In 1865 he found fault with the fact that Arnold's criticism was not coolly logical and rational. Now he praises its quickness, lightness, grace, and flexibility—critical virtues which by now James himself most highly prizes. James's greatest objection to Arnold in 1865 lay in what he considered the latter's faulty judgment. In 1884 he says nothing of Arnold's "judgment" directly, but he certainly could not have found it faulty, since its pronouncements and ideas have become "part of our common stock of allusion."

Finally, James remarks on what might be called the "irreplaceability" of Arnold:

> Yet I have wished to praise, to express the high appreciation of all those who in England and America have in any degree attempted to care for literature. They owe Matthew Arnold a debt of gratitude for his admirable example, for having placed the standard of successful expression, of literary feeling and good manners, so high ... When there is a question of his efficacy, his influence, it seems to me enough to ask one's self what we should have done without him, to think how much we should have missed him, and how he has salted and seasoned our public conversation. In his absence the whole tone of discussion would have seemed more stupid, more literal. Without his irony to play over its surface, to clip it here and there of its occasional fustiness, the life of our Anglo-Saxon race would present a much greater appearance of insensibility.[73]

IV

Arnold began his career talking about the French, but he concluded it by talking about the Americans. At all times he talked to and of the English. In a rough way James follows the pattern, and certainly in his estimate of all cultures he was influenced by Arnold. In the matter of England, he was admittedly prepared by Arnold for his own personal reaction, to come later. And, like Arnold, he could not leave America alone; his last works are concerned with assessing "civilization in the United States."

As a self-baptized Englishman, James himself was aware that Arnold had somehow prepared him in his attitudes toward his new homeland:

... [Arnold] speaks more directly than any other contemporary English writer, says more of these things which make him the visitor's intellectual companion, becomes in a singular way nearer and dearer.... He discharges an office so valuable, a function so delicate, he interprets, explains, illuminates so many of the obscure problems presented by English life to the gaze of the alien.[74]

Thus it is not surprising that for James, English sights should call up Arnoldian images and phrases. Of sight-seeing in Westminster he wrote: "The air always seems to me heavy and thick, and here more than elsewhere one hears old England—the panting, smoke-stained Titan of Matthew Arnold's fine poem—draw her deep breath with effort."[75] Or of London itself:

She doesn't pretend to attach importance to the lesson conveyed in Matthew Arnold's poem of "The Sick King in Bokhara," that,

> "Though we snatch what we desire
> We may not snatch it eagerly,"

London snatches it more eagerly if that be the only way she can get it.[76]

Or at the beginning of an essay on the London theaters James introduces his subject by quoting Arnold's famous declaration, from *Mixed Essays,* that the British theater was "probably the most contemptible in Europe." Admittedly, says James, this was a harsh judgment; but it still held true, and no one acquainted with the contemporary British stage could gainsay it.[77]

Moreover, James's general attitude toward English culture was analogous to that of Arnold, who, probably more than any other English critic, was a curious blend of captious patriot and affectionate detractor. To his sister "K," on January 6, 1865, Arnold wrote concerning his real purpose.

Indeed, I am convinced that as *Science,* in the widest sense of the word, meaning a true knowledge of things as the basis of our operations, becomes, as it does become, more of a power in the world, the weight of the nations and men who have carried the intellectual life farthest will be more and more felt; indeed, I see signs of this already. That England may run well in this race is my deepest desire; and to stimulate her and to make her feel how many clogs she wears, and how much she has to do in order to run in it as her genius gives her the power to run, is the object of all I do.[78]

But his task would not be easy. He wrote to his mother on May 19, 1863, "However, one cannot change English ideas so much as, if I live, I hope to change them, without saying imperturbably what one thinks and making a good many people uncomfortable. The great thing is to speak without a particle of vice, malice, or rancour."[79]

James's attitude toward England was an amalgam of a reverential awe, more monumental than that of Arnold, for England's past and historic continuity, and of a distaste for the Philistine present and a fear that England was losing out in the cultural race of the nations. And in "London at Midsummer," written in 1877, James described the historic pull: "The greatness of England; that is a very off-hand phrase, and of course I don't pretend to use it analytically. I use it romantically, as it sounds in the ears of any American who remounts the stream of time to the head waters of his own loyalties."[80]

But he was as severely critical of the present, the actuality, as was Arnold. Arnold had said that the great sin of English society was "inequality," which had "materialized" the upper class, "vulgarized" the middle class, and "brutalized" the lower class; and to Mr. Roebuck's "I pray that our unrivaled happiness may last" Arnold had answered, *"Wragg is in custody."* So with James: when St. George, the "Master" of "The Lesson of the Master," describes London social life to the young novelist, Paul

Overt, he calls it, "The clumsy conventional expensive materialized vulgarized brutalized life of London."[81]

James in his own person, in darkest London and writing of
Arnold's lower class "brutalized," said in *English Hours* that
the London poor, that stunted and pallid race of subhumans,
had reached a depth, a degradation, unparalleled in the civilized
world.[82] Of Arnold's upper class "materialized," to which *What
Maisie Knew* is his testimony, James wrote to Norton in 1886,
apropos of a "hideous" divorce case that was then convulsing
English society, that the English aristocracy was as rotten as
the French aristocracy was before the Revolution and that it
wanted "blood-letting."[83] And of the general level of intellectual
life in England, dominated by the Philistine and middle-class
interests and pieties, "the middle class vulgarized," James wrote
in 1888 to Stevenson:

Nothing lifts its hand in these islands save blackguard party politics.
Criticism is of an abject density and puerility—it doesn't exist—it
writes the intellect of our race too low. Lang, in the D.N., every
morning, and I believe in a hundred other places, uses his beautiful
thin facility to write everything down to the lowest level of Philistine
twaddle...[84]

And to Stevenson again in 1893, James lamented: "The vulgarity
of literature in these islands at the present time is not to be
said..."[85]

Like Arnold, the self-styled "liberal tempered by reflection,"
James saw that if the future were in the hands of the masses, the
past still possessed all the poetry. Against the "Dissidence of
Dissent"—"Higginbottom, Stiggins, Bugg!"[86]—Arnold upheld
the beauties of established religion, of conservatism, of history—
Cardinal Newman gliding down the aisle of the historic chapel
at Oxford. In the same vein James said:

Conservatism has all the cathedrals, the colleges, the castles, the gardens, the traditions, the associations, the fine names, the better manners, the poetry; Dissent has the dusky brick chapels in provincial by-streets, the names out of Dickens, the uncertain tenure of the *h*, and the poor *mens sibi conscia recti*.[87]

Both Arnold and James, unlike many English and American liberal Protestants, experienced deeply the historic and poetic sway of Catholicism. For Arnold its future was "immense," because of its "poetry." And James in his novels often propels his protagonists—from Newman in *The American* to Densher in *The Wings of the Dove*—into a cathedral for moral reflection at crucial moments.

Both writers were convinced that the future was in the hands of America; and James, like Arnold, made his "tour" and recorded his findings in *The American Scene*. Indeed, there is no place in James's later works where one can look without finding an analysis of the problems of culture in the only country that had begun as a democracy and was attempting to make this democracy permanent—the United States. In his last three completed novels, James returned to his primary theme: the American in Europe. In one of the last unfinished novels, *The Sense of the Past,* he posed the American-in-Europe theme at its most bizarre and fantastic, allowing a character to do actually what his Americans had always done figuratively, to dive back into the European past. In *The Ivory Tower* he was concerned with the theme that was to possess him more and more in his late years and that received its fullest expression in *The Jolly Corner*—the idea of "what-might-have-been," which in James's case means the subjective possibility of what he would have become had he remained in the United States and the objective fact of what had happened to American society and character since the Civil War.

In a sense James was, like Arnold, a "foreigner" paying a visit to a strange land, when he returned to America in 1904. First, he had been living in Europe for decades and had, despite occasional visits to the United States, become completely absorbed in the European scene; second, it is doubtful that any culture in recorded history had changed so much and so rapidly as had the United States of 1904 from the ante-bellum America of James's memories. For the later James, America had become "Europe"—the strange, romantic, unfathomable land:

It was American civilization that had begun to spread itself thick and pile itself high ... Nothing could be of a simpler and straighter logic: Europe had been romantic years before, because she was different from America; wherefore America would now be romantic because she was different from Europe.[88]

James's critique of the United States in *The American Scene* is in some ways that of Arnold all over again. Admittedly, America had solved the problems of politics and of "machinery," but the aesthetic distinctions of beauty, grace, and individuality were still lacking. Yet, because it is founded on memory and love and is filtered through an extraordinarily subtle sensibility, *The American Scene* is much more complex than is *Civilization in the United States,* which finally had to resort to such abstractions as "uninteresting."

James would never have said that America was "uninteresting," for, indeed, he was fascinated by it. Far from being merely prosaic, the United States was infinitely complex and could bear an infinity of interpretations.[89] Moreover, it was unique and therefore was finally incalculable.[90] There were, however, certain specific and positive things that could be said about American culture: there was amiability; there was "readiness"; there was the common decency, the "possible *serenity,*" and the quiet cohesion of a vast commercial and professional bourgeoisie that had been left to itself.[91]

James, however, would agree with Arnold's contention that American culture failed to produce a genuine individuality ("distinction," Arnold called it), and this deficiency constitutes one of the main themes of *The American Scene*. Contrasting England to America, James sets up two quite different visages: "... massive and square-shouldered, yet rather battered and mottled, chipped and frayed, at last rather sceptical and cynical, in fine, in the English figure—thin and clear, consistently sharp, boldly unspotted, blankly serene, in the American."[02]

For character is dependent on the friction and pressure generated by a dense society: "Character is developed to visible fineness only by friction and discipline on a large scale, only by its having to reckon with a complexity of forces..."[03] So, "Individuality and variety is attributed to 'types' in America..."[04] The result is, the "jealous cultivation of the common mean, the common mean only, the reduction of everything to an average of decent suitability..."[05] Although America has space and freedom in the collective sense, it has the tendency to invalidate the individual. Accordingly, there are no "forms" and "manners," for these depend precisely on privacy. On "... the question of manners: the fact that in such conditions there couldn't *be* any manners to speak of; that the basis of privacy was somehow wanting for them...."[06] There was not so much, said James, as a lodge at any gate.[97] Despite the great wealth there was no real society, and the enormous power that the wealth had created existed in a social void.[98] The men were completely devoted to the pecuniary endeavor; and social activity, left to the women, was therefore completely feminized.

What most struck James about America was the almost unprecedented velocity of change. The distance between the America of the early twentieth century and that of his youthful memories, crossed—or "cursed," as he said—with his elaborate historical sense, added a temporal dimension to *The American Scene* that was completely absent from Arnold's estimates of America. There is a law in America, said James, "under which, the material permitting, the decades count as centuries and the centuries as aeons";[99] and "what was taking place was a perpetual repudiation of the past..."[100]

It was not that America was without a past. Standing by the "flood" and bridge at Concord or looking at Mount Vernon, James recalled the great political events that had launched the United States and thought of the "huge bargain they made for us..."[101] Concord itself was "the biggest little place in America,"[102] the American Weimar, permeated with the "rarity of Emerson's genius, which has made him..., for the attentive peoples, the first, and the one really rare, American spirit in letters..."[103]

Of this great intellectual heritage, the Puritan heritage, there was left, however, only a residuum:

Therefore had I the vision, as filling the sky, no longer of the great Puritan "whip," the whip for the conscience and the nerves, of the local legend, but that of a huge applied sponge, a sponge saturated with the foreign mixture and passed over almost everything I remembered and might still have recovered.[104]

What past there was, was being pushed aside as rapidly as possible. Seeing a couple of Indians in modern dress in Washington, James, who had grown up on the Leatherstocking tales, felt that the "bloody footsteps of time" had been reduced to a "single smoothe stride."[105] It was as if the Past, with all its great riches, were a pitiful poor relation to the Present. As James phrased it in powerfully elaborate metaphor:

...the slight, pale, bleeding Past, in a patched homespun suit, stands there taking the thanks of the bloated Present—having woundedly rescued from thieves and brought to his door the fat, locked pocket-book of which that personage appears the owner. The pocket-book contains "unbeknown" to the honest youth, banknotes of incredible figure, and what breaks our heart, if we be cursed with the historic imagination, is the grateful, wan smile with which the great guerdon of sixpence is received.[106]

V

There is finally—and we are certainly out of the realm of direct influence now—a commonality of purposes and values in the total work of Arnold and James. The ultimate plea in Arnold's work is that man be "civilized," that he cherish "sweetness and light" or exercise "sweet reasonableness," and that against the dark hideousness of his age he hold up an image of human life that is graceful, bright, supple, urbane. James's novels are in a sense a tribute to this ideal, and his heroes and heroines are an embodiment of it. Isabel Archer, for example, is endowed with "perception," "spirit," and "intelligence"; she is "open to impressions," has "an immense curiosity about life," is alive to the sense of the poetry of tradition and history; she goes forth to meet her dark fate nobly. Watching her, helplessly, is Ralph Touchett, "a bright, free, generous spirit." One is reminded of descriptions of the youthful Matthew Arnold (minus the "flippancy" often ascribed to him), the "beautiful" young man of Max Mueller's memory or the "young Milton" of George Sand's. On a moral level, Arnold's man of culture is, like a character out of James, a seeker after the light.

James Russell Lowell, writing of Thoreau, described Transcendentalism at its most general level as just, simply, a desire for fresh air:

...the reaction and revolt against *Philisterei,* a renewal of the old battle begun in modern times by Erasmus and Reuchlin and continued by Lessing, Goethe, and, in a far narrower sense, by Heine in Germany, and of which Fielding, Sterne, and Wordsworth in different ways have been the leaders in England. It was simply a struggle for fresh air ...[107]

Of this tradition, each in his own way, Arnold and James were inheritors and continuers.

CHAPTER II

ARNOLD IN AMERICA: 1865–1895

IT WAS A GREAT LOSS to American criticism when, in 1875, James abandoned the American scene to go to Europe, where he remained, except for short visits to this country, for the rest of his life. With his decision to turn from criticism in order to concentrate on creative writing there can be no quarrel. Nevertheless, with that act of expatriation and with that emergence of a great novelist, American criticism lost one of its most serious and complex minds at a time when seriousness and complexity were most needed. The particular tradition of criticism that James was trying to establish, however, was not abandoned. This tradition, which took over the Arnoldian concept of a cosmopolitan culture in preference to what was considered the provinciality of the American cultural heritage, found another champion in the 1880's in the person of William C. Brownell, who was to be the most thoroughgoing Arnoldian of all American critics. Brownell considered James's criticism the best that had been written in the United States, and if he sought any sanction for his own criticism in America's past, it was in the work of James.

James and Brownell were not isolated in their admiration for Arnold. Throughout the latter part of the nineteenth century, a whole generation of intellectuals, who were coming of age in the 'eighties and 'nineties, seized upon the doctrines of Arnold as gospel. Older literary figures such as Whitman, Lowell, Twain, and Howells, would have none of Arnold or his teachings, but, in spite of their opposition, Arnold's critical writings inspired in some of Brownell's contemporaries a devotion that practically assumed the form of a "cult." The situation has been described as follows by Robert Morss Lovett.

Those were the days in which Matthew Arnold was recognized as the head of English criticism. "The Function of Criticism at the Present Time" and "Culture and Anarchy" had appeared, it is true, in the 'sixties, but post-Civil War America had little leisure or taste for them then. It was in the late 'eighties and 'nineties that his influence was at its height in these states.[1]

I

The general course of the reaction to Arnold in America follows, roughly, the development of his career and interests. He was known first as a poet, then as a literary critic, next as a social critic, then as a religious controversialist, and finally as a figure encompassing perhaps all these roles, the diagnoser of human ills and the apostle of culture. But framing practically his whole career in America—the reputation as poet excepted—is an image of a literary critic, whose first *Essays in Criticism* were published in 1865 and whose *Essays in Criticism,* Third Series, came out in 1910. Between these two dates Arnold's initial impress upon American culture began, developed, and, before the first World War, declined.

As the breadth of Arnold's interests—from literary critic to religious and social prophet—increased, so did the intensity of American reaction to him. The general approval that met the 1865 essays soon became split into the extremes of admiration and disdain, and this fervor and furor steadily rose in the late 'seventies and was climaxed during Arnold's visit to America in the early 'eighties. After his death in 1888 Arnold became part of the general heritage, and a more serene image of him and his work became possible; and before many years had passed, the strictures disappeared and hagiography reigned.

In a rough way the divided reaction on the part of Americans toward Arnold follows the familiar schism between nationalism and cosmopolitanism, between the idea of the Virgin Land and the idea of the Atlantic community, that has always underlain most of the cultural theorizing and practice in the United States. Within this general over-all pattern there are individual variations on specific strains of thought. Thus, while Arnold was considered by some Americans to be a "decadent," "effete," and "sterile" European in his attitude toward American life, he was considered by others to be a "savage" and "dangerous" radical in the sphere of religion. Some condemned his "supercilious" coldness, while others applauded his "warmth" and "humanity." To some he was "morbid" and "doubting"; to others "flippant" and "iconoclastic"; to still others he was "harsh" and "angry." But under all this variousness runs a simple antithesis, the simultaneous, alternating, and conflicting impulses toward nationalism, on the one hand, and toward cosmopolitanism, on the other.

Even before 1865 the *North American Review,* in notices of Arnold's works, introduced themes that were to be developed and repeated over and over again in the American reaction to Arnold. In 1853, in a review of *Empedocles on Etna and Other Poems* and *The Strayed Reveller and Other Poems,* the reviewer, who was Arthur Clough, charged that the poet was too introspective, self-searching, self-doubting: "There is a disposition to press too far the finer and subtler intellectual and moral susceptibilities; to insist upon following out, as they say, to their logical consequences, the notices of some single organ of the spiritual nature ..."[2] But in 1861 Arnold's *The Popular Education of France,* which had enjoined the state to organize and administer the educational system of England, was applauded. There was, however, a significant reservation in the reviewer's mind:

The book, otherwise worthy of the highest praise, is disfigured by gratuitous sneers at American civilization, which betray more ignorance than ill-nature, and which on that account are the more unworthy of a volume professing to give the results of actual research and inquiry, and of a scholar whose cosmopolitan culture ought to have raised him above vulgar national prejudice.³

In the matter of Homer, and thus in the area of literary criticism, C. C. Felton, a *North American* contributor, found Arnold unexceptionable; in a review published in 1862 he said that Arnold handled the subject "not only with learning, but with taste and good sense,"⁴ and that "with most of Mr. Arnold's remarks we heartily agree."⁵ In 1863 the *North American* returned to the poet and, in the person of William R. Alger, a Unitarian clergyman and author, found him beautiful and worthy of more attention: "This volume of freighted verse [*Poems,* Boston, 1856]—precious with costly experience, breathing deep passion and lofty wisdom, and finished in forms of serene beauty—has been six years before the American public without attracting extensive notice."⁶

Here, in the *North American* and in the earliest notices concerning Arnold that appeared in America, we have in embryo some of the antitheses which were to develop in American attitudes toward him. He was a morbid sceptic, who made gratuitous criticisms of the United States; but he was also a vigorous social reformer who wrote "lofty" poetry.

In his initial role as literary critic, a role safely out of the realm of social or religious criticism, Arnold met with almost universal approval, James's 1865 review being only one of several enthusiastic assessments. The *Atlantic Monthly,* one of the most respected of American periodicals, *The Nation,* soon to be one of the most authoritative, *The New Englander,* the self-styled voice of New England, *Hours at Home,* the evangelically inclined publication of Charles Scribner and Company, the Calvinist *American Presbyterian Review,* and the Congregationalist *Boston Review,* all joined James, of the venerable *North American,* in almost unqualified praise of the Arnold essays.⁷ Arnold's matter and manner were equally exalted in a barrage of superlatives. And although *The Nation,* which prided itself on its balanced and objective criticism, noted a tendency in Arnold toward "superciliousness," and although *The New Englander* drew attention to what it called his "capriciousness," practically all these periodicals urged upon Americans the adoption of the ideals and the spirit of *Essays in Criticism. The New Englander* claimed that Arnold had been a healthy influence in England and hoped that he would be, too, in America, "which of all things stands most in need of intelligent, bold, and well-considered criticism in literature." Common to all these reviews was the feeling that James had experienced on first reading the *Essays in Criticism,* the feeling that Arnold was distinctive, enlightening, and compelling, that in cultural matters he had held up a bright torch that illumined the surrounding darkness.

This general attitude toward Arnold as a literary critic—one of almost unreserved praise for his ideals and aims and of admiration for his style, tempered occasionally by objections to his personal mannerisms—was to prevail in American periodicals for the next few years. Arnold's poems, and his essays on Homer,[8] on Celtic literature,[9] and on the schools and universities of the Continent,[10] were all favorably reviewed. If Arnold had confined himself to the field of literary criticism or to that of education, he would no doubt have enjoyed a high and uncontested status in America as a literary figure. By 1870 the image of Arnold was so genial that the popular *Appleton's Journal,* in a general essay on him, speaking familiar sentiments, wished for his American counterpart:

We cannot but wish, in conclusion, that we had a writer like Mr. Arnold in this country (even if a poet were spoiled in making him),... who would devote himself to the examination of our authors, and to the destruction of their present low ideals, and their thousand faults of temper and taste. We must have an American critic, if we are to have an American literature; ... there can be no literature without criticism."[11]

But Arnold had always, even in his purely literary criticism, applied literature to life and hence to institutions; and with the publication of *Culture and Anarchy* he had become, avowedly, a social critic. Thus, as the image of the masterful literary critic was taking form in American periodicals, there was emerging also, in scattered references here and there, the image of a contentious social, and later religious, critic. Even as early as 1867, before the publication of *Culture and Anarchy,* Arnold was generally known as the apostle of culture and the contemner of the Philistine. In that year an enlightened workingman wrote a letter to *The Nation* entitled "A Plea for the Uncultivated."[12] After all, said this intrepid soul, all culture, since it is the product of leisure, ultimately rests on the backs of the workers; furthermore, if you asked a scholar or a cultivated gentleman "What is a dollar?" he would not be able to reply, because he does not know how a dollar is made or where it comes from. But this "Philistine," as he signed himself, was stoical about his plight: "We, the uncultivated, the Philistines, as Matthew Arnold calls us, have become so accustomed to this classification that we accept it without protest..." He was hopeful for the future, however, and he concluded by describing true culture: "... as it has been well defined by Arnold, sweetness and light, diffused among all, and not monopolized by a few." In a leading article entitled "Sweetness and Light," published in the same issue, *The Nation,* objective as ever, attacked *both* Arnold and the "Philistine." Arnold is a "fault finder" and his talk is often "loose"; and a classical education, far from being a hindrance in the management of practical affairs, is a positive asset, as witness Gladstone. Again, in 1868 *Lippincott's* published a defense of "American culture," principally against Arnold, and observed: "Matthew Arnold has said much of sweetness and light, but less of another essential element of culture—*strength*."[13]

In that same year George Percy, in a lengthy general essay on "The Prose of Poets," published in *Hours at Home,* remarked, in passing: "Matthew Arnold writes brilliant nonsense about 'culture' in prose as refined and finished as his verse."[14]

The following year, attention was focused on another side of the "controversial" Arnold, that is, Arnold the religious critic, in *The Nation*'s discussion of *St. Paul and Protestantism,* which was then appearing in England in the *Cornhill Magazine.* Although approving of Arnold's analysis of St. Paul's character and of his strictures on English Protestantism, *The Nation* said that the essays were disfigured by "the consciousness of self," and that certainly religious conditions in America, where belief is held less rigidly than in England, were not analogous to those in England. But then, "Knowledge of America is not his strongest point."[15] At this same time, however, Arnold's fame as an educational reformer had penetrated to Congress itself, and he was cited by Congressman James A. Garfield in a ten-minute speech on the floor of the House on February 16, 1872. Garfield was arguing against a bill to provide federal support for education. According to a summary by his biographer Theodore Smith:

Garfield ... gave in admirably condensed form the forces making for American education, enumerating the state and municipal governments first, and voluntary enterprise second. To emphasize the idea that the conservation of these two sources of strength was the first object of statesmanship, he quoted fully from Matthew Arnold's celebrated report on education made in 1868, which laid down the doctrine that "the public school for the people must rest on the municipal organization of the country."[16]

Arnold made his first great impress as a socioreligious critic with the publication of *Literature and Dogma* in 1873. Signifi-

cantly, it was through *Literature and Dogma* that Arnold in-
curred the disapproval of the *Overland Monthly,*[17] which had
first published Bret Harte's "The Luck of Roaring Camp" and
which regarded itself as the voice of the American West, and
also lost the approval of *The New Englander,* because its orthodox religious sentiments were disturbed by what it termed the
"pantheism" of the book.[18] Likewise, the Episcopalian *American
Church Review,* the Baptist *Christian Union* (for which Noah
Porter wrote two lengthy onslaughts), the *Baptist Quarterly,*
and the acrimonious religious weekly, *The Independent,* attacked Arnold's religious liberalism.[19] These two elements of
the national consciousness, the drive toward an indigenous culture and the conservative voice of religion, were to be precisely
the two forces that most objected to the Arnoldian program.
But even among the favorable reviews—in *Lippincott's, The
Nation,* the *Atlantic Monthly, Scribner's Monthly,* the *North
American Review, The Galaxy,* and *Old and New*[20]—there
were reservations concerning Arnold's manner, which was
thought to be somehow irreverent. *Scribner's,* for example, approved of a liberal interpretation of the Scriptures, but it added:
"... we may well dread an ally so savage in his sarcasm, so
destructive in his negations, and so lacking even in good taste,
as Mr. Arnold shows himself."

The most unqualifiedly enthusiastic reviews came from three
organs whose point of view was farthest from that of *The Overland* or *The New Englander,* namely the Unitarian *Old and
New,* a spokesman for religious liberalism, and the *North American Review* (for which T. S. Perry reviewed the book) and the
Atlantic Monthly, representatives of Eastern seaboard culture,
with its complex ties to England in particular and to Europe
in general. By 1873, then, the image of Arnold as a literary
critic had been complicated by the conception of Arnold the
controversialist; he was now not only the apostle of culture and

the stigmatizer of the Philistine, but also the vigorous—for some too vigorous—prophet of a liberalized, literary Christianity, which was attacked by an aroused American clergyman, Charles Aiken, as "one of the three or four chief gospels offered to our times in lieu of the old gospel that is to be taken from us ..."[21]

It was discerned very soon that Arnold's liberalism was unofficial, nonorthodox, perhaps even paradoxical. *The Nation* remarked disapprovingly on the apparent contradictions in Arnold's politico-social attitudes in a review of *Last Essays on Church and Religion,* in which Arnold had accused English liberalism of wordmongering and of setting up a hue and cry over such superficial issues as the Burials' Bill:

> To this reform Arnold is opposed, and at first glance his conservative radicalism seems a curious and inconsistent position. No doubt this mixture of liberal intellectual instincts and conservative moral motives is common and growing commoner, but is it sound? ... his position is an anomalous one, after all, by any intellectual standard—a position only reached by one other, the great French positivist [Comte], with whom Arnold would so dislike to be coupled.[22]

By 1879, with the publication of *Mixed Essays,* Arnold, though still revered as a poet and literary critic, had become a controversial figure in other respects. *Mixed Essays* was genuinely "mixed"; its subject matter ranged from George Sand to such uneasy topics as equality and democracy. In the essay entitled "Democracy" Arnold said, among other things: "What influence may help us to prevent the English people from becoming, with the growth of democracy, *Americanised?* I confess I am disposed to answer: ... the action of the State"[23] (which, according to Arnold, should henceforth play the social-political role that the aristocracy once did).

T. W. Higginson, who embodied in his own person the ambivalent American attitude toward Arnold, admiring the literary man, distrustful of the sociologist, expressed the duality of feeling in his review for the *North American:*

No one can compare "Mixed Essays" with "Essays in Criticism" and not see that, with increase of power, there has hardly been a corresponding increase of that sweetness which the author of both volumes has long represented to so many minds. Yet the purely literary portion of this later work is as delightful as ever, its knowledge as large, its criticism as delicate, its touch as sure. Mr. Arnold still wields the polished sword of Saladin, and it is hardly fair to complain if he brings from rougher contests the added ornament of some notches on the blade.[24]

Reactions to Arnold's politics were varied, according to the point of view of the magazine and the reviewer. The *Literary World* of Boston, through Arthur Verner, expressed a by now familiar objection to Arnold's manner: "... Mr. Arnold has a genius for hating; not, of course, in a blind, rude, animal fashion, but gently, sweetly, in the enlightened manner of a man of culture."[25] The *International Review* of New York objected to the strictures on America, although it was consistently respectful of Arnold's ideas: "The book [*Mixed Essays*] throughout is able, original, and full of thought..."[26] W. C. Brownell, an avowed follower of Arnold, regretted, in *The Nation,* that the Master had abandoned literary activities for missionary work in social and political fields.[27]

Some reviews were strongly favorable, and *Scribner's* singled out Arnold's "Equality," agreed with its admonitions on the ill effects of inequality and with its proposals to enlarge the functions of the state, and described Arnold as "one of the truest and most intrepid writers of the time."[28] The *Atlantic Monthly,* which in that same year had printed ecstatic reviews of Arnold's poems and of his *Johnson's Lives,* even accepted without cavil Arnold's horror of being *Americanised:* "But let us at least show that we have the nobility which can rise above personal pique, and recognize and respect truth under whatever disguise it comes to us."[29] The *Atlantic* saw hope, however, and added that not *all* Americans were boors. Proof positive of this was the fact that "Mr. Matthew Arnold's own poems (the best and daintiest of them) have been reprinted in a fifteen-cent edition by the canniest publishing house in the country for railway circulation, and have had an uncommonly good sale."[30]

By 1882, Arnold and America had established a special and uneasy relationship. More than any other foreign critic he spoke of and to the people of the United States. It had always been his habit to consider America his province as well as England, and he had consequently developed in America a large and divided audience. Samuel McCall remarked in an account of "English Views of America" written for the *International Review*: "The Boston *Advertiser* reminded Mr. Arnold that his works were more popular here than in England..."[31] E. S. Nadal, in an essay on Arnold in *The Critic,* recently founded in New York under the editorship of R. W. Gilder and not noted for its generosity to English writers, observed: "Mr. Arnold's writings have been widely read here. They have a natural relationship to this country..."[32] Although not agreeing entirely with Arnold's views on America, Nadal concluded, "...I would say that the example of Mr. Arnold's unconventional and persistent thoughtfulness is needed in this country. It does not seem to me that truthfulness is the especial characteristic of our literature."[33]

Then, in 1883–84, Arnold brought all the issues that clustered about him to a head by making his celebrated tour of America.

II

The reaction to Arnold's visit, which epitomized and brought into sharp focus the continuing reaction to him throughout the last part of the nineteenth century, divides itself roughly into three levels: the response of newspapers, the response of literary journals, and the response of prominent individual writers, both creative and critical. On the popular or journalistic level, which will not concern me here,[34] Arnold became a national joke. This reaction, touched off by the lecture tours, was as short-lived and ephemeral as is the interest in most daily news items, and Arnold was forgotten by the American press (although he did not forget *it*) as soon as he returned to England. At the other end of the scale, among most of the chief literary figures of the day—men such as Lowell, Stedman, Whitman, Twain, and Howells—Arnold generated a more well-bred but an equally negative reaction. The only two great voices of the so-called American Renaissance who were enthusiastic Arnoldians were, significantly, the pure polar types of the American mind, the "optimist" and the "pessimist" respectively of the national experience, Emerson and Melville. But most of the preëminent literary figures of the 'seventies, 'eighties, and 'nineties were against the visiting Englishman, either because of his manner or because of his opinions, or sometimes both. In this they repeated two of the three major charges against Arnold that had been made in the periodicals in the 'sixties and 'seventies, that his manner was offensive, and his opinions on America more so. Beyond these explicit objections, Arnold would have inevitably encountered in America a reflex action of distaste to which the country had been conditioned by previous English travelers who had toured the country, had been applauded, financially as well as vocally, and had then returned home to England to say unpleasant things about the sister country. Moreover, the ill feeling that had arisen in the northern United States against the pro-Southern sympathies of some members of the English upper class—and middle class—during the Civil War still persisted in the 'eighties.

The extreme negative reaction to Arnold, both as man and as thinker, was that of Walt Whitman, who professed that he could hardly bear to read Arnold, much less take him seriously. To Whitman, Arnold was an object of antipathy as a poet, as a critic, literary, social, and political, and as a man. In all branches of endeavor Arnold represented genteel aristocracy and ineffectuality, twice removed from life. In 1883, in an essay in *The Critic* ironically entitled "Our Eminent Visitors," Whitman extended mock welcome to Arnold and to Henry Irving, the actor, who was likewise about to make an American tour: "Welcome to them each and all! They do good—the deepest, widest, most needed good—though quite certainly not in the ways attempted—which have, at times, something irresistibly comic..."[35] These visitors, said Whitman, come and talk complacently of things they know nothing about to an upper-class audience equally ignorant of the masses of the people. Whitman's disdain was not a result of provincialism or a feeling of insularity, for he said in the same essay that "the noble and melancholy Tourgueneff," Carlyle, Castelar, Tennyson, and Victor Hugo would all have understood America. Nor was it specifically Anglophobia, since he had included Carlyle and Tennyson in his preferred list. It was rather that Arnold, with his "civilized" manner, seemed somehow ineffably effete to Whitman; and at the root of the poet's distaste there was undoubtedly a profound revulsion from the so-called "genteel" tradition, which, in Whitman's eyes, included not only Brahmins of Boston but the Stedmans of New York.

Some years later, in his talks with Horace Traubel, Whitman took up all aspects of Arnold's career and found this effete quality in everything. Arnold's poetry was fine, "wonderful fine," but it was fragile, like porcelain, and lacked substance.[36] As a writer who gloried in his own looseness and individuality of style, Whitman objected to what he thought were Arnold's poetic preoccupations; the critics who objected to his own poetry because of its style he designated as being like Arnold in their preoccupation with rules and canons and their neglect of the substance of poetry.[37] On the question of style Arnold further irritated Whitman by denigrating Emerson as a poet because of his stylistic deficiencies. "I can easily see how a stylist like Arnold should find Emerson below the mark ... But there's a higher thing than the pure stylist can ever know."[38]

Arnold's criticism, like his poetry, was distasteful to Whitman.

My own criticism of Arnold—the worst I could say of him—the severest ... would be, that Arnold brings coals to Newcastle—that he brings to the world what the world already has a surfeit of: is rich, hefted, lousy, reeking, with delicacy, refinement, elegance, prettiness, propriety, criticism, analysis: all of them things which threaten to overwhelm us.[39]

Arnold was the man of books, incapable of understanding real life; and Whitman spoke disparagingly of "the Arnolds," whom he stigmatized variously as lovers of art for art's sake or as pure scholars or as "second-" or "third-hand" men.[40]

Finally, it is difficult to see how Whitman could ever have approved of Arnold as a person, whatever Arnold's views might have been. For Whitman confessed to a personal antagonism: people like Arnold "riled" him,[41] and to them he was "constitutionally antipathetic."[42] Or, as Whitman put it more picturesquely, when asked by Traubel whether he would use vellum for the cover of his new book of poems: "Vellum? pshaw! hangings, curtains, finger-bowls, chinaware, Matthew Arnold!"[43]

Whitman's deep disapproval was lessened slightly by the more favorable opinions on Arnold of his friend John Burroughs. Whitman thought it possible that Burroughs had been slightly corrupted by the New York literary circle of Stedman and his friends, but hastened to add that John was not "one of 'em."[44] "We must be in no haste to dismiss Arnold," said Whitman, for Burroughs has given him "great place."[45] Whitman once talked with Mrs. Florence Coates, whom Arnold had visited at Germantown and who was an avowed "Arnoldian." Mrs. Coates tried to convince the poet that the Englishman was to be taken seriously. Whitman said later of this interview: "Mrs. Coates gave me the other side of him—the social side, the personal side, the intellectual side—the side of deportment, behavior— the side of which I ought perhaps most to hear about and did willingly and gladly hear of from her."[46]

But these judgments of friends were not enough to bridge the deep and irreparable gap between the prophet of egalitarian democracy and the apostle of culture. At Arnold's death, Whitman noted that he would not be missed, as were Carlyle, Emerson, and Tennyson.[47] Arnold was, said Whitman in summation, "one of the dudes of literature."[48]

And this was the man who in 1883 came to lecture to America. Whitman sputtered his indignation at that "damned set of roosters," like Arnold and Gosse, who had the gall to come to America in order to tell Americans what they are.[49] Arnold in particular always gave the impression that he hated to touch the dirt, "—the dirt is so dirty!" "But everything," protested Whitman, "comes out of the dirt—everything; everything comes out of the people, the everyday people, the people as you find them and leave them: not university people, not F.F.V. people: people, people, just people."[50] Such a man, who knows nothing of "the real things here," of the "elements," could never understand the United States.[51]

James Russell Lowell, the colossus of American criticism at that time, expressed this same personal distaste for what was thought to be the superrefined chilliness of Arnold. In a letter written in 1888, he remarked that the weather had been as "cold and clear as a critique of Matt Arnold's."[52] Throughout his works, whenever he referred to Arnold it was invariably to disagree, and usually to disagree with one of the essentials of

Arnold's thought. Of the Arnoldian thesis that Shakespeare, genius and all, had finally an ill effect upon later English poetry, Lowell asserted: "Mr. Matthew Arnold seems to think that Shakespeare has damaged English poetry. I wish he had!"[53] Of the "touchstone" theory, Lowell said, "But I question the validity of single verses, or even of three or four, as examples of style..."[54] Arnold's effort to imitate the Greeks was attempting the impossible and resulted in "pseudo-classicism," the fruit of which was something like "Merope": "It is dull, and the seed of the dullness lay in the system on which it was written."[55] And Arnold's design to augment the dignity and authority of the state was dismissed with: "Ill fares the State in which the parental charge is replaced by an abstraction."[56] When Arnold, in a lecture in Boston in 1883, relegated Emerson to the second rank, Lowell's personal distaste combined with his patriotism produced a judgment akin to Whitman's. In a letter to James B. Thayer, Lowell said:

...I greatly doubt whether Matthew Arnold is quite capable (in the habit of addressing a jury as he always is) of estimating the style of one who conversed with none but the master of his mother-tongue... I think that Matthew Arnold, like Renan (who has had an evil influence over him) is apt to think the *super*fine as good as the fine, or better even than that."[57]

If Whitman may be said to have represented the continental United States, and Lowell the New England tradition, then Stedman may be said to have headed the culture of New York literary life, which was attempting to carry on, in its own way, the genteel tradition. And to Stedman, as to Whitman and Lowell, Arnold was no prophet for America, although he had been a good one for England. Like them, Stedman felt a personal distaste for Arnold—although he once mentioned meeting and liking the apostle of culture—and at Arnold's death he began a generally favorable obituary for the New York *Herald*

by speaking of Arnold's "arrogance."[58] In *Victorian Poets* Stedman maintained that Arnold was, although a good poet, only a
minor one anyway.[59] Arnold's gift for phrasemaking, which had
been so greatly admired by many people, annoyed Stedman: "Is
not Arnold making an *ad captandum* point of shrewdness in
coining so many new words—'remnant,' 'lubricity,' etc. Is it not
getting to be almost a trick, or trademark?"[60] Of Arnold's criticism as a whole Stedman was equally distrustful; it was, he
wrote to Gosse, too "eccentric," "subjective," "adroit."[61]

When Arnold criticized Emerson and America, Stedman re-
acted just as had Whitman and Lowell. Why, Stedman wrote
to a friend, did "Professor Arnold" rate Emerson, whose sentences were each "a flash of beauty," lower than Montaigne,
whose sentences were largely made up of quotations from the
classics?[62] Furthermore, Arnold was incapable of seeing America
steadily and seeing it whole: he saw only its coarseness and completely missed its beauties and distinctions,[63] because he had
"preconceived opinions" on the subject that distorted his view.[64]

Even more vehement than Whitman on the subject of Arnold
was Edwin P. Whipple, who had begun reviewing for the *North
American* in the 1840's, and, by the time that Arnold's critical
essays were being published in this country, had become an
authoritative and well-known critic. The discussion of Arnold
in Whipple's *Recollections of Eminent Men* is essentially similar
to the discussions by Whitman, Lowell, and Stedman, except
that the condemnation is more severe and is not set forth in the
extravagant language that mitigates the harshness of Whitman's
critique. Arnold's leading characteristic, according to Whipple,
is "moral and intellectual scepticism and despondency."[65] An
inherent feebleness in Arnold's constitution prevents him from
generating any real power, for the "soul is wanting."[66] Arnold
has purchased an "expanse of his intellectual powers at the ex-

pense of weakening his will, and the heart of his being is not thoroughly sound and strong."[107] All this emptiness, according to Whipple, is characterized by a godlike propensity to condescend and a "superb superciliousness."[108] Nothing is sacred to Arnold; all institutions and people are fair game for this superciliousness. Arnold is so overrefined that the slightest trace of vulgarity repels him. Whipple admitted that Arnold had a minor power of "suggestiveness" and was a good phrasemaker, but declared that he had no magnetic power and therefore really had influenced nobody.

There remains, finally, the opinion of an eminent Westerner to complete the major American writers' disavowal of Arnold, and it is provided, appropriately, by Mark Twain. The two men met on Arnold's visit, and, according to contemporary testimony, Arnold was dazzled by this man who was so energetically nonserious. But when Arnold, after his return to England, offered some criticisms of America, Clemens, who had always felt it his own right to assail American institutions, erupted and filled pages in reply. He later used parts of this reply in *The American Claimant*. In the story, Parker, the assistant editor of the *Daily Democrat,* makes a speech to a group of workingmen which specifically answers Arnold's charges that Americans lack "reverence" and that their newspapers are scandalous. For what is precisely the distinctive aspect of the American press, according to Parker, is its "frank and cheerful irreverence ... ," "by all odds the most valuable of all its qualities."[109] The visiting English aristocrat, who is hearing these strange sentiments for the first time, exclaims to himself: "What right has Goethe, what right has Arnold, what right has any dictionary to define the word irreverence for me? What their ideals are is nothing to me. So long as I reverence my own ideals my whole duty is done ..."[110] But, it should be added, this wholesale repudiation of the past and its forms and this celebration of American individualism are in large measure offset by the total effect of the novel, in which Twain presents to the inquiring eyes of Lord Berkeley anything but an idyllic picture of American institutions themselves. Again, in one of his speeches Mark Twain took humorous issue with Arnold over General Grant's grammar (Arnold had remarked on some deficiencies in Grant's *Memoirs*) and pointed out an obscure passage from Arnold himself: "To read that passage a couple of times would make a man dizzy; to read it four times would make him drunk."[71] In reply to "foreign criticism" in general, Twain said in 1889 that there was but one civilization, meaning a place where dirt, poverty, and ignorance had been banished, in the whole world, "and it is not yet thirty years old. We made the trip and hoisted the flag when we disposed of slavery."[72] There were, of course, some partial civilizations "tottering" around Europe, but whatever democratic instincts they possessed were provided by the impetus of the American Revolution. "We" invented civilization. Twain summed up all his arguments against Arnold in particular and foreign criticism in general in *A Connecticut Yankee in King Arthur's Court*.

Of all the major American critics, Howells was, as might be expected, the most temperate on the subject of Arnold. He expressed no distaste for Arnold personally, but, every bit as firmly as Whitman, Lowell, Stedman, Whipple, and Mark Twain, he deprecated the Arnoldian influence. Howells, writing retrospectively in 1888, regretted that the daily press had made such a circus of Arnold's tour: "Upon the whole, the impression which Americans had received from him personally was not one of great dignity ... He had become, in a certain degree, one of our national jokes ..."[73] Furthermore, said Howells, "Even while we perceive that his observation of our life wanted breadth and depth and finality, we must acknowledge that in its superficial way, and as far as it went, it was mainly just."[74] Arnold said, in

Civilization in the United States, that Americans were loud, vain, and boastful. This Howells admitted.[75] But Arnold's chief criticism of the United States was that it lacked "distinction." And here he ran counter to the entire American tradition. For it was just this lack of "distinction," according to Howells, that Americans most highly valued and upon which they pinned their hopes for a great future—in the maintenance of a democracy where all men are equal.[76]

Furthermore, the very fact that Arnold was English made him undependable as a guide. If any influence was to be cultivated, let it be the Continental one of the French and Russian naturalists. American writers, said Howells, should cultivate "Americanisms." Englishmen in general had argued for generations that Americans were corrupting the language. On the contrary, argued Howells, American was, in a sense, a new language, and should be used, as the Elizabethans had used the developing English language, with novelty and imagination. If writers started worrying about correct "English," they would only succeed in becoming priggish and artificial.[77] In critical matters as a whole, the English tradition is amateurish, as was Arnold, and should be avoided.[78]

The misfortune rather than the fault of our several or individual critic is that he is the heir of the false theory and bad manners of the English school. The theory of that school has apparently been that almost any person of glib and lively expression is competent to write of almost any branch of polite literature . . .[79]

Such, then, were the opinions on Arnold expressed during, before, and after his visit by some of the leading American literary figures of the last part of the nineteenth century. Howells excepted, there was in all these men a certain dislike for Arnold as a person, variously pictured as the ineffectual dilettante, the cool sophisticate, or the supercilious destroyer. It must be remembered that these men were all, roughly, contemporaries of

Arnold. Arnold's converts, James and Brownell, were young and still maturing when Arnold's critical writings first began to be circulated in the United States. Whitman, Lowell, Stedman, Whipple, Mark Twain, and Howells were firmly established literary figures and would brook no certain condescension from an Englishman. Furthermore, they each represented some geographical or psychological unit which almost automatically deprecated the English influence. They did not look upon Arnold with any awe, as so many of the lesser literary people did; they considered themselves perfectly capable of standing on their own American feet in matters cultural. Finally, most of them foresaw, each in his own way, the development of a native culture and an indigenous tradition, which, though by no means ruling out foreign influences, ran counter to the cosmopolitanism that Arnold advocated.

The independence of these major writers was decidedly not characteristic of the general literary milieu of America in the 1880's, as it is revealed by the periodical literature concerning Arnold during his visit. In anticipation of the lecture tour, all the great metropolitan centers extended a welcome; and the *Literary World* of Boston, *The Dial* of Chicago, *The Nation, Harper's Weekly,* the *Christian Union, The Century,* and *The Critic* of New York, and *The American* of Philadelphia published full-scale articles on Arnold. Only Boston, perhaps with a dark intuition of what Arnold was to say of Emerson, was dubious, and the *Literary World* editorialized nautically: "Mr. Matthew Arnold has never had any faith to speak of; and the man without faith is the ship without a rudder. He may shape a course, and never fetch it; he may sail the seas, but never make a port."[80] *The Dial,* in contrast, went "overboard," so to speak. In its columns Horatio N. Powers, Episcopal clergyman and poet and, so far as I know, *the* most fervent Arnoldian that

America has ever produced, searched for the adequate superlative:

> I cannot express my admiration of his fluent, virile, precise style, his scope and insight, his wisdom, moderation, catholicity, and illuminating interpretation, without seeming to exaggerate his quality as a writer and his virtues as a man. Amid a Babel of noises and factions, he stands calm, judicial, self-contained; and minds that hate shams and love truth and beauty are reassured by his example and inspiration.[81]

The American was almost equally enthusiastic.[82] James H. Morse in *The Critic*[83] and Henry Beers in *The Century*[84] extended a more tempered and judicious welcome; *Harper's Weekly* printed a brief favorable notice of his coming, but added, "He holds positive opinions."[85] H. W. Mabie, in the *Christian Union,* professed great admiration for Arnold as a literary critic, but expressed doubts on the soundness of his religious outlook.[86] *The Nation* said that Arnold was mistaken in his notions about America, but that he was welcome anyway, because the critical spirit was much needed in the United States.[87]

The climax of Arnold's visit to America occurred in Boston, in which city, of all places, he chose to criticize Emerson. In the "Emerson lecture," as it was called, Arnold said that Emerson was neither a first-rate poet, philosopher, nor prose writer, but that he was an inspiring writer and "a friend and aider of those who live in the spirit." The rest of the country did not seem to be particularly shocked by these opinions; in fact, other sections rather enjoyed Boston's discomfiture at seeing its idol publicly smashed. As a Boston reporter picturesquely described the lecture, "It was like spitting in the prophet's beard." And the *Literary World,* although admitting it considered Emerson no god, thought that Arnold showed bad taste. "He threw stones at the Concord philosopher and bruised him badly.... What a blow at Emerson! What Matthew Arnoldese is this! Did we not say that Mr. Arnold had no faith? He is forever pulling down."[88] But *The Critic* of New York, clearly amused at Boston's chagrin, said:

New England, I am told, will have none of Matthew Arnold. His lecture on Emerson has utterly destroyed him in the sight of the good people of that quarter of the globe ... Fortunately, the rest of the country does not take the Emerson lecture so to heart, and the new edition of Mr. Arnold's prose and poetry has been nearly all disposed of—in the Middle and Western states.[89]

Still, *The Critic* itself, sectionalism aside and patriotism to the fore, likewise firmly disagreed with Arnold on Emerson: "Probably Mr. Arnold is right in what we may call his negative criticism of Emerson. Few admirers of our great man of letters would call Emerson a great poet, a great philosopher, a great writer—laying stress, as Mr. Arnold does, on *form,* on evolved or dramatical development of his themes."[90] But Arnold lays too much stress on form, for Emerson's greatest virtue was his substance: "Mr. Emerson's literary art consisted mainly in packing his *sentences* full. He never rounded the *essay* or the *poem;* he rounded the single *thought.*"[91] The general reaction of Emersonians to Arnold's estimate is probably best summed up in a poem, printed in *The Critic,* by Emma Lazarus, a devoted follower of Emerson.

Critic and Poet
an apologue
("Poetry must be simple, sensuous, and impassioned; this man [Emerson] is neither simple, sensuous, nor impassioned; therefore he is not a poet.")

No man had ever heard a nightingale
When once a keen-eyed naturalist was stirred
To study and define—*what is a bird,*
To classify by note and book, nor fail

> To mark its structure and to note the scale
> Whereon its song might possibly be heard.
> Thus far, no farther;—so he spake the word.
> When of a sudden,—hark, the nightingale!
> Oh deeper, higher than he could divine
> That all-unearthly, untaught strain! He saw
> The plain, brown warbler, unabashed. "Not mine"
> (He cried) "the error of this fatal flaw.
> No bird is this, it soars beyond my line;
> Were it a bird, 'twould answer to my law."[92]

The protests of proper Bostonians notwithstanding, Arnold's critique, because of its incisiveness and because of his authority as a critic, carried practically everyone before it and set a stamp on Emerson criticism which prevailed until very recently, and by which Emerson was considered neither a great poet, essayist, nor philosopher. *The Nation,* which viewed Boston's provincial reaction with disdain, proclaimed the lecture "a beautiful and delicate piece of criticism, such as no other Englishman or American, save perhaps Lowell, could have produced..."[93] Moreover, even many of those who found fault with the lecture did so not on the grounds that Arnold was wrong, but rather because in their judgment he lacked "tact." "Standing upon his right to speak the truth," said *The Critic,* "the whole truth, and nothing but the truth, as he saw it, he opened his lips and gave oracular utterance to his iconoclastic views."[94] There followed from this statement a brief flurry of "letters to the editor" of *The Critic* claiming that Arnold *did* have tact and that he was right to speak out. The debate ended in a limp, summarizing doggerel:

> "I say he lacked
>   Literary tact"
> "Tact he had
>   The truth is, he was mad"
> "No, not mad; he coolly came

> To overthrow a greater name"
> "Therein you wrong him sadly
>   He would have spared us gladly"
> "True, and as for tact—
>   That's what his audience lacked?"
> "I have proved this whole thing in my article;
>   He has style, but of tact—not a particle!"
> "Oh, my head is sorely racked!
>   What is, what is not, the fact?
>   One thing, just one thing is plain—
>   He'll never, no never, come back again!"[95]

There was, too, something heroic about Arnold's intrepid analysis, especially in view of the known admiration of the Concord prophet for the apostle of culture. In 1876 Joel Benton, in an article published in *Appleton's Journal* and already referred to, related that Emerson had been strongly taken with the *Essays in Criticism,* that he "not only welcomed it with high praise, but used it as a sort of touchstone for determining the mental condition and calibre of those young men who so often flock to him . . ."[96] In 1884 *The Critic* referred to a forthcoming article by Mrs. James T. Fields in *Harper's* which was to stress the admiration of Emerson for Arnold. According to Mrs. Fields, the first question that Emerson would ask a returning visitor from Europe was, "Have you seen Matthew Arnold?" If the answer was negative, he was disappointed. Also, he had defended Arnold's essays on Homer against a friend who said they were "all nonsense." "No, no, no," said Emerson, "it is good—every word of it."[97] Emerson himself, in a letter to James Fields, the publisher of the *Essays,* said: "I have never thanked you for the valued book of your 'Arnold,' which you sent me,—which is a treasure . . ."[98] And in his journals he mentioned Arnold's "critical superiority," and his "excellent ear for style," although he thought Arnold's poetry of a "singular poverty."[99]

With all this, faced with a Boston audience, knowing Emerson personally and knowing that Emerson had expressed admiration for his own work, Arnold was being courageous to say what he said, and the courage was recognized as such. The *Andover Review* said in 1884: "To speak of Emerson as he does among the friends and worshipers of the American seer requires an heroic temperament."[100] Writing retrospectively in 1893 in the *Methodist Review,* A. B. Hyde, who as a college student had been both dazzled and confused by hearing Emerson lecture, said:

His views of Emerson were certainly free from illusion, at least such as Americans may have ... How many ... have lauded poems incoherent and essays incomprehensible. And now Mr. Arnold, in his fearless effort to get at the best that is known and thought in the world, showed to a Boston audience why Emerson was not a great poet, not a great writer, not a great propounder of philosophy ... "He is the friend and aider of those who would live in the spirit." Just what we average boys thought, but we dared not assume to say it.[101]

Arnold's Emerson lecture and the reaction to it were crucial, because they brought together two of his roles, that of the literary critic and that of the commentator on America, for the Boston reaction was as much a patriotic response as it was a literary one. Yet Arnold's prestige as a critic was so high that his estimate of Emerson finally prevailed and was indeed welcomed, as by Mr. Hyde, as a formulation and utterance of forbidden thoughts.

Besides bringing to a test his reputation and influence as a literary and social critic, Arnold's American tour involved his religious role as well. In certain official and conservative circles Arnold was openly regarded as "dangerous" in his religious views, much as a man of unorthodox politics would be regarded today. Arnold's experience at Princeton is illustrative of his notoriety in this respect. As might be expected, some of the students in the 'eighties were enthusiastic readers of Arnold's advanced opinions and were determined to have him appear at Princeton to speak. The college officials, however, refused to give their sanction; and so the students themselves, under the leadership of George McLean Harper, had to raise the money and make the necessary arrangements for Arnold's appearance off campus.[102] The lion, however, seems to have turned out to be quite lamblike. The *Daily Princetonian* reported that the lecture was "a fine specimen of polished English...,"[103] but said that the speaker was hindered by defects of oratory[104] and that "the lecture was entirely devoid of any systematic analysis."[105] In fact, Arnold's oratory moved the students to amusement: "Prof. E. declares that he can improve Matthew Arnold's delivery one hundred per cent in five lessons. Who couldn't?"[106] After the lecture the students were invited to meet the speaker. To the majority he was either a stranger or only a faintly known name. Someone said that his father was the famous Arnold of Rugby, and so the apostle of culture spent his interview with the young Princetonians answering questions about the game of rugby.

In spite of all this general levity, however, the heresies of Arnold were not forgotten, and it does not appear to be merely coincidental that in the following month an anonymous article, entitled "Scepticism and Literature," appeared in the college literary magazine:

Matthew Arnold is the product of an age whose religion belies its convictions. As a mariner upon a shattered wreck, from which is torn more planks and beams with every surge that sweeps over it, so Arnold standing upon religion, sees its supports one by one give way, and gives utterance to a cry of despair.[107]

By implication the young Princeton students were urged to remain strong and sturdy in the faith of their fathers. Bliss Perry in his autobiography tells of hearing Francis Patton, who became President of the College in 1888, "in the Princeton Chapel

describe Christian truth as a securely locked safe with the bur-
glar Matthew Arnold trying in vain to pick the lock!"[108]

At Haverford College too the authorities refused to allow the
noted heretic to address the students. But, as Rufus M. Jones
records in his autobiography: "The cancellation of the lecture
of course sent us all with new enthusiasm to Arnold's writings,
and he accordingly became a greater hero to us than he otherwise would have been. Thus the would-be guardian of orthodoxy
often promotes the heresy he fears."[109] How deep the feeling
against Arnold went in certain academic circles is revealed by
an anecdote related by William P. Trent.

"When Arnold was on his first lecture tour in America . . . a
professor in a large university announced that he would not
shake hands with such an infidel if the latter were invited to
address the students of the institution."[110]

In orthodox church circles too Arnold aroused opposition, as
he had prior to the visit. The *Andover Review,* the *Unitarian
Review,* and *The Critic*[111] all joined in dispraise of Arnold's theology. The *Unitarian Review,* as might be expected, applauded
Arnold's efforts, but said that Arnold lacked positiveness and
"system." *The Critic,* nondenominational, published "A Theologian's Estimate of Matthew Arnold," which, while approving
his aim, nevertheless said: ". . . he does not possess the instincts
and training of a theologian. The application of the literary
method in judging the Bible and the works of theological
science has landed him in bewildering inconsistencies with himself."

In spite of all this opposition, however, Arnold's religious
writings seem to have taken hold, at least in literary circles. In
this respect, of course, he was but a single voice in the multi-
tudinous discussion concerning a great and complex crisis which
Western Christendom was enduring. To Americans, however,
Arnold could speak, if only for linguistic reasons, as no French

or German thinker could; and in the English-speaking world itself he was regarded as one of the leading speakers for the emergent liberal Christianity. To the older generation who were of Arnold's mind, those who wished to salvage the poetry and morality of Christianity, Arnold came, not as destroyer and infidel, but as saver and reconciler. To the younger generation, as Rufus M. Jones attested, he was the voice of the future. Ten years after the visit, in 1894, Mrs. Florence Coates, writing a memoir about her friend Arnold, said: "Matthew Arnold was always, and clearly, on the side of religion, virtue and the ideal. The last years of his life he devoted to the salvation of men from their *doubts,* and some he saved."[112] Arnold himself noted, happily, that his religious work was being circulated and appreciated in America, and in a letter to his sister he said: *"Literature and Dogma* has certainly done good here in New England; at a critical moment it has led many back again to the study of the Bible, and has given reality to the study of it."[113] To his younger brother Arnold related this anecdote:

At Newport they showed me the following in a newspaper: "The Baptist Union recommends all good Christians to give at least two hours to reading their Bible for every hour they give to hearing Matthew Arnold. This shows that in the judgment of the Baptist Union Matthew Arnold's doctrine is very nearly twice as powerful as that of the Bible."[114]

In later years, after the visit, there were many to testify to the accuracy of Arnold's own observations. William P. Trent, after telling the story of the professor who declared he would refuse to shake the hand of the "heretic," added: "That such a speech would scarcely be possible in this country today [1902] is partly due to the diffusion of Arnold's writings."[115] And thus: "As intellectual solvents 'Literature and Dogma' and 'God and the Bible' are still doing useful work among classes of people that a generation ago anathematized the author."[116]

Amid all the pros and cons surrounding Arnold, as literary, social, and religious critic, there was emerging a figure called "The Apostle of Culture," who was always right and could do no wrong and who was discussed in a kind of incantatory hagiography. This was the Arnold of Horatio N. Powers, and he was evoked again in 1884 by Louis J. Swinburne in *Lippincott's:*

Consider for a moment the thoughts and the kind of thoughts we owe to him. The necessity of a true and simple culture, tolerance in all things, disinterestedness in mental judgments, the seeing a thing as it is itself, or lucidity of mind, temperance in expression, amiability in life and character, the endeavor to know the best that is known and thought in the world,—here, indeed, we seem to have the heads of so many sermons; but what delightful sermons they have been! The first of all English critics (I do not limit it by the qualifying adjective "living"), he writes with exquisite fineness of perception and delicacy of feeling and insight, with a charm of style and language peculiarly his own. How it has flowed into our own ears, this strong, supple, simple diction, at once full of amenity and light irony, wrapping fold within fold the subtility of his thought, and letting us into the secret recesses of a beautiful and finely-tempered mind! And the matter of these essays, I need hardly say, has become in a peculiar way the common stock of all who love letters and desire to further themselves in knowledge and right feeling.[117]

III

It was only four years after his return from his American tour that Arnold died, in 1888. Once more before his death he was to become a controversial figure in this country because of the various comments he made about America upon his return to England. Underneath this short-lived controversy there were three things happening to the image of Arnold in America in the latter part of the nineteenth century: first, objective assessments by a new generation of critics; second, a positive fervor about him developing among the young people who had been brought up, so to speak, on Matthew Arnold; and third, a more abstract and more inclusive picture forming in the American literary mind, now that his career was complete and he had become one of the "saints" of English literature.

In 1882, before his first visit, Arnold had written "A Word About America," for the *Nineteenth Century,* and after his return he wrote "A Word More About America" for the same magazine. *The Dial* (whose editors were always enthusiastic Arnoldians) was rapturous about this second essay, since it said that America had solved the political problem (although not the "human" one). *The Dial* admonished all those who thought Arnold had nothing good to say of the United States to read the essay.[118]

But Arnold's paraphrase and estimate of Grant's *Memoirs,* which were meant to introduce Grant to the English public, were attacked by both *The Critic* and the *North American Review.*[119] The *North American Review* piece, written by James B. Fry, a Civil War general and in Arnoldian matters the polar opposite of Horatio N. Powers, embodied the last explosion, as far as Arnold is concerned, of outraged Civil War feelings, buttressed by Fry's fervent and all-inclusive Anglophobia. Fry's picture—and he was to return to the fray in 1888—was the last American assessment of Arnold which regarded him, in a sense, as a living, breathing "enemy."

"Mr. Arnold has presented a weak and incorrect abstract of our hero's literary as well as of his military work," began Fry; and in the major part of the review he gave a minute exposition of the ways in which Arnold's paraphrase attempted to correct Grant's English according to Oxford standards. But "in no instance does Mr. Arnold's change in General Grant's English improve it." Furthermore, Fry contended, Arnold often distorted Grant's meaning: "Under cover of a statement made by Grant, Mr. Arnold assumes the defense of the sympathy for the South shown by England during the rebellion." Grant had said of the 1856 election that he did not favor a Republican candidate because a Republican could not win. Arnold had expressed approval of this statement, and Fry interpreted this approval as evidence of Arnold's Southern sympathies. Fry then went into a long defense of the North and an attack on slavery, its evils, and the Southern government, "which Mr. Arnold admits Englishmen, for whom he now offers a poor excuse, admired and favored, as against the government of the Union, founded upon the principle of human freedom..." Fry finished his review with a rhetorical question, "How deeply are we indebted to him?"

In 1888 Fry renewed his attack on Arnold,[120] the occasion being the publication in an English periodical, the *Nineteenth Century,* of Arnold's "Civilization in the United States," in which he said that the United States lacked "distinction" and "beauty," physically as well as spiritually.

While the *North American* was in press, the news of Arnold's death was announced. It was too late to delete or soften Fry's attack, but the editors inserted a laudatory obituary on the first page of the issue.

To Arnold's charge that America was not "interesting," Fry, his martial instincts quivering, replied: "Surely we have been interesting to British sovereigns from Victoria all the way back to George the Third, and to British statesmen from Gladstone to Pitt; and it is beyond dispute that we have proved interesting to the British Army and Navy wherever we have met them..." Arnold had also charged that Americans were undisciplined and lacked a sense of awe. To this charge Fry replied, proudly: "There may be some truth in this. We stand in awe only of God and His works, and, therefore, we are not *aw-fully* disciplined as people who are thrilled all their lives by the presence of 'Majesties,' 'Lords,' and other born aristocrats." Fry finally dis-

missed Arnold completely as a writer and thinker and ended in
a burst of patriotism.

Other reactions to "Civilization in the United States" were
more temperate, but questioned Arnold's strictures nevertheless.
A number of journals, including *Our Day,* the *Andover Review,*
the *Literary World, The Critic, The Nation, The Dial, The
Independent,* and the *Christian Union,* took up the subject.[121]
The Critic and the *Andover Review* voiced the old objection of
distaste for Arnold's tone, its "flippancy" in particular. *The
Critic* responded to Arnold in a patriotic vein; it reprinted a
piece from the *Philadelphia Daily News* which purported to be
shocked at the fact that a Hellene like Arnold could not see the
close analogy between ancient Greece and the United States and
which insisted that "human destiny" was working itself out
in this country. Still another attitude represented was that of
cool dismissal, as shown, for example, by *The Nation,* which
would have no truck with amateur political thinkers and proclaimed, "... there is no department of human activity in which
progress in the United States is not constant and steady, though
at particular points not always very perceptible." But the ubiquitous Horatio N. Powers wrote a letter to *The Critic* on "Mr.
Arnold's Right to Criticize," and the *Andover Review* and the
Literary World admitted that much of what Arnold said was
true. The most balanced judgment was that of the *World:*

> What we find in these American judgments by Mr. Arnold is very
> clear-headed criticism based on very insufficient data, and criticism
> which accordingly misses the mark.... Still Mr. Arnold, as regards
> America, was walking toward the light. He saw some things, if he
> did not others, clearly and accurately.[122]

Only *The Dial,* always faithful, came out without reservation
for the English critic, and Melville B. Anderson asked:

> Which is the more patriotic course: to join the brutal mob of
> nameless journalists who affect to deem it American to be impervious

to all foreign comment; or, on the other hand, to weigh thoughtfully every suggestion that may tend to render us personally and nationally worthier of the "society of the future"?[123]

But Arnold ended the argument by dying abruptly in 1888 and thus inviting the unequivocal tribute of the obituary, many of these being combined with an estimate of *Civilization in the United States*. The most significant of the obituaries was that written by Charles Eliot Norton for the American Academy of Arts and Sciences, of which Arnold had been a member. Norton said, "... not one has done more to affect the course of the deeper currents of thought in his time than Matthew Arnold."[124] Other reactions were more emotional; and the stricken Horatio N. Powers composed for the *Literary World* a poem of seven stanzas called "Memorial Verses," the first stanza of which I quote:

> Dazed with sudden shock I stood,
> As if stealthily struck in the dark,
> Conscious only of strangeness and pain—
> A gnawing and desperate pain,
> As I grasped in the awful void.
> Arnold dead! O soul-searching woe!
> The elect of the Muses fled!
> Great voice of the century dumb!
> Arnold dead! Lordly pattern of man,
> Oracle, charmer of souls,
> Compeller of strenuous life,
> Revealer of secrets untold,
> Consoler, interpreter, friend![125]

Francis F. Browne in *The Dial* and Helen Gray Cone for *The Critic* were also moved to verse, heartfelt, prosaic, ephemeral.[126]

Along with the obituary tributes there also appeared the first, sometimes hazy, attempts to "place" Arnold and assess his final significance. The most objective of these appraisals was an

article in *The Nation* which undertook to account for the phenomenon of Arnold's success on historical grounds:

What brought him most of his popularity as an essayist and social
philosopher was undoubtedly his opportuneness. He appeared just as
John Stuart Mill, Darwin, Tyndall, and Huxley had taken hold of
the young men, and destroyed their interest in theological discussions
which perturbed the previous generation, without furnishing them
with anything very solid in the nature of a solution of the moral
problem of the universe. To tens of thousands who could not worship
science, and had but a poor head for facts of any kind, and yet felt
that they must give up their old religious belief, it seemed for a
moment as if Arnold had hit on a way of proving something which
would take the place of a creed, and cultivate the faculty of reverence,
and keep alive the faith in the final triumph of righteousness.[127]

T. W. Hunt, in the *New Princeton Review,* tried to explain
Arnold more as an individual phenomenon, who had done
"invaluable work" in minimizing the distance between creation
and criticism in literature; who had brought "thought to bear"
on literature; and who had instigated "the wide diffusion of
the literary spirit, the emphasis of literature as a most important
department of education, and an essential factor in all progress."[128] Even more indicative of the fact that Arnold had passed
on into history were two comparative studies, "Tolstoi and
Matthew Arnold" in the *Andover Review,*[129] and a two-pronged
attack on Emerson and Arnold entitled "Two Prophets of This
Age" in the *Catholic World.*[130]

Meanwhile another generation of critics, younger than Whitman or Lowell, was assessing Arnold without either the sense
of personal reaction or the jangled patriotism of their elders.
George Woodberry (1855–1930) is a good example. Woodberry
was by no means a partisan of Arnold, whom he considered
too "sceptical" and too far removed from real life.[131] Nevertheless,
Woodberry thought that Arnold stood for intelligence and respect for ideas in matters of literary criticism[132] and that Arnold's

tenets of "disinterestedness" and keeping one's eye "steadily upon the object" were sound and valuable critical guides.[133] And Whitman's younger disciple John Burroughs, an exact contemporary of Howells, was, although no Horatio N. Powers, also an admirer of Arnold. Burroughs confessed that he could not see much value in Arnold as a general force.[134] But in literary matters:

We have had a much needed service from Arnold; he has taught his generation the higher criticism, as Sainte-Beuve taught it to his. A singularly logical and constructive mind, yet a singularly fluid and interpretive one, giving to his criticism charm, as well as force and penetration.[135]

At Arnold's death Burroughs recorded in his journals: "I look upon Arnold as the greatest critic of English literature; such steadiness, directness, sureness of aim and elevation, we have never before seen."[136] Thus Arnold's reputation as a literary critic, high since 1865, still remained high in the latter part of the nineteenth century, even with men who were not sympathetic to his other roles.

To other literary people growing up in the post-Civil War period Arnold's words and works were gospel. Sarah Orne Jewett wrote in 1889 to a friend, "I have been reading Mr. Arnold's 'Essays in Celtic Poetry' with perfect reverence for him and his patience and wisdom. How much we love and believe in him, don't we?"[137] Evidently Arnold's pronouncements carried a godlike sanction for Miss Jewett, and his detractors annoyed her:

Doesn't it seem as if it must fret a man like Arnold to the quick to go on saying things as he has and seeing people ignore them, then dispute them, then say that they were God's truth, when the whole thing has become a matter of history and it is too late to have them do the immediate good he hoped to effect?[138]

Philip Littell, who was born in 1868 and was thus nineteen years Miss Jewett's junior, wrote in the *New Republic* in 1915 about his first reading of Arnold with an equal enthusiasm: "It would have been difficult for me at that time to measure my gratitude to him. I was eager to part with what he took away, eager to receive what he gave."[139] Arnold's conception of the Greek spirit seemed to Littell quieter and more edifying than the scholarly one of Murray and Zimmern. Moreover, Arnold lived his own precepts with serenity and brightness: "It is pleasant to remember what Matthew Arnold did for some of us who were young in the last century's 'eighties. He bettered our enjoyment of books. He made us feel, rather intimately, the presence or the absence of the grand style, natural magic, fluidity and sweet ease, the lyrical cry."[140] Brander Matthews, in 1916, paid Arnold a similar tribute:

Those of us who are now sexagenarians and who had the good fortune to make acquaintance with *Essays in Criticism* in our undergraduate days and read the successive collections of Matthew Arnold's later criticism as they appeared one by one ..., can never forget the debt we owe to the critic who opened our eyes to the value of culture, to the purpose of criticism and to the duty of "seeing the thing as it is." We felt an increasing stimulus as we came to know Arnold's writings more intimately, as we absorbed them, as we made their ideas our own, as we sought to apply their principles and to borrow their methods. The influence of Arnold's work upon the generation born in the middle of the nineteenth century was immediate and has been enduring.[141]

Between obituaries and youthful enthusiams, the general image of Arnold in the American literary milieu continued to develop in the 'nineties and the early part of the twentieth century, as posthumous works of his were published and as critics and scholars attempted to assess his position and significance. If anything, his prestige as a literary critic soared even higher; his social criticism began to lose its immediate sting for Americans, as its author joined the ranks of the illustrious dead; and the religious criticism, except to the strictly orthodox, appeared less and less controversial, as the immediate issues with which it was concerned died with the passing of time and Arnold's own attitudes became, in truth, the attitude of the great majority of Christian believers. The guiding and inclusive image, that of the apostle of culture, became even brighter for those who still meditated upon it, and became, in fact, equipped with a halo.

Arnold the religious critic was the first, and the only, aspect of Arnold to fade into near-oblivion and become merely a historical fact. It is true that orthodoxy, for a while, continued to frown on this side of his thought. In 1888 the *Andover Review,* in a study of R. H. Hutton, F. W. H. Myers, and Arnold, stigmatized Arnold's religious liberalism: "Matthew Arnold, indeed, scorns to acknowledge Christianity as standing in any relation whatever to thought. He glories in his metaphysical inconsistency... surely never was boast better founded."[142] Again, in 1889, in a laudatory article on Arnold's influence on literature, which was admitted to be great, the *Andover Review* deprecated *Literature and Dogma* for its underestimation of the powers of the supernatural.[143] Arnold's real and continuing opponent in the sphere of religion was Catholicism, avowedly a dogmatic and unliberal form of belief; and as late as 1896, in a review of Arnold's letters, the *Catholic World* charged: "Arnold's influence upon the religious views of English-speaking Protestants it would be difficult to exaggerate,... [it is] widespread and distinctive." Arnold, said the *World,* represents the penultimate phase of Protestantism, a shade removed from no religious belief at all.[144] Many Protestant believers, however, still regarded Arnold as a savior. Mrs. G. Van Rensslaer, in an essay published in *The Century,* took Arnold to task for his misunderstanding of American architecture, especially Richardson's, but said:

Upon many of the younger generation in America [Arnold's writings] have had an extraordinary tonic, stimulating, illuminating effect—not merely furnishing the mind but opening the eyes of the soul. For my part I rejoice in this opportunity to say that to no book do I owe so much as to "Literature and Dogma" unless it be the great Book with which it so largely deals.[145]

In 1897 Louise S. Houghton in the *New World*[146] undertook to prove that Arnold had been finally the preserver of orthodox Christianity, which "owes much to him. . . . How great is Matthew Arnold's service to orthodoxy is perhaps chiefly shown in the fact that all thoughtful believers now see what he first made clear,—that the Bible is to be criticized as a literary, not a scientific work." Finally, Arnold's religious doctrines were paid the ultimate tribute, before they disappeared into the limbo of lost, impossible causes, by being embraced by science itself, in the person of John Fiske, the resolute though Christian evolutionist, who was in most respects an enthusiastic admirer of Arnold's doctrines. In *The Unseen World* Fiske repeated with approval Arnold's analysis of St. Paul: "Faith, in Paul's apprehension, was not an intellectual assent to definitely prescribed dogmas, but, as Matthew Arnold has well pointed out, it was an emotional striving after righteousness, a developing consciousness of God in the soul, such as Jesus had possessed . . ."[147] Fiske likewise, in *Excursions of an Evolutionist,* in an essay on "Evolution and Religion," quoted with approbation Arnold's root definition of the twin bases of the religious instinct:

Matthew Arnold once summed up these two propositions very well, when he defined God as "an Eternal Power, not ourselves, that makes for righteousness." This twofold assertion, that there is an eternal Power that is not ourselves, and that this Power makes for righteousness, is to be found, either in a rudimentary or in a highly developed state, in all known religions.[148]

Meanwhile, posthumous writings of Arnold's—his second series of *Essays in Criticism* and his letters—were published. The *Essays in Criticism,* literary in concern, were praised unstintedly. *The Dial,* as might be expected, was the most rapturous. Concerning the programmatic "The Study of Poetry," with which the volume began, Melville B. Anderson, spiritual brother of Horatio N. Powers, announced: "I think many will join me in the opinion which I unhesitatingly express, that there is nowhere else to be found an essay on this subject of anything like the same educational value."[149] *The Critic,* which had always expressed reservations about Arnold, rejoiced in the return of Arnold to a sphere in which he had always been, and unquestionably so, a master: "Perhaps, however, he had more of sweetness and light in literature than in politics, for assuredly his literary essays are his best, though by the side of them may be placed a few chapters from the books on religious subjects." Arnold's literary opinions themselves, said *The Critic,* were "too well known to make it necessary to discuss his estimates..."[150]

The signal event that modified the general image of Arnold, however, was the publication of his letters, which had the effect of removing from the American literary mind one of the chief objections to Arnold, an objection that went back as far as Whitman and Lowell, namely that he was cold or flippant or supercilious. The letters, with their record of the strict fulfilling of dreary tasks, of warm devotion to family ties, of the love of nature and animals, of a consistent humility, punctuated only briefly by a disarmingly genuine delight in local triumphs and successes, laid forever the ghost of snobbery. Although there were complaints that the carefully screened and edited letters were dull, no one of the many reviews used the word "arrogance" in connection with them. George Woodberry correctly appraised the situation when he said in *The Bookman:*

The effect of the publication of Matthew Arnold's letters will be to increase respect for him, by supplementing the impression of his books with more direct and various knowledge of his personality in certain aspects that found imperfect reflections in either his verse or prose. He was believed to be supercilious, hard, and narrow; but the first of these two epithets will no longer be applied to him in an un-qualified way, and the question of his narrowness becomes sim-plified.[151]

The Dial, its devotion only increased by absence and time, waxed lyrical, characterizing him as "this kindly lover of beasts and birds and flowers, this affectionate son and tender father, this gentle critic who dealt so urbanely with every form of rhetorical and political and ethical humbug..."[152] Thus had the supercilious fop become a godly figure.

CHAPTER III

WILLIAM BROWNELL

THE "most discerning literary critic of our day is dead," wrote Edith Wharton in an obituary of William Crary Brownell in 1929. Mrs. Wharton elaborated: "Since Mr. Paul Bourget's early 'Etudes de Psychologie Littéraire,' since Henry James's 'French Poets and Novelists' and his later 'Notes on Novelists,' I know of nothing in modern French or English literary criticism possessing the range, the substance, the quality of being at what Matthew Arnold called 'the centre,' to the same degree as William Brownell's three or four volumes."[1]

In truth, Brownell had written eight volumes, but some of them were so slim, and they had appeared at such stately intervals and over such a long period of time (1889–1927), that Mrs. Wharton, a friend of Brownell's (he was one of her editors at Scribner's), may perhaps have made a natural slip. But certainly, her constellation of Brownell, James, and French culture, with a concluding reference to Matthew Arnold, sums up remarkably well the influences, traditions, and areas of thought in which Brownell worked. It was to James that he looked as an American predecessor, to Arnold as a foreign prophet, and to French culture as a great teacher. He was, in fact, to become the most thorough, and maybe the greatest, American disciple of Arnold.

Brownell's life span (1851–1928) embraced what is perhaps the most significant period of American history, and he was interested in all of it. In his last book, published in 1927, he mentioned, approvingly, *Gentlemen Prefer Blondes,* but as a boy he had heard Emerson lecture and he had heard Lincoln in the Lincoln-Douglas debates of 1860. His first three literary passions were *Robinson Crusoe,* the Bible, and Bunyan, those three cornerstones of the post-Renaissance English-speaking world. In his last work he discussed the comic strip. He was born in 1851 in New York City, the only child of cultivated parents, whose ancestry, on both sides, reached far back into the New England past. As a boy, he seems to have been precocious and serious, although not at all unhappy, and he was a reader of the Bible from an early age. He entered Amherst College at the age of sixteen, and after graduation in 1871 he became a reporter for the New York *World,* of which, at the age of twenty-one, he was made city editor. From 1879 to 1881 he was on the staff of *The Nation,* and he spent the years 1881 to 1884 in France. The fruit of this experience was his first book, a remarkable study in comparative culture entitled *French Traits* (1889). After his return to America in 1884, Brownell was employed for nearly two years by the Philadelphia *Press.* In 1888 he was appointed editor and literary adviser for the publishing firm of Scribner's, a post which he held until his death in 1928. From 1889 to 1927, carefully and unhurriedly, Brownell brought out a series of distinguished volumes of criticism, which earned him, if not the agreement, at least the respect of the American critical world.

Like James, although not so intensely, Brownell was tradition-minded, and like his predecessor he thought he could see little to build on, in his early days anyhow, within the American scene. Like James, too, he explicitly rejected Poe, Emerson, and Lowell, while at the same time he regarded James himself as the most promising critic yet developed in America and agreed, even more emphatically than James, that Arnold was the best guide for any critic.

Poe, for Brownell, was a quintessential provincial who had been romanticized by literary historians into a legend: "And this verdict has naturally been relied on by the extremely *un*-professional many who possess those 'primitive tastes' to which says Mr. Henry James—decidedly our most competent critical authority in such a matter—Poe particularly appeals."[2] Poe's reviews, with their acrimonious comments on other American writers, seemed to Brownell to be a product of the "polemical" rather than the "critical" temper. Preëminently Poe lacked discipline, which, for Brownell, meant that he lacked culture. Once more Brownell echoed James when he said that Poe's genius was that of a "charlatan." Above all, and as might be expected, Brownell deplored Poe's ejection of truth from the province of art. Brownell's bent was ethical, and he could see only vacuity and morbidity in Poe's mystical "supernal beauty."

Brownell's analysis of Emerson, despite his approval of Emerson's religious force, indicates that he thought this predecessor likewise unsound. Emerson's doctrine of individualism had gone astray, thought Brownell. Emptied of imagination, it served only to give license to flagrant individualism, the chief flaw, in Brownell's opinion, as in Arnold's, of the Anglo-Saxon world. The only effective countermeasure is culture, which Brownell always conceived of as a disciplinary force: "Culture and nothing but culture is precisely the cure for the mental condition illustrated in these and other eccentricities of the spirit of nonconformity."[3] But culture itself, says Brownell, did not enter into Emerson's philosophy, and Emerson considered literature of a secondary nature: "One follows easily the trend of his predilection: Art in his view . . . is chiefly valuable as recording history; history is of value so strictly as fuel for his own intellectual combustion that it is of small importance in even this regard."[4] In short, Emerson and culture were at war, and this rejection of culture was but an index of provincialism. Emerson's literary quirks (in particular, his expressed dislike of Shelley, Aristophanes, and *Don Quixote*), his lack of interest in France, his disregard for social questions—all appeared to Brownell to make "his philosophy . . . provincial, and, however vital, barbaric."[5] Finally Brownell thought, as did James, that

Emerson's criticism most needed the cosmopolitan touch. Although Emerson's *English Traits* was one of the most objective portrayals of a foreign society ever written by an American, even here Brownell saw the provincial mind at work, and he described the book as "distinctly less penetrating and sound than it might have been had [Emerson] had even a touch of cosmopolitanism . . ."[6]

One might expect that in Lowell, with his love of the classics, respect for tradition, and essentially humanistic point of view, Brownell would have found an emulable predecessor. But he was no less positive in his rejection of Lowell than he was in his rejection of Poe and Emerson. In general, Brownell dismissed Lowell as a dilettante, for Lowell's culture was too exclusively belletristic and uninformed by science, theology, art, philosophy, and history. In addition, Lowell's criticism was essentially impressionistic, guided only by emotional temperament: ". . . the truth is that Lowell's eminently scholarly tastes were wholly directed by his temperamental predilections, and he followed these, I think, with an enthusiastic docility that limited his culture to a degree unfortunate for the importance and endurance of much of his work in prose."[7] Lowell lacked, according to Brownell, a pervading central and philosophical conception of literature, and he lacked too the critical spirit and the critical temperament. Brownell also disliked the fact that Lowell always stayed on safe ground, with the admitted classics of the past, thus ensuring himself against error. Finally, as in his analysis of Emerson, Brownell regretted in Lowell the absence of interest in and understanding of the French. And the critic to whom Lowell is invariably contrasted, to Lowell's detriment, is Matthew Arnold. Arnold was steeped in "history," but Lowell knew only literary history. Short Arnoldian pronouncements on both Shakespeare and Dante are adduced by Brownell to show that Arnold could say more in a phrase about a subject than

Lowell could in an essay, as in the instance of Dante, whom Lowell had spent twenty years in studying. Arnold did not have to spend twenty years, said Brownell.

His greatest predecessors, then, in American criticism were for Brownell either provincial or, in the case of Lowell, too far removed from experience. It was James alone, of all the "American Prose Masters," who had a temperament eminently "critical."[8] But there were objections to James also: he was too much inclined to the esoteric, too exclusively concerned with aesthetic values, and hence did not give a complete and rounded characterization of his subject from a central point of view, as did Arnold. Nevertheless, James was the greatest American critic. In his last book, *Democratic Distinction in America,* Brownell was to speak of James's "matchless essay"[9] on Emerson; and in his treatment of James in *American Prose Masters* (1909) he declared:

The two volumes "French Poets and Novelists" and "Partial Portraits" stand at the head of American literary criticism and "Essays in London and Elsewhere" next them. The "Life of Hawthorne" is, as a piece of criticism, altogether unexcelled and for the most part unrivaled in the voluminous English Men of Letters series...[10]

And we know from the testimony of Brownell's second wife, Gertrude Hall Brownell, who in her reminiscences of her husband tells of a meeting between James and Brownell, that James himself was somewhat surprised at how seriously Brownell took him:

My unqualified admiration for Henry James made me deplore insufficient ardor in his essay on James, whereupon he told me that at the time of his writing it the fact itself of his making James one of his prose-masters was regarded as a significant tribute by James himself, who said that up to that date [1909] he had never been considered and analysed with such seriousness. They had a good talk together, and James at leave-taking wound up, with a smile, "Don't despair of me. I may do something yet!"[11]

In James's subtlety, seriousness, critical acumen, European-looking attitude, and general distress at American provinciality, Brownell saw not only the greatest potential American critic but also a kindred spirit. Brownell had no intention, however, of following in James's path to Europe, for he was always unqualifiedly committed to America and American democracy. Furthermore, James had not been interested in immediate social issues; he had no "program"; and, finally, he was not primarily a critic throughout most of his career. For a guide who was most certainly interested in the social issue and who had a most complete "program," Brownell turned, as had James before him for different reasons, to Matthew Arnold. Brownell was in fact one of that post-Civil War generation that, as Robert Morss Lovett remarked, was to be the most deeply influenced by Arnold.

Of this group Brownell was the most powerful and distinguished critic. It was not that Brownell was a mere carbon copy of Arnold, for he was a man of originality and wit in his own right; and he disagreed with Arnold on many specific issues, especially those relating to American society. Furthermore, Brownell was a formidable person: the adjective most often used to describe him was "austere." His professional air, his dignity, and his high seriousness, not unbroken by irony and wit, invested American criticism itself with an elevation that perhaps it had never before possessed. Appearing on the scene precisely when American criticism was becoming genuinely self-conscious, Brownell lent a professional dignity to that self-consciousness, which had previously tended to be either blusteringly provincial or pallidly apologetic.

Nevertheless, Arnold was indubitably *there* by the time Brownell arrived on the scene. He had said many of the things that Brownell wanted to say, and he had said them, in Brownell's estimation, incomparably well. Thus Arnold became a permanent *point de repère* for the younger American. No other critic is cited so often and so favorably in Brownell's work. In addition, Arnold became Brownell's philosopher, for he was, said Brownell, "not merely nor even mainly an artist . . . but an apostle as well."[12]

I

Like James, Brownell had explicitly recorded his debt to and estimate of Arnold, for Arnold, along with Thackeray, is one of the culture heroes of Brownell's *Victorian Prose Masters*. The essay on Arnold is divided into seven parts, and takes up successively Arnold's literary and cultural influence, personality, literary criticism, social and political criticism, religious writings, style, and poetry. Brownell was only lukewarm on the subject of the poetry, but in later years, according to his wife, "he regretted not having estimated Matthew Arnold more highly as a poet, not having penetrated himself more, perhaps, with his poetry."[13] On all other counts Arnold is, in Brownell's estimation, unrivaled.

Brownell begins the first section, dealing with Arnold's influence, with an acknowledgment not unlike that of James in the *English Illustrated Magazine*:

How different in a critical aspect from its condition when Arnold began to write is the England of our day—England and its literary dependency, ourselves! And how largely the difference is due to the influence of Arnold's writings. Thirty years ago [Brownell is writing about 1900] he was deemed a dandy and a dilettante in literature. Today his paradoxes are become accepted commonplaces.[14]

Arnold's poise, good temper, "curiosity," flexibility, and serenity have shifted the point of view of criticism as a whole. Where once there was only truculence, there is now urbanity.

Beyond this general influence, Arnold had taught particularly that the real method of criticism must be persuasion, the instillment of conviction. Brownell continues, offering a proof of Arnold's effectiveness in "lifting" Anglo-American criticism:

And if one seeks a concrete instance of the great advance made in English critical writing in the past twenty-five years, mainly through the urgency of that culture for which Arnold was always contending and in whose triumphs he is surely entitled to share, a very striking one is furnished by the contrast between the state of things at present and that existing when he inquired, "Why is all the *journeyman-work* of literature, as I may call it, so much the worse done here than it is in France?"[15]

Arnold has been fortunate in that he has received "abundant notice" from his own generation, and there is no doubt that he will go on receiving notice from succeeding generations. Brownell attributes this efficacy to that quality which James admired in Arnold, his ethical bent, and to the fervency with which he preached his gospel. "To have one's gospel so promptly accepted demonstrates that it has been preached. He had, in a word, a mission. And he has fulfilled it."[16]

Arnold's personality, for Brownell, as for Philip Littell, possessed a singular charm in that he practiced what he preached: "The pursuit of perfection that he preached he practised with equal inveteracy."[17] The quality of "sweet reasonableness" which Arnold found in St. Paul was, says Brownell, Arnold's own chief trait: "His reasonableness was tinctured with feeling, his stoicism was human, his temper affectionate, his aim benevolent, and his manner gentle."[18] Withal, Arnold was realistic and hard-headed, as his adverse judgments of many of his contemporaries indicated. Emerson's inimitable optimism, for instance, seemed to Arnold particularly insubstantial. Brownell mentioned Arnold's letters as revealing the essential simplicity and charm of the man: "The 'Letters' leave the impression of a singularly elevated soul, living habitually on a high plane."[19]

But this idol had his weaknesses as well. Arnold was lacking in the aesthetic faculty; while in Italy, the home of so many works of art, he occupied himself with, of all things, botany. Also, Arnold lacked a real sense of humor although he had wit. Arnold's most serious flaw, however, was his lack of genuine energy, which is the very stuff of genius, as Arnold himself had said.

These flaws, said Brownell, were far outweighed by Arnold's merit and his aim: "To the advocacy of these ends he brought an essentially critical spirit. He was in endowment and in equipment the first of English critics. Among English critics, indeed, he stands quite alone. No other has his candor, his measure of disinterestedness..."[20] Indeed, Arnold had turned his own defects into virtues, for what he was, weaknesses and all, was exactly what his age needed: "For the consideration of his public and his era he deemed energy less important than light, earnestness less needful than sweetness, genius less beneficent than reasonableness, erudition less called for than culture."[21]

Turning to Arnold's literary criticism, Brownell observed, shrewdly, that the much-advertised "disinterestedness" was in the method only, for Arnold was biased and had, like all men, his own idiosyncrasies: "One may say, in fact, that his motive is didactic and his method disinterested."[22] This type of criticism, with its underlying didacticism, was the very antithesis of the "impressionism" which Brownell, like James and Arnold, so disliked. Moreover Arnold was preoccupied with ideas: "Arnold passed his intellectual life indeed, whatever his didactic strain, in the world of ideas. No English writer, certainly, is richer in them."[23] Arnold is at the same time completely nonscientific and occupied with a nonscientific consideration—personality. However, although Arnold's critical analysis is ultimately personal, it can claim exactness because it is framed and controlled by a rich culture and by constant comparison to classic examples. This method, as opposed to Taine's "man, moment, milieu," does not "account" for writers, nor does it wholly "depict" them, but rather it sets forth their salient qualities and their personalities:

They [writers] are considered in the light of their relation to literature, but nevertheless distinctly as personalities whose relationship to literature, too, is a personal relation. Arnold's criticism may be loosely characterized as literature teaching by examples, just as history has been called philosophy so teaching.[24]

Arnold's services to literary criticism proper are as signal as those he performed for culture in general. The dictum that literature is a criticism of life revealed even to the "unreflecting the essentially critical nature and function of the truly creative 'thought of thinking souls'—to recall Carlyle's definition of literature itself."[25] Arnold had done great service to prose criticism itself by showing that, although it lacks the creative element of beauty, it has a definite and necessary function as expositor and interpreter:

And real criticism, criticism worthy of its office—criticism such as Arnold's—contributes as well as co-ordinates and exhibits. It is itself literature, because it is itself origination as well as comment, and is the direct expression of ideas rather than an expression of ideas at one remove . . .[26]

In matters of politics and sociology Arnold could, at times, go wrong, as witness certain of his misconceptions concerning the United States and his obsession with Irish Home Rule. Americans, said Brownell, were not merely Englishmen on the other side of the water, but a new race that had broken with the European tradition. However, even when they dealt with America, Arnold's general principles were, as elsewhere, stimulating and cogent.[27] If they were not absolutely conclusive, they were always suggestive.[28]

In educational matters Arnold was invariably right, and never touched upon this important subject without "illumining" it.[29] On the Arnoldian thesis that culture is the great educator, Brownell was in complete agreement.[30] Arnold urges the salutary application of education

to the phenomena of the large mechanical and external element in modern civilization, of our Anglo-Saxon individualism, of our want of flexibility, our concentration upon one aspect of a thing and our blindness to its other sides, our faith in "machinery" as an end in itself...[31]

The fifth section of Brownell's analysis deals with Arnold's religious writing, another area in which Arnold exercised a decisive influence on the American critic. Brownell was especially anxious to absolve Arnold of a charge of "heresy" or irreligion: "His distinction as a religious writer has been imperfectly perceived, which is singular, considering the very great religious influence he has exerted. It consists in the way in which he has brought out the natural truth of Christianity."[32] He did this by his dismissal of miracles and by his interpretation of the Bible as literature. How deeply this affected Brownell can be seen from the fact that he adopted Arnold's religious approach as his own.

Finally, in his estimate of Arnold, Brownell takes up and praises the master's literary style: "The virtue of all his criticism—literary, social, and religious—is revealed, not to say enhanced, by the limpidity of his style."[33] Brownell elaborates considerably his paean to Arnold's style, noting particularly its clarity, beauty of diction, and felicity of vocabulary—not remarkable in range but unerring in choice. On all counts Arnold is one of the masters of English style.

In this summary of Brownell's sometimes extravagant praise of Arnold, one can see stated succinctly the enthusiasm which Arnold aroused among his admirers in the late nineteenth century. It will be noticed that Brownell's picture of Arnold is larger, fuller, and more detailed than that drawn by James, since by Brownell's time Arnold's career was more nearly complete and a more general image was beginning to form. It will be noticed too that within the broad Arnoldian tradition inherited by James and Brownell, there is a shift in emphasis. The aesthetic interest of James has, in Brownell, become metamorphosed into a more philosophical and sociological one, and Arnold the man has begun to emerge as a great and revered figure out of the past. Like James, however, Brownell saw in Arnold a complete and exquisite embodiment of his own preoccupations, and in the broadest sense Brownell adopted the Arnoldian program: the concept of the nature and function of culture as it should apply to the Anglo-American world; the idea of the high, creative, intellectual function of criticism; the "natural truth of religion"; the theory of education as a social and political cure-all. Above all, of course, Arnold appealed to Brownell as the high apostle of culture. In a sense Brownell's career is like a prolonged dialogue, sometimes Socratic, between himself and Arnold. All the salient points of Arnold's doctrine became part and parcel of his own equipment. He often, it is true, disagreed with and corrected his mentor's statements, but, over all, he was faithfully carrying on the Arnoldian tradition in America through the last part of the nineteenth century and the early part of the twentieth century.

II

Arnold, it will be remembered, insisted in his first book of literary criticism, *Essays in Criticism,* on certain excellencies in French culture, especially the habit of rationality, and brandished these excellencies at his countrymen. Brownell's first book was likewise concerned with the French and with the educative example of the French.

To a certain degree Brownell had inherited his contrasting

views of French and Anglo-American culture from Arnold. As
he said in *The Genius of Style:*

... [Arnold] maintained that English prose had something to learn
from French measure, restraint, clearness, and conformity to recognized standards of tone and taste. All this was so sound and at the
time so impressive ... and has since become so thoroughly a part
of our thinking and feeling upon this extremely central and consequently widely suggestive subject, that it has quite generally been
accepted as final.[34]

But Brownell did not need Arnold to interpret the French;
his *French Traits,* based on the personal observations he made
while living for three years in France, has been generally recognized, by Americans and Frenchmen alike, as one of the finest
studies in comparative culture ever written.[35] Indeed, Brownell
surpassed Arnold in his study of and understanding of the
French. For Brownell, moralist that he was, would have nothing
to do with "Goddesses of Lubricity." The French, he said, have
not our sense of sin nor our conscience; and for this reason their
errors never leave quite the scars that ours do. What would be
a vice among us, is merely a social irregularity with them.
Actually, they are less liable to become addicted to major vices
than the Anglo-American is. It was on this point, the question of
French morality, that Brownell most emphatically disagreed
with Arnold, showing not only his independence but a remarkable objectivity for his time. Brownell warned his readers, quoting Arnold's famous phrase, to avoid condemning the French
without first trying to understand them, "To avoid misjudg-
ments in this matter, to avoid talking of the French being 'given
over to the worship of their Goddess Lubricity'..."[36]

By and large, however, Arnold and Brownell discovered in
French culture the same virtues and used their discoveries for
the same end—to preach to their respective countrymen. Neither
of them desired to Gallicize the Anglo-American completely.

Arnold, patriot at heart, said, "Genius is mainly an affair of energy, and poetry is mainly an affair of genius; therefore, a nation whose spirit is characterized by energy may well be eminent in poetry;—and we have Shakespeare."[37] As Arnold implies, such a nation need not apologize for itself; and when he was eulogizing the French, it was only in the hope of adding their admirable traits to those of the English, in order to produce in his own country a fuller, more balanced, and more harmonious culture. The French, for Arnold, were an embodiment of the "stock of new and fresh ideas" which were to be injected into the English "stream of thought."

So, too, Brownell always had one eye on America when he wrote of the French, and he subtitled his book "An Essay in Comparative Criticism." In the closing pages of *French Traits* he adjured his countrymen as follows:

…one's last word about the America emphasized by contrast with the organic and *solidaire* society of France, is that, for insuring order and efficiency to the lines of this advance, it would be difficult to conceive too gravely the utility of observing attentively the work in the modern world of the only other great nation that follows the democratic standard, and is perennially prepared to make sacrifices for ideas.[38]

For both Arnold and Brownell, French culture possessed an aesthetic value—beauty—and a social value—order—with all the accompanying virtues. To Arnold America had been, in great part, "ugly." Even the rural areas were unattractive. Similarly, on his first sight of New York, after returning from France, Brownell felt an almost physical revulsion:

Emerging into West Street, amid the solicitations of hackmen, the tinkling jog-trot of the most ignoble horse-cars you have seen since leaving home, the dry dust blowing into your eyes, the gaping black holes of broken pavement, the unspeakable filth, the line of red brick buildings prematurely decrepit, the sagging multitude of telegraph wires…[39]

In retrospect, "Paris never looked so lovely, so exquisite to the sense as it now appears to the memory. All that Parisian regularity, order, decorum, and beauty . . ."[40] Thus Arnold in *Culture and Anarchy:*

The modern spirit has now almost entirely dissolved those habits [subordination and deference], and the anarchical tendency of our worship of freedom in and for itself . . . is becoming more manifest. More and more . . . this and that man, and this and that body of men . . . are beginning to assert and put in practise an Englishman's right to do what he likes; his right to march where he likes, meet where he likes, enter where he likes; boast as he likes; threaten as he likes; smash as he likes.[41]

Arnold looked to the Continent, and especially to France, for a correct sense of duty, where peoples have a concept of "the . . . nation, . . . of the State,—the nation in its collective and corporate character, entrusted with stringent powers for the general advantage, and controlling individual wills in the name of an interest wider than that of individuals."[42] This same lack of discipline and worship of individualism, thought Arnold, permeated all levels of English society, and in the arts it bred provinciality and eccentricity.

Brownell, putting France and America side by side, came to the same conclusion; and he added the charge that the individualism itself had not even the imagined virtues—color and variety—of its defect, but issued, paradoxically, in monotony: "The monotony of the chaotic composition and movement is, paradoxically, its most abiding impression. And as the whole is destitute of definiteness, of distinction, the parts are, correspondingly, individually insignificant."[43] Brownell found the root of all these faults in one of America's most cherished tenets—"individualism." The Emersonian doctrine of self-reliance had been carried too far, thought Brownell, and now obstructed the integration of any semblance of social order.

In France, by contrast, there was everywhere discipline, moderation, a solid "centre," coupled with liveliness, flexibility, and intelligence. Brownell found the secret of French character in what he called the "social instinct," which makes France the most homogeneous and civilized race in the world, because with them relationships, not individuals, are stressed:

The social instinct which subordinates the individual and suppresses eccentricity, and the social and tolerant nature of morality which dictates conformity to general rather than personal standards, a highly developed intelligence and the absence of that sentimentality in conjunction with which it is impossible to find the refinement of manners which is based on reason, however it may inspire that *"politesse de coeur"* in which Prince Bismarck finds the French lacking, afford precisely the conditions for producing in perfection an impersonal, artificial, graceful and efficient medium of social intercourse.[44]

The French thus had made a civilized art of everything, including manners and conversation. Conversely, Brownell noticed a lack of delicacy in English criticism as a whole—including that written by Arnold himself:

We ... are all familiar, Mr. Arnold reminds us, with the notion of "hewing Agag in pieces" and our ungentleness of manners proceeds largely from the astonishing way in which this Teutonic and Puritan passion has penetrated our very nature. How English literature witnesses this from the time of Milton to the very latest number of "The Saturday Review" we all know ... Not only is the hewing done with the grandiose strokes of Carlylean brutality, but it is amiably and dextrously performed by the advocate *par excellence* of "sweet reasonableness" and the chief critic of the custom, Mr. Matthew Arnold himself.[45]

Arnold was more delicate in dealing with literary personalities than were most English critics, Brownell added, but the impersonality of the French he could never achieve. Arnold was but representative of his race in having the basically personal attitude that inevitably leads to the *argumentum ad hominem* type of criticism so familiar in the English-speaking world; thus a fairly good-sized Dunciad might be culled from Arnold's critical writings. In contrast, the social instinct of the French gives a remarkable lightness and delicacy to their literary criticism; hence "hewing Agag in pieces" is done in France with civility and grace.

Brownell agreed with Arnold's distinction that, as compared with the Anglo-Saxons, the French were characterized by intelligence rather than energy. Like Arnold too he saw that this French passion for intelligence and reason manifested itself in the national passion for clarity in all things. The respect for the intellect, in its turn, tended to elevate the general critical tone of the nation and had the effect of making the average French essay greatly superior to the average English essay.

But the French were *too* sane, thought Brownell, and he regretted their lack of indulgence in that quality which the Anglo-Saxons so abundantly indulged—sentiment:

So, amid all the gayety and brilliant *"verve"* of French life at its flood, we feel inevitably with Arnold, exclaiming in Montmartre, that "amiable home of the dead"—

> "So, how often from hot
> Paris drawing-rooms, and lamps
> Blazing, and brilliant crowds,
> Starred and jewell'd, of men,
> Famous, of women the queens
> Of dazzling converse—from fumes
> Of praise, hot, heady fumes, to the poor brain
> That mount, that madden—how oft
> Heine's spirit, outworn,
> Long'd itself out of the din,
> Back to the tranquil, the cool,
> Far German home of his youth."[46]

Yet France was still the light of the world. In commenting on her political greatness Brownell cited approvingly Arnold's statement in *Friendship's Garland,* " 'Till modern society is finally formed, French democracy will still be a power in Europe.' "[47] In his conclusion Brownell again quoted Arnold, in calling France " 'the country of Europe in which the people is most alive'—according to Matthew Arnold's acute synthesis of the results of the Revolution . . ."[48]

Brownell began his literary career with a sociological essay on France, simultaneously accepting and correcting Arnold's ideas, and he was to end it many years later with a sociological analysis of the United States, which once more uses Arnold as a starting point but again one not to be accepted uncritically. In between he was preoccupied with the practice and theory of criticism and, secondarily, with the problems of culture in general. Once more Arnold played a seminal role in these activities.

III

Robert Morss Lovett, commenting upon Brownell's criticism, remarked, ". . . Mr. Brownell's view of the function, and of the methods, standards, ethos of criticism is, in large degree, Arnold's."[49] This acceptance extended from innumerable specific pronouncements of Arnold's on various writers to Arnold's theories, or what Brownell thought were Arnold's theories, on the nature and function of criticism.

In literary criticism proper both Arnold and Brownell worried at the two problems which have bothered critics from time immemorial but which have been especially exacerbated from the nineteenth century on: first, the justification for criticism itself, and second, the problem of objectivity in the practice of criticism. The art of criticism is, in a sense, as its more objective practitioners have always felt, presumptuous. No matter how many times it is said that one does not think the hen a better judge of the egg, or the architect of the house, than oneself, there still persists an uneasy and undefined relationship between the creative and the critical act. The ambiguities have become even more pronounced since Arnold's time (and indeed he is one of the great exemplars), with the ever-increasing phenomenon of men of creative talents turning critic or devoting themselves in great part to criticism. Thus Goethe's classic short way with reviewers—"Kill the dog!"—might in our time, if acted upon, eventuate in a wave of suicides.

It was and is one of Arnold's abiding charms for subsequent critics that he elevated the critical act itself. He had begun the influential essay "The Function of Criticism at the Present Time" by defending criticism on the ground that since not all men have the creative genius, at least they can and should exercise their faculties by criticism. Furthermore—and this is the heart of the matter—criticism per se is not to be disdained, for, as Arnold said in his tribute to Sainte-Beuve: "first-rate criticism has a permanent value greater than that of any but first-rate works of poetry and art."[50] Brownell, at the beginning of his book *Criticism,* first expressed a defensive attitude: "Criticism itself is much criticized—"[51] and he mentioned the common assumption of the alleged "inferiority to books of the books about books."[52] In his discussion, however, he sharply separated the two functions, creative and critical—"Criticism [is] the statement of the concrete in terms of the abstract"[53]—and, remembering Arnold's services, which he had remarked on in his essay on Arnold, he continued, "criticism is enabled to extend its field while restricting its function, and to form a distinct province of literature, while relinquishing encroachments upon the territory of more exclusively constructive art."[54] Much of the distaste for criticism in England and America arises, according to Brownell, from a confounding of the essentially separate functions of criticism and reviewing. In France, as usual, they do these things better. There the Academy, as Arnold had said, provided a "centre" and a competent body of critics supplied a norm.

There was no Academy, nor was there a norm, in the American world of Brownell, nor did he think it desirable that there should be. The problem then remained for the individual critic to achieve objectivity and distance from the thing criticized and to restrain personal eccentricities and quirks. Brownell thought that the individual critic worthy of the name should have his own standards and a solid center of reference for them: "A work of criticism is in fact as much a thesis as a theme; . . . its unity is to be secured only by the development in detail of some central conception preliminarily established and constantly referred to . . ."[55] Brownell here was attacking the particular brand of Crocean "expressionism" that Spingarn was then propounding. But at the same time Brownell was setting up a critical ideal, which was "concentric and constructive work,—such as *par excellence* that of Matthew Arnold . . ."[56] To have this adequate center of reference the critic must have knowledge, although not specialized knowledge, a precept that recalls Arnold's contention that "knowledge, and ever fresh knowledge, must be the critic's great concern for himself."[57] More explicitly, Arnold had said that the critic must have an adequate knowledge of at least one other great literature and must regard Europe as one great confederation. Brownell's ideal critic also must be knowledgeable. "The mere function of examining and estimation can hardly be correctly conducted without illumination from the side-lights of culture."[58] Brownell mentions, characteristically, three French critics, Sainte-Beuve, Taine, and Scherer, as examples of men who possess this "cognate culture."

Arnold had warned in "The Study of Poetry" that too much learning in history or philosophy was liable to be dangerous, and, elsewhere and in passing, he had consistently derided the metaphysical tendency. Taine's historical approach was not necessarily right, since an abundance of learning might lead to overvaluing the past as past. This type of judgment was as bad as the purely personal one, which tends to overvalue moderns, and so Brownell, who would only allow his ideal critic a "tincture" of philosophy, approved this middle-of-the-road philosophy of Arnold's as regards historical and other learning, on the one hand, and pure impressionism, on the other. "Neither history nor physiological psychology," he said in his essay on Arnold, "ever engaged Arnold's attention in dealing with literature."[59] Taine had said that out of a right understanding of the writer's character and age a right understanding of his work "spontaneously" issues. Brownell disagreed by quoting Arnold:

... Arnold aptly remarks: "It cannot be said that Macaulay had not studied the character of Milton and the history of the times in which he lived. But a right understanding of Milton did not 'spontaneously issue' therefrom in the mind of Macaulay, because Macaulay's mind was that of a rhetorician, not of a disinterested critic."[60]

For to Arnold, and Brownell after him, criticism was an infinitely delicate process, involving sensitive perceptions and perfect balance. Brownell says of the perfect critic, again quoting Arnold:

He [the practitioner] may quite conceivably profit by Arnold's caution: "To handle these matters properly, there is needed a poise so perfect that the least overweight in any direction tends to destroy the balance ... even erudition may destroy it. Little as I know therefore, I am always apprehensive, in dealing with poetry, lest even that little should ... prove too much for my abilities."[61]

What, then, are the criteria for criticism? Whatever Arnold's were, nobody, so far as I know, has ever been able to spell them out exactly. Moreover, both James and Brownell had noted that Arnold's perceptions were more important than anything else and that they were more precise than his explicit categories of criticism. Brownell ultimately came to the conclusion that the final criterion was taste, its quality being determined by both the individual and the environment. Criticism, then, becomes the rationalization of an emotional perception. Any "rational exercise of the mind" is but the "checking of sensation by thought." Tastes are various and difficult to rationalize, however; hence absolute criteria are rare. One of these rarities is, in fact, Arnold's definition of a successful translation: "Matthew Arnold's measure of a successful translation: that is, the degree in which it produces the same effect as the original to a sense competent to appreciate the original, is an instance of a sensible appeal to taste . . . But such instances are rare . . ."[62] Taste can neither be invoked by command nor controlled by decree, and thus, since taste is so indefinable, the rational powers alone constitute the stable and predictable elements in criticism. Furthermore, reason not only can interpret the primary emotional perception, but can relate the result to life as well. Since all literature is but a "criticism of life," it is always necessary to establish and state this relationship.

In practice Brownell's critic must search out, as did Arnold, the "characteristics" of a work rather than its "causes," which are the concern of the Taines. Without neglecting ideas, the critic must put his perceptions to work discerning the "personal" element in an artist. Of Arnold's method itself Brownell said:

His subject, indeed, although as I have intimated almost always an idea or a number of associated ideas, is often ideas illustrated or exemplified in some personality. It is what Joubert, Keats, the Guérins, Heine, Byron were themselves and what, in relation to ideas, they stand for, in each instance.[63]

In other words, Arnold's criticism, according to Brownell, reads the man through the works. Brownell stated the creed, later to be considered a "fallacy," clearly enough when he said: ". . . in criticism of the larger kind as distinct from mere reviewing or exact commentary, by example, we mean, practically, personalities. That is to say, not *Manfred* but Byron, not the *Choral Symphony* but Beethoven."[64]

This method, which was to be utterly disdained by a generation that was nascent when Brownell wrote his book, was called by him "synthetic" and was attributed to Arnold and Sainte-Beuve. In his summing up of the critical process Brownell hedged in his "personality reading" with all kinds of provisos and proposed bulwarks of objectivity by calling criticism

... the initial establishment of some central conception of the subject, gained from a specific study illuminated by a general culture, followed by an analysis of detail confirming or modifying this, and concluding with a synthetic presentation of the physiognomy whose features are as distinct as the whole they compose—the whole process interpenetrated by an estimate of value based on the standard of reason ...[65]

Whatever Arnold's first principles in literary criticism may have been in fact, they had become in Brownell's mind the drawing of a physiognomy, a method that was to prevail generally in Anglo-American criticism throughout the first decade of the twentieth century. This same concept of criticism was to be carried further by Stuart P. Sherman, the next major disciple of Arnold, who frankly recorded his adventures among the souls of the masters and who made of Arnold himself a "saintly" figure.

IV

Brownell, in everything but politics, was frankly and avowedly a conservative, but, just as Arnold was a liberal with a difference, Brownell was a conservative with a difference, as his politics, if not his religion and sociology, attest. Surveying the twentieth century, as it girded its loins for various battles in various spheres, in the cultural milieu, in religion, and in politics,

Brownell thought he saw, always, the need for the brakes of conservatism, for the setting up of standards, in life and in art. Once more Arnold was an authority of power, in matters of culture, in religion, and in politics.

Speaking of her husband's religion, Gertrude Hall Brownell remarked:

> One has heard it said that Matthew Arnold, who had to his account all those clear-headed books, "Literature and Dogma," "God and the Bible," "St. Paul and Protestantism," was yet at the end of his life a simple communicant of the Church of England. Mr. Brownell in the same way was modern in his thinking, with a heart full of old-fashioned religion ...[66]

In Brownell's opinion, Arnold's religious writings, especially *Literature and Dogma,* were his most important works. In 1927 Brownell claimed that Arnold's theological writings had become the very texture of the religious thinking and feeling of the time, and that they were as timely in the twentieth century as they had been for the nineteenth. Arnold's great service consisted of removing dogma from religion, on the one hand, and uniting religion and culture, on the other: "... at the present day ... nearly the whole thinking world, save that portion of it committed to the defense of dogma, has practically, if insensibly, come to adopt his view that the sanction of religion is its natural truth."[67]

Above all, Arnold had made religion morality, which was the heart of the matter for Brownell. In his last book Brownell asked: "Why ... need taking the 'exemplary' rather than either the 'sacrificial' or a 'scientific' view of the Life that closed on Calvary, impair the sentiment which unites those who feel its force?"[68] Asked in 1927, this question, it is needless to say, expressed an implicit conservatism, although it merely echoed Arnold's old argument, which, in its day, was considered revolutionary.

In the broader sphere of culture at large, Arnold was also for Brownell a conservative force. In the introduction to *Popular Education of France* Arnold had said:

The difficulty for democracy is how to find and keep high ideals. The individuals who compose it are, the bulk of them, persons who need to follow an ideal, not to set one . . . Nations are not truly great solely because the individuals composing them are numerous, free, and active; but they are great when these numbers, this freedom, and this activity are employed in the service of an ideal somewhat higher than that of an ordinary man, taken by himself.[69]

Thus throughout his *Standards,* published in the apocalyptic year of 1917, Brownell kept insisting upon the need of a higher ideal for democracy than pure individualism.

Standards, said Brownell, are the products of sensibility rather than reason and therefore are produced by culture rather than by philosophy. All that the modern age possesses, he was convinced, is a kind of crude vitality. This anarchy may well be one of the inevitable consequences of the extension of the electorate and thus the inevitable consequence of democracy itself, which, in Brownell's mind as well as Arnold's, could not be called into question, at least in its political manifestations. Yet in both men, although they remained political liberals, there were aristocratic apprehensions that democracy would finally lower everybody and elevate nobody; thus not only would the masses be no better off, but the cultured few, Arnold's "remnant," would be dragged down as well.

But Brownell did not think that the extension of the "intellectual and aesthetic electorate" was the basic cause for the disappearance of standards; he felt that the blame lay more properly in "our ingrained individualism." Even the colleges and universities can no longer provide a community of educated tastes and interests, for the "classics have disappeared before the universal passion for preparing, as Arnold observed, 'to fight the battle of life with the waiters in foreign hotels.' "[70] The great public, on its part, asks only for sensation and novelty; and neither novelty nor sensation, by definition, can have any standards. The only saving group is, in Arnold's phrase, the "remnant," which, says Brownell, "cannot be too largely increased at whatever sacrifices; and the only way in which it can be increased is by the spread of its standards."[71]

This general lack of discipline in society has devastating effects on the individual, breeding in him utter egoism, with no center of reference save the dictates of his own untutored psyche. But

When Arnold observed that "man worships best in common; he philosophizes best alone," what he had in mind was that it is best to do this thinking in solitude—solitude rather than independence. Thinking for oneself meant to him that neglect of the thinking of others which produces less the thinker than the thinkist...[72]

Thus modern society is caught in a whirl, ever flying out from an unstable center. The only hope is that the age may not last, that it may crumble in its own dissatisfaction at so much un-crystallized energy. Arnold perhaps was ultimately hopeful: "Arnold himself employed a short and easy formula of consolation when depressed by the way the world was going. 'The instinct for self-preservation in humanity' would, he thought, ultimately reorient it."[73] Brownell himself was not so sanguine. The "ideal of service" is gone, he said, and people now obey only "the law of human life"; the inner life has disappeared, and "natural man" has been unleashed. In morals and in religion, the "sense of awe" has gone; humanitarianism has completely usurped love of God. Modern art is "art *sans* taste, in fact, and what is still more striking, *sans* virtuosity."[74] Art and letters have been sentimentalized out of their accepted standards by "militant" democracy and are now directed at the "crude" or "un-cultured." The modern writer, like the Byron and Wordsworth of Arnold, does not "know enough." The cure for this is "authority," but one arising naturally and not autocratically, from native culture.

> Not the authority of an autocracy certainly; nor even that of criticism whose function, as I said, is the exposition of the principles that are the tests of standards, so much as the standards themselves which arise insensibly in the mind of the cultivated public and spread in constantly widening circles.[75]

Many of the expressions and phrases used by Brownell in *Standards* echo those of the New Humanists, with whom Brownell is commonly but mistakenly grouped. For their frankly antidemocratic bias was not his, as it was not Arnold's; and always, in matters of politics, Brownell, like Arnold but more fervently than Arnold, remained a political democrat and a nondoctrinaire liberal.

Certainly there are many aristocratic sentiments to be found throughout Arnold's writings, and the author himself has been taken by many to be a snob. In his lecture on "Numbers" he stated specifically that the political majority was unsound and that its political rule would lead to destruction if it were not curbed by the saving "remnant." Yet in the long run he remained a political liberal, for he thought that "inequality" was the real villain and the source of all vulgarity, and that there could be no perfection that did not involve a "general expansion," reaching to all the people. And America by its practice of political equality had solved the political and social, although not the "human," problem. Finally Arnold had been at least touched by some of the optimism that animated certain peoples and classes of his world. With social equality established and material progress increasing the leisure of all people, he looked to the future, at times anyway, with hope: "But then the ideal life is, in sober and practical truth, 'none other than man's normal life, as we shall one day know it.' "[76]

Brownell, we know from his own testimony, had great admiration for and trust in Arnold's political pronouncements. In *French Traits,* for instance, he said that Arnold's "political and social observations will certainly someday obtain the recognition hitherto denied them by our Anglo-Saxon inability to conceive of sound social and political criticism as emanating from the Nazareth of mere culture . . ."[77] So Brownell was a devotee of democracy, and he said of French democracy that its chief virtue was that it gave more happiness to more people than any other nation in Europe. He would not have sacrificed political democracy for the virtues of an aristocracy: "We are not going to cease being democratic because a few of us aim at being superior— . . ."[78] And *Democratic Distinction in America* is his testimony to his faith.

V

Both Arnold and James had begun their careers by talking about the French but each ended by talking about the Americans. Brownell, ever faithful, if unconsciously so, followed the pattern: *French Traits* in 1889; *Democratic Distinction in America* in 1927. But here the resemblances cease, for *Democratic Distinction,* while taking its starting point from Arnold's *Civilization in the United States* and while agreeing with parts of Arnold's critique, is essentially a criticism and a correction of Arnold's estimates.

Democratic Distinction is a charming book, urbane, witty, and, surprisingly enough for the author of *Standards,* light-hearted. It is one of those "reconciliations" that some long-lived writers write as codas, in which the antitheses are reconciled, the darkness gives way to the light, and Prospero arranges a happy ending, bland and benign. Its author has been customarily called "austere" and "forbidding," yet it would seem that this judgment has arisen more from a general glance at the gray shroud with which the twentieth century, in its youth, was pleased to bedeck its elders than from a specific reading of such a document as *Democratic Distinction in America.* Speaking himself, with approval, of the passing of certain conventions relating to the sexes, Brownell said that in his own lifetime the "leg-show" had passed from the stage to the street and that this was good, for, "In the too casual glance of Victorian days women must have felt the lack of something [in the discreet male glance] guaranteeing real interest..."[79]

Democratic Distinction in America is an answer to *Civilization in the United States,* and like that book and like *The American Scene,* and like the work of Sherman, and like Eliot's *Notes Towards the Definition of Culture,* it addresses itself to the problems of culture in the modern world. In some ways, in the area of sanity and balance, *Democratic Distinction* is superior to both its predecessors and its successors. Certainly, in the contrast with Arnold at least, Brownell knew more of what he was talking about. Moreover, he had never indulged in the kind of "racialism" that often got in Arnold's way and overbalanced his social instincts and insights. From *French Traits* to *Democratic Distinction in America* Brownell never relaxed his grip on his central thesis: that individuals are not shaped and formed by heaven nor yet by a mysterious chemistry of the blood, but are rather the products of a social situation:

It is the converging and coöperative forces, the forces of concert, that exert the cultural pressure which moulds man into mankind by modifying his habits and conforming his nature in order to fit him for a functional place in the organism they are ceaselessly building and rebuilding.[80]

Also, Brownell expressed a persistent humility throughout his book. Speaking of Arnold's distaste for the "common man," Brownell made an admission that few intellectuals before and after have been willing to make: "... who and what are 'we,' and how far removed from him?"[81] Arnold's "remnant," said Brownell, was in America small and uninfluential, because, among other things, it was "too much inclined to generalize about [its "poor relations"] unchecked by a view of 'the object as in itself it really is.' "[82] Furthermore:

Our "remnant" in fine has neither enough "magnetism" nor enough "contacts" to extend its virtues widely if it would, and could hardly produce any great extension of "an ideal commanding popular reverence" such as Arnold considered essential to "national dignity and greatness"...[83]

And finally, admitting that a certain kind of "distinction" was lacking in American society, Brownell placed the blame on himself and other critics and intellectuals.

It is possible, of course, that we shall collectively fail of distinction not because it is attainable only by the few, but because it is antipathetic to the many. The fault—if in the future any one is to be at fault at all—will be the "remnant's." If distinction cannot be made a conjoint and universal ideal it had better be replaced.[84]

In and of itself, *Democratic Distinction* is a survey of American culture, past and present, with a final glance at prospects for the future, from the Arnoldian perspective: the antagonism, interplay, and possible reconciliation of mass civilization and minority culture. It should be added that Brownell consciously separated his argument from that of the New Humanists, with whom he was most generally though incorrectly identified. The ideals of Babbitt and More are dismissed concisely and distinctly because of their "commending to an energetic people in an expansive age a purely inhibitive ideal."[85]

Arnold's basic mistake about America, argued Brownell, was twofold. First, he had, like Europeans before him, translated the American phenomenon into a European setting. He had missed the two salient and unique facts about American democracy, namely that, first, it was the only great democracy that had always been so, and, second, it had developed, as a society, "laterally," without the pressure of either immediate foreign influences from without or an institutionalized aristocracy from within. These two circumstances had produced a social mobility and freedom that Europeans overlook, or misunderstand: "To the Englishman maintaining that American women were spoiled one of them replied: 'We have the kind of women you like, only we call them "squaws." ' "[86] Brownell demonstrates by giving a specific example:

When Arnold calls Channing's works "the flower of moral and intelligent mediocrity," he is very likely reflecting that an English divine of Channing's eminence would have a higher quality of talent, instead of remembering that in England a divine of Channing's talent might perhaps be forced for lack of popular demand to bury it in a napkin.[87]

The result of this freedom, says Brownell, has been that the "sky above has not been made of brass, and that much, much less among us than in 'reverential' societies do

'Shades of the prison-house begin to close
Upon the growing boy.' "[88]

Arnold's second basic misapprehension was to confuse the social power with the aesthetic. Admitting that America lacked aesthetic "distinction," as Arnold had complained, Brownell argued that it had its own "brand of distinction," which it should be reluctant to exchange for a "purely aesthetic one."[89] And this brand of distinction was the "fraternal" one of "amiability," that *politesse du coeur* which Thackeray and Chesterton had said was the salient characteristic of American society. Against Arnold Brownell quotes Santayana, who after a satiric enumeration of the number of things and causes, from "Mother" to "Business," that America enveloped in love-cults, speculated that America may yet "breed beauty out of love."[90] In any case, adds Brownell, amiability is a national ideal,[91] and "distinction of the heart" is "not a poor thing."[92] Democracy has conferred on education *"its* greatest distinction in making it general...,"[93] and has made of education "democracy's answer to Plato's and— at the other end of a long argument—Bagehot's contention that the work of the world must be done by a class that thinkers may have leisure to think."[94] This religion of equality, with all its drawbacks, is still the best that the world has yet produced: "... we have had the religion of equality, which religion for religion is surely more religious—whatever strain it may impose on the wise whose task, some cynic has observed, is largely to undo the harm done by the good."[95]

This "distinction of the heart," operating within a society that has developed along political and ethical lines and has been guided by these concerns rather than social and aesthetic ones, has not failed either to produce "aristocrats." Arnold was perhaps right in denying Lincoln the kind of "distinction" he had in mind, but Lincoln, according to Brownell, had a "moral" as contrasted to an "aesthetic" distinction which is, in the last analysis, superior.

Moreover, Brownell noted, as Constance Rourke was to document later, that the "natural aristocrat"—the "democratic aristocrat," as Brownell called him—was one of the great national myths, cropping out at the lowest level of popular culture and in the work of America's most sophisticated novelist, Henry James. "He [the natural aristocrat] figures impressively, as nowhere else with the same distinction, in the fiction of Henry James—most definitely and brilliantly represented, perhaps, by the felicitously named Cockerel of 'The Point of View.' "[96]

"Other portraits by the same ingenuous hand," continued Brownell, "are positively chauvinistic...,"[97] and he mentioned Isabel Archer, Milly Theale, and Christopher Newman. For "if we have less grace," said Brownell, "we also have less ungraciousness."[98] Also, "The aristocratic democrat is certainly one of our best cards—character refined, reflected in manners, kindly even when crude."[99] In the future we can hope perhaps for even more of the quality of deference," which is "the quality with which ideal democracy replaces the 'ideal commanding popular reverence' that Arnold deemed the 'security for national dignity and greatness' supplied by 'aristocratical institutions.' "[100] The fabled "good society" of America had been, all things considered, truly "good": "It preserved its innocence long enough after the Civil War to merit with the rest of the country James's much later characterization of American society in general as the most innocent in the world."[101] It was the innocence of "sophistication" that was made capital of by both Henry James and Edith Wharton. Thus, in Brownell's eyes, did America have her "distinctions" and her "aristocrats."

Brownell agreed with Arnold that, politically, America had thus far solved its problems successfully, because, through all vicissitudes, it still pursued the ideals of the Declaration of Independence, which had replaced classes with people and thus constituted "The Sermon on the Mount" for the American people. According to Brownell, its "political misadventures have been due to the conflicts of majorities and minorities unaffected by considerations of classes and masses as such."[102] Writing in 1927, Brownell saw two possible threats to the functioning of the political system, Communism and Big Business. But genuine Communists were in a distinct minority and the idea itself has been "at least scotched by its own recent demonstration that an indefinitely prolonged tyranny of the proletariat is a necessary preliminary to its own establishment—even nominal."[103] Big Business, he thought, would be held in check by the public power of taxation.

Although American culture had "distinction of the heart" and a viable political system, it did want that "aesthetic" distinction that Arnold talked of, and it missed this precisely because the aesthetic power was a social or cultivated grace, which required a complex and organic society for its flowering. Although we may produce gentlemen in the rough, yet "it is quite probable that in the ordinary acceptation of the term the *distinguished* gentleman in the rough is rare . . ."[104] The root trouble, said Brownell, who was still preaching the sermon of *French Traits,* was a social immaturity that either vaunted a pure individualism or, when it did value unity, enforced a kind of mass homogeneity or conformity, a pure "herd instinct": "It was early discovered that it was not good for man to live alone. Neither was he combined with his fellow men on the principle of mere aggregation."[105] We need, in short, "concert" along with "initiative" and "enterprise"; but we need also less of the "booster" spirit. Most of our crudities, extravagances, and eccentricities result from this basic lack of social "concert." According to Brownell, these extravagances are not ascribable to any inherent defect in democracy or to any lack in popular political sagacity, but merely to social immaturity.[106] This immaturity tends to vulgarize the mass and to make of the superior a "solitary," compounding his superiority in solitude. The "superior," on his part, would find it particularly salutary if he would do more about the situation and complain less.[107] Thus in all things what American democracy needs most is the "spirit of society";[108] The "democratic road to distinction" lies through "the modification of our acknowledged individualism . . ."[109]

Brownell then takes up various spheres of American culture and shows how the lack of social concert tends to weaken or thin them. For example, Americans have made their humor capricious and have weakened the power of the sentiments by their eccentric anarchism. Wit, said Brownell, is eminently a social quality, and lacking the social connection, American humor tends toward the frivolous, even toward continued mockery of seriousness: "Left to itself, the irrepressible spirit of levity, obviously individualistic however contagious, inevitably honey-combs our seriousness—itself not generically suggestive of the 'high seriousness' preached (at one epoch) to subsequent soci-eties by Greek example."[110] Our national comic figure is not a wit, but a clown: "Mockery of seriousness, indeed, is the staple basis of much of the humor in which ... we 'tell the world' we altogether excel it."[111] But the rest of the world, except in its response to Mark Twain, Artemus Ward, Will Rogers, and a few others, is, like Queen Victoria, "not amused." And thus arises, in part anyway, our national touchiness to the foreign charge that we are essentially a lightweight people and culture: "I think our touchiness itself, which is undeniable, is a mark of the immaturity that distinguishes us from older societies and that if we seem 'slight' it is not because we are 'essentially' but because we are socially so."[112]

At the same time, in the Western world at large and not in America alone, pragmatism and the emasculation of religion were drying up the wellsprings of emotion, which had once so flourished in the religious sentiment. Poetry, it is true, had taken over the cry of the heart, but still, ". . . the soul's ascendancy has greatly dwindled."[113] The sense of sin had become metamor-phosed into a sense of righteousness, and the emotional force that had once enforced morals was disappearing. Thus it was that "morality should have, so to say, lost touch with emotion, . . . that social ethics should have so largely replaced personal moral-ity, and that, accordingly, sin must be transformed into crime to receive the attention it could once safely count on."[114]

In matters of tradition, Brownell claimed that Americans had more than they realized, and that the political tradition itself stretched back to the Magna Charta. But again, Americans are, in the main, indifferent to the "awakening and deepening senti-ment" of tradition that makes it such a binding social force. We have "such an interest in the contemporary and in ourselves as unconsciously to have disassociated them a little from our tradition."[115] In literature the tradition was indeed incomparable: it was both broad and deep, for it included English literature as well as American. Nor was native literature lacking in a rich tradition, and he noted how Sherman had "so copiously" and "so conclusively" demonstrated the importance of and the need for study of the indigenous literature.[116]

The penultimate civilizing forces, then, are society, sentiment, and tradition, but "education is the chief, and education, ideally considered, is distinction itself."[117] "As a social force education is the great leveler—inevitably also leveling up, not down."[118] In America education is general, which is an unmixed blessing, but the innovations made in recent attempts at its liberalization—the elective system, the switch in emphasis from cultural content to "student thinking" and "statistical facts," the emphasis on student activities—were all lessening its centrality and force. Nevertheless, it still remained the brightest and surest hope for the promotion of social cohesion. At its best—and Brownell was thinking of his own well-remembered days at Amherst—there is a "poetry of college life." The college is a "microscopic adumbration of George Sand's 'ideal-life as we shall one day know it,' and points the way to a distinction to which not only is democracy confined but of which it is, here and thus, shown to be capable."[119]

Brownell turns, in the last chapter of his last book, to consider popular culture, both "general" and "aesthetic," and, after a lifetime of rather stringent criticisms of American culture and in the middle of the mournful "hue-and-cry" being raised by other lay preachers, such as Babbitt, in the 'twenties, Brownell found that all was not quite so grim as most of his fellow critics would insist.

In what he called the "general" aspect of popular culture and in the field of education, Brownell said that, although the vocational was overcoming the cultural ideal and thus was leading the college graduate to desire to conform to rather than to ameliorate his group, still, through the agency of the university extension department and the summer school, the "influence of the extended professorate as a whole has become a wide-spread and powerful social force."[120] Broadly speaking, the American scene was alive with all kinds of cultural activities and though "we are still conducting an experiment in its cultural justification [that of our political success] ...,"[121] yet the "promise of our cultural progress is bright for, especially, the reason that it has broadened its basis."[122]

Concerning "aesthetic" culture, so called, Brownell, still a Victorian in great part, took an exceedingly dim view of its modern manifestations. He thought, however, that its failure likewise resulted from the lack of cohesiveness in the culture itself and that there should be a closing of the gap between the aesthete and the mass. Not everyone who aspires is a genius, and the unsuccessful aspirants might well devote themselves to mediating between the minority and the mass: "... if the practise of art among us were to become less general and indiscriminate and at the same time its discriminating public ... were to expand in proportion, the result would be nearly ideal."[123]

But he concluded with two optimistic prophecies that, although seemingly rather fanciful in 1927, have become more and more of an actuality in our own time—the increased use of and respect for good architecture and the more extended interest in good music. Brownell could not have foreseen, of course, what radio and the phonograph would accomplish in this sphere; nevertheless he perceived that music, of all the arts, would most readily approach a popular status. "It is nearer to more people," he said, and could be appreciated without having to be fully understood. The growth of the music-loving public was, it seemed to him, an advance manifestation of that "democratic distinction" that he hoped would someday prevail more generally in a more cohesive American society. (Unconsciously but consistently, he had chosen the word "concert" to describe his ideal social organism.) And at the end of his last book—and of his public career—he said:

Music, in fine, demonstrates the achievement of distinction in appreciation which in one way or another is an inseparable ally in the development of art and, as the field in which perhaps our general aesthetic cultivation has made most progress, best proves the pertinence of popular culture to the distinction which is at once democratic and unimpeachable.[124]

PART TWO

EBB

CHAPTER IV

ARNOLD IN AMERICA: 1895–1930

BESIDES REMOVING the charge of superciliousness from the image of Arnold in America, the reviews of the letters indicated the three main routes which the over-all Arnoldian reputation and influence in America were to travel.

I

The least conspicuous route was that pointed out by Hamilton Wright Mabie in an extraordinarily acute psychological analysis of Arnold as revealed in his letters.[1] Mabie's estimate, which granted Arnold's complexity and attempted to account for it, was an approach that was not to be followed up by critics and historians of literature until the middle part of the twentieth century, particularly with the publication of Trilling's *Matthew Arnold*. Majority criticism in the early twentieth century was generally to take Arnold as a rather vague symbol, luminous or dark, as the case might be.

In 1895 Mabie, of all the reviewers, regarded Arnold as a complicated human being with a many-sided program, rather than as a monolithic museum piece. He mentioned, for example, Arnold's high spirits, which had been lost sight of generally in the welter of rather lugubrious tributes. "A well known English critic," wrote Mabie, "has spoken of [Arnold] as the 'larkiest' writer of his time; and it is certain that he got immense enjoyment out of life and his work." But, Mabie added, the tonic of irony was always there, and usually self-directed, and at bottom there was a profoundly serious, a religious attitude toward experience. "He had great tenacity of temper and a genuinely English ability not only to hold his own but to stand alone." Thus in Arnold's make-up there was a consistent dialectic between an inner strenuous temper and a magically felicitous exterior, between seriousness and gaiety, and underneath both was a unique and inviolable "self." The letters, said Mabie, contain "all the other books in solution," for they reveal "that magic of expression which made him not only one of the most attractive and influential writers of his time, but one of those phrase-makers who give a criticism or a generalization universal currency by packing it into a sentence." Mabie discussed Arnold's methods of attack and concluded that the secret of his success lay in his assumed stance of deprecating ingenuousness. He was the master of tactics and of the flank attack; and with all the attacking he did, it was "astonishing" that he was not more hated than he was. But he always assumed the "light touch." Mabie concluded by remarking upon a trait of character in Arnold that is perhaps at the root of both his life and his writings, that is, the desire, simply, that man have dignity: "[Arnold was] a man who, in holding himself high, invested all his occupations and relations with dignity and sanctity."

A second route for Arnold's reputation was pointed out by *Poet Lore,* an irreverent journal, dedicated, so it said, to manliness and clarity in the arts. Although the attitude of *Poet Lore* toward Arnold was, like that of Mabie's, a minority opinion in the 1890's, it was to become, unlike Mabie's, a majority opinion as the twentieth century unfolded. For to the Butlerian editors of *Poet Lore* Arnold, along with his fellow Victorians, was merely a "stuffed shirt." The reviewer spoke of glimpses of Arnold "mouthing a bun between school inspections."

To the bun side of Arnold these letters plenitudinously bear witness, with their tireless chronicling of every shade of weather and every kind of dinner . . . Juxtapose this Arnold of the bun and the Arnold of the literal fastidious verse, and straightway, as in a thumb nail mirror, the cool-poised critic appears, who well knew how, with just enough adroitness, to lash "Philistine" and "Barbarian" of his supremely beloved Britain toward the particular variety of safe, conservative progress which his own taste approved.[2]

Bidding good-bye to the nineteenth century, *Poet Lore* said: "both Coleridge and Arnold seem already, before the close of the nineteenth century, to belong ... to that antiquated provincial world where the fences are up." Even style is an indication: "The formal, ponderous diction of Coleridge, the pure, colorless exactitude of Arnold, betray the presence of the dawn and high noon of the century ..."

The central Arnold of the late nineteenth and early twentieth century in America, however, was that of the avowed "Arnoldians," who had little opposition in 1895 but who were, within a decade, to be regarded as anachronistic. This Arnold was a great spiritual force, called "The Apostle of Culture," and tributes to this force ranged from the mawkishly sincere to the dignifiedly sincere. Mrs. Florence Coates, in *The Century* in 1894, spoke of her last letter from Arnold. It had been written shortly before he died, and in it he had mentioned the tulip-tree beside her house, where he had stayed. "Five years have passed since those words were written," said Mrs. Coates, "and it is June. Once more I see the maple green, and the tulip-tree in flower—but Lycidas is dead, and hath not left his peer!"[3] Minnie E. Hadley, in a magazine essay on Arnold published in 1902, exclaimed: "A first acquaintanceship with Arnold is like the acquirement of a new soul."[4] More restrained, but still striking the lofty note, was the estimate written by Joseph Henry Crocker, for the *New England Magazine:*[5] "All friends of clear thinking and right living rejoice that Matthew Arnold lived." Also: "He leads us to a mount of vision from which we see how large an estate is true manhood, and how mighty a power is manly religion." John Burroughs said in 1897, in an article on the rereading of books: "There are probably few readers of the critical literature of the times who do not recur again and again to Matthew Arnold's criticism . . .'"⁶

This central traditional image of Arnold was in its way taken over by various peoples and sects for various purposes. For example, it became the guiding star and the central symbol for "culture in the provinces," at its best the ideal for serious effort and thought, at its worst the property of genteel married ladies and clergymen, banded into clubs for the worship of the English heritage.

One of the most interesting of these was the "English Club" at Sewanee, organized in 1885 under the direction of the Reverend Greenough White, Professor of Ecclesiastical History in the University of the South.⁷ The club, "mostly ladies," began with the study of linguistics, but by 1886 was concentrated on literature. After various vicissitudes, suspensions, a brief excursion in 1890 into Browning (where, White says, the members lost their way in the mazes of *Sordello*), the club found itself once more in the study of Tennyson in 1895, and in 1896 studied Elizabeth Barrett Browning. "When at the end of the year," said White, "a subject was sought for ensuing study, which should lead into the heart of our times, . . . none presented itself more eligible than Matthew Arnold."⁸ It turned out to be a good year, and "It was felt that at last, after years of discipline, the Club had reached a point where it might make a little contribution to the culture of the country."⁹ In this project Arnold was central: ". . . ours is an age much given to criticism; its spokesman, naturally, has been the finest critic of his day—Matthew Arnold. As such we have studied him . . ."¹⁰ With Arnold as a "nucleus," the club systematically studied the age: religion, ethics, politics, and literary criticism, with other papers on such subjects as Clough, Meredith, and Mrs. Humphrey Ward. The point of view of the club was Arnold's, namely that what the age needed was good criticism, "the sore need of our time."

The results of the club's efforts were published in book form as *Matthew Arnold and the Spirit of the Age*. The attitude toward Arnold evinced by the individual papers was by no means always admiring. Arnold was deficient in the "fine arts"; he lacked "faith"; he was inferior to his master Sainte-Beuve in objectivity; he was not critically sound in dealing with his own contemporaries (that is, he was not enthusiastic about Browning and Tennyson). Nevertheless, and with all these weaknesses, Arnold was "the last great representative of criticism"[11] and "the master spirit in the literature of the years that have just passed."[12] Above all, his example and his precepts are sorely needed in these days when criticism is in such a pitiably low state, and there is "no master; no lion's roar silences the braying of these critical asses."[13]

Both the recently founded *Sewanee Review* and the New York *Outlook,* whose boast it was that it stood for "righteousness" (it had formerly been the *Christian Union*), looked with approval on Greenough's club. It was, said the *Sewanee,* "an indication of a promising outlook for general culture, especially in the South..."[14] And *The Outlook* mentioned Sewanee as not only "one of the most thriving and promising of our younger universities, but the home of a circle of very cultivated people."[15] To the *Sewanee Review* itself, founded under the editorship of W. P. Trent, a judicious appreciator of Arnold, Arnold seems to have been a symbol and a guide. In a long article on Arnold it said, "He was a great literary critic, doubtless the greatest and safest that the English-speaking race has yet produced..."[16] The author of the article, C. F. Smith, remarked especially on Arnold's persuasiveness: "Arnold's essays on 'The Study of Poetry' and on Wordsworth made me a Wordsworthian."[17] Later, the *Sewanee Review* was to be edited by William A. Knickerbocker, a student and admirer of Arnold, and was to publish articles on Arnold by Ludwig Lewisohn, another critic who had been greatly influenced by Arnold.

Besides being a symbol and a guide for a nonurban cultural center in the South, Arnold was likewise a symbol and a guide for an isolated cultural effort in the urban North, that is, *The Dial* of Chicago. *The Dial,* which was still in its early, conservative, New England-loving, Whitman-hating stage, waved Arnold like a flag in defiance of "low" tendencies in literature and criticism. When Vida Scudder, in her *Social Ideals in English Letters,* ventured to say that Arnold's "message," which for her meant the training of the intellect and nonparticipation in practical affairs, was all right for his own time, 1870 to 1890, but not appropriate any longer (1898),[18] *The Dial* publicly chastised her. W. H. Johnson, in "The 'Passing' of Matthew Arnold," declared, "We are not willing to give up Arnold without a struggle." Arnold had had many detractors in America, said Johnson, "but such attacks really did more good than harm, since they convinced the judicious that the critic's verdict, 'Thou ailest here, and here,' was timely and well-grounded; and an increasing number of Americans went on reading Mr. Arnold's works with profit and enjoyment." So that, far from being relegated to the dustbin of the unusable past, Arnold will become "the reformer of reformers." It is true that the working classes, in their ignorance, are devouring Bellamy's *Looking Backward,* "but here and there will be one of a thousand among them, with keener power of discernment, who will loosen with disgust his hold upon the air-castles of Bellamy and drop to the solid ground of the apostle of *culture . . .*"[19]

Miss Scudder replied to this charge by letter,[20] and claimed that she was trying to point out "the remarkable breadth and depth" of Arnold's social criticism, but she finally equivocated: "The contemporary power of Arnold is rapidly passing away; but already, for some of us, he is uplifted among the illuminating stars."

Meanwhile, in the literary setting of the East, the apostle of culture continued to receive his due, especially as the various books about him, mostly by Englishmen, were published and reviewed. Saintsbury's *Arnold* was violently attacked by *The Nation*[21] for precisely the same reason as that for which Arnold had formerly been attacked by American critics: an air of superiority. "He [Saintsbury] is extremely jaunty and Tory and superior," said *The Nation,* and he had no right to do a book on Arnold since he did not genuinely understand his subject and since he writes so badly. It was not that Arnold was without his detractors in America, but they were in a distinct minority. Only *The Critic,* in a review of Brownell's *Victorian Prose Masters,*[22] questioned the prestige and efficacy of Arnold and revived the old charge that Arnold did not understand America. It was Whitman's picture once more, and for the last time, of an effete, remote "literary dude."

Herbert Paul's book on Arnold, widely reviewed, excited the same comment that Saintsbury's had. For the wheel had come full circle, and the "flippancy" of Paul was deemed unworthy of his august subject, who had become by now one of the untouchables. *The Outlook,*[23] indeed, saw a certain poetic justice in Arnold's having been overtaken by a man who assumed the same "superior attitude" toward him that Arnold had once assumed toward others. But W. P. Trent in *The Forum*[24] characterized the book as "the criticism of nagging." The *Atlantic Monthly,* as always faithfully Arnoldian, said, in the person of H. W. Boynton: "Mr. Paul has undertaken to dispose of Matthew Arnold with the same jaunty confidence which may no doubt have proved a useful asset to the London Daily News."[25] Brownell felt the hurt most deeply, and he said in a review for *The Bookbuyer:* "Foreknowledge of it [Paul's book] might not seriously have disturbed his [Arnold's] Olympian serenity, but must momentarily have made him wince. The fact seems subtly and cunningly, however unjustly, to minimize his importance."[26]

But Edith Wharton, in a review for *The Lamp* in 1903, refused to be disturbed: "Matthew Arnold needs no avenging; he can no more be patronized than he can be snubbed."[27]

The virulence of these reactions to the books of Saintsbury and Paul is hard to understand when one takes into account what the two Englishmen had said about their fellow critic. Saintsbury said that the *Essays in Criticism* was one of the great books of English criticism; in their way Dryden, Johnson, and Coleridge had done "greater things," but nothing more important for us today. Arnold was freshly new and original and was by all odds the most "impressive" voice of his era; "and a great deal of what followed was directly due to him."[28] The *Essays* was an "epoch-making book, as the manual of a new and often independent, but, on the whole, like-minded, critical movement in England."[29] It is true that Saintsbury denigrated Arnold's social and religious excursions as years spent "in the wilderness," but he only rejoiced in Arnold's return to literature in *Mixed Essays,* describing the preface to that work as having points of the highest value:

The opening passage about the *point de repère* itself, the fixed halting-place to which we can always resort for fresh starts, fresh calculations, is one of the great critical *loci* of the world, and especially involves the main contribution of the nineteenth century to criticism if not to literature altogether.[30]

All in all, as critic and poet combined, only Dryden and Coleridge can rank with Arnold.

Paul, likewise, deprecated Arnold's religious and social ventures, and was, indubitably, "flippant," but his praise for Arnold in many respects was almost unqualified. Arnold was, said Paul, "our English Goethe." "Matthew Arnold may be said to have done for literature almost what Ruskin did for art. He reminded, or informed, the British public that criticism was a serious thing."[31] The *Essays in Criticism* was one of the "indispensable books. Not to have read it is to be ignorant of a great intellectual event."[32] Although Arnold's social analysis was over-simplified, and although his religious views were "peculiar,"[33] and although he had his critical limitations, still his criticism was "original, penetrating, lucid, sympathetic, and just. Of all modern poets, except Goethe, he was the best critic."[34]

For the American admirers of Arnold, however, the accompanying disparagement and flippancy was painful, especially when Arnold's social and religious teachings, which had stirred up so much controversy and won so many adherents in the United States, were attacked.

Dawson's *Matthew Arnold and His Relation to the Thought of Our Time* announced in its preface: "There is today a cult of Matthew Arnold; it is growing; it must grow. It will grow.... Briefly the cult of Matthew Arnold is the cult of *idealism* ..."[35] Dawson spent the bulk of his book on Arnold's religion, which he did not like, but his book, being neither crochety nor flippant, was received with great favor by American critics, as was G. W. E. Russell's eminently respectful *Matthew Arnold*. *The Nation*[36] doubted whether there could ever be a "cult" of Matthew Arnold, but *The Dial*,[37] in a review of Russell and Dawson, maintained that there *was* in fact a "Cult of Matthew Arnold." "Few writers," said Edith Rich for *The Dial*, "have been so beloved and appreciated by the literary men of their own time. Their regard was a continual source of wonder, even to him." To the rhetorical question "How did Arnold establish a cult?" she replied:

He was, first of all, the great apostle and exponent of culture; he was the man above all men in his generation who knew the best that has been said and thought in all ages, who "saw life steadily and saw it whole." And through this, he was great as a critic and a man of letters.

The review closed with an exhortation to the readers to peruse

their Arnold. The *Contemporary Review, The Arena, Current
Literature, The Outlook,* the *Atlantic Monthly* (through H. W.
Boynton), and *The Critic,* all reviewing either Dawson or Russell or both, agreed more or less with Dawson's thesis.[38] Both
The Outlook and *The Arena* later explicitly took issue with
Dawson's views on Arnold's religious work and claimed that he
had been a great and beneficent religious force.[39] Robert T. Kerlin, for *The Arena,* said that "while the Churches do not accept
and proclaim the views of Matthew Arnold, yet a large part, and
that the really serious and intelligent part of the Christian world,
hold with him in almost all essential respects."

Arnold, then, his canon almost complete (*Essays in Criticism,*
Third Series, was still to come in 1910), his canonization practically complete, became less and less an immediate issue in
American criticism as the century wore on and became more
one of the hallowed figures of the past. In 1905 Peter A. Sillard,
in the *Atlantic Monthly,*[40] spoke of the reverence that now clung
to the one-time controversial critic. In reference to the first
Essays in Criticism, he asked: "Who is not familiar with them?
Do we not return to them again and again to enjoy their perennial freshness? Many of the truths for recognition of which he
pleaded have since become commonplaces; ... he was one of
the greatest intellectual forces of his century." *The Nation*[41] in
1907 disagreed with James Dixon's *Matthew Arnold.* Dixon, a
Scottish-born educator and a Methodist who had for some time
lived in America, accused Arnold of being a doubter and a sceptic. Against Dixon's charge, *The Nation* quoted with approval
R. H. Hutton's assertion that Arnold's religious position had
expressed precisely the dilemmas of his generation: "No one
has expressed more powerfully and poetically its spiritual weakness, its craving for a passion it cannot feel, its admiration for
a self-mastery that it cannot achieve, its desire for a creed that
it fails to accept."

Pronouncements about Arnold now took on a ritualistic flavor, with all specific disagreements forgotten. In 1908 *The Nation*,[42] which had industriously and specifically disagreed with Arnold throughout most of his lifetime, published an essay called "Matthew Arnold Twenty Years After" in which it paid him this tribute:

Arnold, we now see clearly enough, was the most competent English critic of the latter nineteenth century. His strength lay in the fact that he did not deal in mere casual and shallow impressionism: he tried to go back to first principles and build up from fundamentals.

In that same year *The Dial*[43] said that Arnold had been perhaps *too* good for his own reputation: "It may be against the permanence of Arnold's criticism, that it was too effective—that it was caught up and absorbed in the thinking of the day. Once read, Arnold cannot be forgotten..."

Of Arnold's last posthumous work, *Essays in Criticism,* Third Series, *The Nation*,[44] now gone completely sentimental, said in the person of Stuart P. Sherman that here "is a title to wake any reviewer from his lethargy, and, indeed, the volume...is one of the precious things of the season." Even the slightest sketches are "in the master's true vein." But there was not much excitement generally over the publication of the *Essays,* nor were there many reviews. The wave of anti-Victorianism in America had long since gathered its force, and was soon to try to sweep away a century, the nineteenth. Fresh new critics, like Mencken and Brooks, were opening their careers. Huneker had for years been preaching a kind of cosmopolitanism that was avowedly Continental and non-English. New prophets spoke, new sirens beckoned, and Arnold, who had overcome almost every obstacle that had blocked his attempt to speak to the American literary world, at last fell victim to that iron and irrevocable judgment by which each generation, in the strength of its youth, sentences its immediate predecessors—indifference.

II

As Arnold moved back into time, he soared up into space, becoming in that process both exalted and dim, a great misty figure in that long line of saints, the culture heroes of literature. He became *the* preëminent academic critic. All the great Victorian authors had become standard subjects for study in college curricula in the late nineteenth century. Arnold, however, was not only a subject to be studied but a prophet to be heeded, and the professor himself was more likely than not an "Arnoldian." Yet even in this academic domain, Arnold's preëminence, although it was never wholly lost, was being questioned in the early years of the twentieth century, if not by the professors at least by the students.

Some indication of what had happened to Arnold's reputation among the young during the early years of the present century is indicated by the differing reminiscences of Logan Pearsall Smith, Ellery Sedgwick, and Christopher Morley. For Smith, at Harvard in the 1880's, Arnold was "... the most humane, the most European and least provincial of all English authors, whose outlook is still our outlook, who still speaks to us with contemporary accents."[45] Ellery Sedgwick, just before he entered Harvard in the 1890's, confessed that "... the criteria of Matthew Arnold were secretly woven into all my literary enthusiasms." At Harvard, however, he began to feel "differently."[46] But Christopher Morley, who graduated from Haverford in 1910, remembered Arnold only as a vague collection of undergraduate notes: "... Arnold has never been more than an interesting and gracious wraith in our mind."[47]

At the same time, scholars and critics in their professional endeavors began the long analysis of his work, seeking both to assess him historically and to analyze him objectively, a process which is still continuing and will no doubt continue for some time to come.

In the area of active criticism, the area in which Arnold had played such a predominant role in the 'eighties and 'nineties, he moved from the foreground to the background. The wonder is, not that he moved back as far as he did, but rather that he was actually as relevant to as many differing kinds of critics as he turned out to be. For the forces working against what he stood for, or what he is supposed to have stood for, were considerable.

In a general way he suffered in the all-inclusive demise of the Victorian era itself, although, it should be added, not nearly so much as did some of his eminent contemporaries, such as George Eliot. But Arnold himself suffered the ultimate fate, a portrait by Strachey, who said there should be a club formed for "the hushing up of Matthew Arnold."[48] In this general eclipse Arnold was but one small unit in a vast, multiform change of the Time-Spirit, a profound rejection which the centuries bestow upon one another, in order to render the ancestor harmless and ineffectual. So innocuous had Arnold become that by 1922, on his centenary, even the *Catholic World,* always in the nineteenth century anti-Arnold, could look upon the apostle of culture with benignity. In that year it published two articles which, though making reservations about the Biblical criticism, celebrated the literary and cultural criticism and the poetry of Arnold, and, indeed, held them up as an example for correcting the sins of contemporary criticism.[49]

More specifically, Arnold had become, on one side, a traditional conservative figurehead, associated with England in the world scene and with New England in the domestic scene. Thus when T. S. Eliot wished to evoke the aged Brahmin spirit he chose "Matthew" to stand beside "Waldo" as one of the twin guardians of the "eternal law." For Arnold was by now (*circa* 1917) the patron saint of a class that Mencken described contemptuously, in an attack on Brownell's *Standards,* as "the native, white, Protestant *Gelehrten* ..."[50] It was this side of

Arnold, the Protestant English gentleman, that was to be relegated to the outermost limbo.

In the first place, the rapid immigration in the last half of the nineteenth century of other ethnic strains than Anglo-Saxon had made it more and more possible, as the twentieth century wore on, to think of culture as not something exclusively the property of the English. In the second place, there was, during, before, and after World War I, an outbreak of virulent Anglophobia, which contained some potentialities for an actual conflict between the two nations. Third, on the domestic scene there was a continuing reaction, in cultural matters, against New England, which was commonly supposed to be the closest to the mother country and to be an embodiment of its preoccupations. The moral tradition in criticism, according to Joel Spingarn, "from Sidney to Matthew Arnold, finds its last stronghold today among the American descendants of the Puritans."[51] The "new" literature, both in prose and poetry, came mostly out of the Middle West, and determinedly so; and Macy's significant, if not seminal, *Spirit of American Literature* was avowedly Anglophobic. Randolph Bourne's attack on "This Older Generation" was aimed directly at "... the eternal verities of Protestant religion and conventional New England morality."[52] In the whole reinterpretation of American literature which was to culminate in Parrington's great work, Arnold, along with the New England tradition, suffered an eclipse, like the Victorians. And Arnold became generally associated with that transatlantic Anglo–New England aristocratic world of Henry James and Edith Wharton, reputedly so far removed both from life and from the realities of the American scene and so close to extinction. "All our roots were dead now," wrote Malcolm Cowley in *Exile's Return,* "even the Anglo-Saxon tradition of our literary ancestors, even the habits of slow thrift that characterized our social class."[53]

Huneker, and after him, Mencken, had been for some time preaching a kind of cosmopolitanism which was quite different from that of Arnold, going to foreign authors not for their antiquity but for their modernity, not for wisdom but for iconoclasm, not for a "message" but for aesthetic reaction. Moreover, Huneker's Europe was the world of Strindberg, Shaw, Nietzsche, and Gorky, and not the Europe of Spinoza, Goethe, Joubert, and George Sand. Huneker's critical interests, like Mencken's, were much more catholic than those of Arnold, and included painting and music as well as literature. He seemed to open up a world of color, forms, and sound, such as Arnold with his notorious indifference to the fine arts and his tacit assumption that art *was* the printed page, never could.

The explicit clashes between what Arnold stood for and what the critics of America were up to in the early twentieth century are manifest. In the whole fight against the sexual taboo and for honesty about the private life, Arnold, who had glanced askance at Shelley's peccadillos, not only was irrelevant but was one of the enemy. "The priggish Arnold," V. F. Calverton labeled him, in an ironically entitled chapter "The Viceless Victorians" in his *Sex Expression in Literature.*[54] The exploration of the night side of experience, in life and literature, that was to be conceptualized in the name of Freud was again something utterly foreign to the aims of the critic who had said:

No one has a stronger and more abiding sense than I have of the "daemonic" element—as Goethe called it—which underlies and encompasses our life; but I think, as Goethe thought, that the right thing is, while conscious of the element, and of all that there is inexplicable round one, to keep pushing on one's posts into the darkness, and to establish no post that is not perfectly in light and firm. One gains nothing on the darkness by being, like Shelley, as incoherent as the darkness itself.[55]

Arnold's interest in social matters and his political liberalism were to run into a generation of writers who tended either to

veer away from all social considerations or to plunge, in the
other direction, into a complex sociology which was the avowed
enemy of Arnold's kind of liberalism.

The whole tenor of Arnold's thought, with its emphasis on
discipline, patience, and the recognition of limitation, was foreign to an age that was, both before and after the war, expansive,
romantic, undisciplined, to say the least. Mencken, for example,
was fond of shaking his fist at the deities whom Arnold tried to
propitiate by high thought and right action. Just previous to the
war, and particularly in the so-called poetic Renaissance, there
was a feeling in the American literary world akin to that experienced by Wordsworth and Coleridge on the eve of the French
Revolution. Old worlds had died, and a new one was being born
to which the old gods were irrelevant. Huneker said in 1910:
"The artist who turns his face only to the past—his work will
never be anything but an echo. To depict the faces and things
and pen the manners of the present is the task of great painters
and novelists. Actualists alone count in the future."[56] Coupled
to this attitude, in the Huneker-Mencken line, was a carefree
outlook that applauded its own vagaries and gloried in its own
prejudices. At the end of *Promenades of an Impressionist*
Huneker proclaimed: "...I have promenaded my dearest prejudices, my most absurd illusions."[57] Mencken, much more in-
fluentially, propounded the same brand of breeziness. Speaking
of the atmosphere of the 'twenties itself, Edmund Wilson
described the literary life of the period as a curious blend of
"nonsense and inspiration, reckless idealism and childish irresponsibility..."[58] In this kind of atmosphere, it hardly needs
saying, the sober, if ironic, spirit of Arnold was of little consequence. And later, after World War I, was to come the explicit
and telling attack of Eliot on Arnold, rejecting "spirit" in the
name of "letter."

With all these forces at work against him, it would seem that

Arnold's very survival would be problematical, yet exactly the reverse is true. More than any other nineteenth-century critic he was relevant to the issues of American criticism during the early twentieth century, and more than any other nineteenth-century critic he was invoked as authority and archetype. And if he had seemed to have departed by the main entrance, he kept coming back through the side doors. For example, Christopher Morley, who, as noted, had only the vaguest recollection of Arnold from his college days, was struck with a "shock of excitement"[59] upon accidentally coming across *Civilization in the United States* in later years. Although he disagreed with much of what Arnold had to say, he quoted a long and highly complimentary description of Arnold, supposedly written by a "mysterious correspondent," and concluded: "If a man, one hundred years after his birth, still evokes such graceful and pensive homage, he has evidently some durable claim upon our hearts."[60]

The most remarkable aspect of Arnold's career at this time is the number of different, often diverse, routes that he traveled: toward Impressionism, toward its opposite, Humanism, and toward *its* opposite, Liberalism. Everybody, it seems, could find some kind of sanction or implication in the Arnoldian doctrines. As Ludwig Lewisohn said in *The Nation,* in 1922: "We all talk Arnold, think Arnold, preach and propagate Arnold."[61] Although this blanket assertion may be an overestimation, one can hardly begin to explore the individual critics of the time or analyze the larger patterns without finding Arnold as either percept or precept.

It was Paul Elmer More who first noticed the biological line, later reëmphasized at greater length by Eliot, between Arnold and Pater. Although More had a great respect for Arnold generally, he thought that Arnold's method, when used by less moral critics, was insidious. Arnold's dictum to know the best, with its emphasis on "appreciation," was a step in the direction of Pater's epicureanism and refined sensationalism: "Yet withal it remains true that the Epicureanism of Pater and the hedonism of Oscar Wilde were able to connect themselves in a disquieting way with one side of Matthew Arnold's gospel of culture."[62] As early as 1900 it seems to have been supposed by some American critics that Arnold had furthered, although not wholly practiced, impressionistic criticism. Arnold's avowed dislike of philosophizing and theorizing supplemented this conception.

Lewis E. Gates, Harvard professor and critical theorist, was the first American critic to attempt to formulate a serious and complete theoretical basis for what he called "appreciation," which was essentially Impressionism with the historical factor added. Gates, who was an admirer of Arnold, published a selection of Arnold's prose in 1897, and in his introduction said: "It is, then, as an appreciator of what may perhaps be called the spiritual qualities of literature that Arnold is most distinctly a furtherer of criticism."[63] In *Studies and Appreciations* (1900) Gates issued his theoretical manifesto of "appreciative" criticism, in the essay "Impressionism and Appreciation." Pater, of course, was the real hero in Gates's eyes, and Gates regretted the fact that Arnold had so busied himself with political and social preoccupations. Nevertheless, Arnold's advocacy of "detachment" was essentially sound, and, in general, he was on the right track: "The popular legend that places Matthew Arnold at the head of this critical tradition in England is at least partly true; he certainly cared more for the shade and sought more patiently to define it, than any earlier English critic."[64] But Gates thought that the efforts of Arnold and Pater and other Impressionists were miniscule compared to the profound urge in the human psyche itself, which aspired in an ever-increasing fashion toward "appreciation" of art.

In 1910 Spingarn, the student of Croce, ruled out even the historical consideration when he set forth the principles of his "expressionism" in *The New Criticism*. Like Arnold, Spingarn was aggrandizing the critical function itself, and went as far as equating it to the creative. In his view, the critical process, which in effect reduplicated the creative process, was a creative act itself. "Criticism can at last free itself from its age-long self-contempt, now that it may realize that aesthetic judgment and artistic creation are instinct with the same vital life."[65] The work of Arnold, along with that of Goethe and Carlyle, had been a step in the right direction in this elevation of the critical process to a "creative function." Unfortunately, Arnold actually "meant merely that criticism created the intellectual atmosphere of the age—a social function of high importance, perhaps, yet wholly independent of aesthetic significance."[66] Like Gates, then, Spingarn thought that Arnold was on the right track, but that his interest in social and political elucidations barred him from the ranks of the true and elect.

At the same time Arnold was being cited as authority and reference, but again not being admitted finally to the inner sanctum, by the Impressionists' enemy, the so-called New Humanists. The arguments, disagreements, and reciprocity between Arnold's ideas and those of the New Humanists are complex and innumerable. In Arnold, because of his strictures on the Romantics and on the Elizabethans, his concern with moral values, his reverence for the classics, his notion that literature is a criticism of life, his analysis of the Philistine and of modern civilization, his concern for the "remnant," his desire for a qualitative rather than a quantitative democracy, and his refusal to confound man and nature, the Humanists saw an ally and proper ancestor. Certainly, as More said, Arnold was in the great tradition, with Cicero, Erasmus, Boileau, Shaftesbury, and Sainte-Beuve:

These are the exemplars ... of what may be called the critical spirit: discriminators between the false and the true, the deformed and the normal; preachers of harmony and proportion and order, prophets

of the religion of taste. If they deal much with the criticism of literature, this is because in literature more manifestly than anywhere else
life displays its infinitely varied motives and results; and their practise is always to render literature itself more consciously a criticism of
life.[67]

There were profound differences, however, between Arnold and
the Humanists.

According to More, both he and Babbitt considered themselves
primarily moralists rather than literary critics or men of letters.[68]
Their preoccupation with ethics had arisen from a study of
Oriental literature in their student days at Harvard. Babbitt's
ethical doctrines, according to More, were arrived at from a
study of Buddhism. Later on, this was to be supplemented by
the study of Aristotle, who, for Babbitt, became the greatest of
ethical teachers. More, on the other hand, derived his ethics
from a study of Sanskrit, particularly the *Upanishads* and the
Bhagavad Gita. Gradually, More worked over to Platonism,
which he supplemented with Christian theology.

Both Babbitt and More had particular objections to Arnold
as a literary critic and as a moral teacher. Comparing Arnold to
his Victorian contemporaries, Babbitt[69] expressed the judgment
that Arnold's criticism was excellent and unique for his age, in
that Arnold's outlook was "positive"—that is, his mind refused
to take anything purely on authority—and "humanistic"—in
that he believed in the dualism of human nature and was concerned with morals. All this was to Arnold's credit. But, thought
Babbitt, Arnold was too vague, in that he never gave precise
or even tenable definitions for his famous phrases, like "grand
style" or "touchstones." This failing was attributable to an underlying Romanticism in Arnold which instinctively shied away
from the precise. Arnold's attempt to make poetry a substitute
for religion Babbitt regarded as "dubious." In his religious writings Arnold was mistaken in ruling out "the pure supernatural
light" of the genuine religious spirit.

More's objections to Arnold were similar. Besides being an unwitting precursor of Impressionism, Arnold failed on the religious side for lack of having any mystical insight and a binding and positive philosophy that would have brought his moral and aesthetic senses together. Arnold's picture of himself as "wandering between two worlds" More regarded as a sign of confusion. Although Arnold expressed the inadequacies of his age perfectly, he should have risen above them with a solution of his own.[70]

Even beyond these specific points of disagreement, the Humanists and Arnold were in many ways worlds apart. Both Babbitt and More were more learned and scholarly than Arnold, more concerned, in More's case anyway, with the supernatural sphere, more philosophical and logical; and, finally, not only were they not liberals, they were consciously antiliberal.

In the eyes of many of the followers of Babbitt and More, Arnold was regarded as almost but not quite one of the saints in the hierarchy. Norman Foerster, assessing Arnold as literary critic in 1922, declared that Arnold's judgment on the Romantics was "conclusive," and, applying the same criterion to American literature, from that of the Transcendentalists to the literature of his own day, he said: "Like Byron, Shelley, Wordsworth, [American writers] do not know enough."[71] But Robert Shafer, the most devout and vociferous follower of More, regarded Arnold as signally lacking in the *sine qua non* for Humanists, a genuinely religious outlook: "The whole weight of human experience,"[72] wrote Shafer, was against him.

If it might be said that the Impressionists took as their heritage from Arnold his sensibility, and that the Humanists appropriated his morality, then the liberal critics—those interested in the "usable" past—assumed the cultural stance of Arnold and adopted or adapted his methodology, and in the great critical debate of the 'twenties Arnold was used again and again by all

parties and factions. In some ways, of course, since he represented Europe and the past, Arnold was the enemy in the eyes
of those who were looking for native traditions. According to
Randolph Bourne, Arnold's call to culture was peculiarly effective in America, much more so than it ever could have been in
England, where a rich traditional culture could be taken for
granted. Americans had next to nothing to take for granted;
and so they avidly seized upon the cultural ideal of Arnold: "It
was Matthew Arnold, read and reverenced by a generation im-
mediately preceding our own [Bourne was born in 1886], who
set to our eyes a definition and a goal of culture which has become the common property of all our world."[73] Bourne attributed
Arnold's efficacy to the clarity of his ideal; there was nothing
vague or shadowy about knowing "the best that has been thought
and said." Moreover, it was a democratic ideal, one which every
man, if he had the will, could realize. Coming as it did when
America was producing a great leisure class hungry for culture,
Arnold's program met with a large and eager audience. According to its progenitor, this magic culture was a process of pure
acquisition; contact with the classics was the only necessity. The
underlying motive in the American mind that attracted the intellectuals to Arnold was what Bourne called our "cultural humility." The breathlessness that young Henry James had felt in
the presence of European civilization was an exaggerated version
of this humility. Bourne concluded that Arnold's influence was
ultimately pernicious, in that it bred in the American mind a
preoccupation with the "best," with the result that Americans
were so busy reverencing the European past that they neglected
the American present. To Arnold, too, Bourne attributed the
reluctance of academic people to deal with contemporary literature; instead they preferred to continue canonizing the "best"
of the past in the Arnoldian manner.

The attitude of Bourne's friend and fellow critic Van Wyck Brooks was likewise colored by the idea of Arnold's excessive gentility and its connection with decaying Protestant Anglo-Saxon–New England culture. "Aesthetic Boston," said Brooks in *New England: Indian Summer,* "preferred to talk about Europe, and especially England. For they agreed with Matthew Arnold that America was not 'interesting' and that for lovers of 'elevation' the sky there was of brass and iron."[74] Brooks also repeated Bourne's criticism of our "cultural humility," played upon by Arnold. But in the last of his pentad we find Brooks using Matthew Arnold as a club against T. S. Eliot, and citing Arnold as being wisely aware of the dangers in the Toryism of the Church of England and of the dangers of general economic inequality; "and," adds Brooks, "his time was not like Eliot's time when the mere existence of inequality had placed the European system in mortal peril."[75]

The early Brooks, the Brooks of *America's Coming-of-Age,* was, as he himself recognized, an Arnoldian. Although a literary man like Arnold, he had turned, like the Englishman, to social criticism, for, as he explained in the preface to *The History of a Literary Radical:* "If our literary criticism is always impelled sooner or later to become social criticism, it is certainly because the future of our literature and art depends upon the wholesale reconstruction of a social life . . ."[76] Like Arnold and Brownell, Brooks was possessed by the root idea of the social cause and nature of everything and was convinced that only a harmonious social background could produce harmonious individuals: ". . . the mind can work healthily only when it is essentially in touch with the society of its own age."[77] Of his own aims and those of his fellow liberals he said, "To quicken and exhilarate the life of one's own people—as Heine and Nietzsche did in Germany, as Matthew Arnold, William Morris, and H. G. Wells have done in England—is to bring, not peace, but a sword."[78]

Moreover, Brooks's own criticism adopted the form, if not the content, of Arnold's, although there are naturally echoes of the latter, too. The central thesis of Brooks in *America's Coming-of-Age* was the very one made familiar by Arnold and his admirers, that American culture had no "centre" and hence was split into divergent extremes. The real villain was Protestantism, equivalent to Arnold's Hebraism, which in its American home and in the name of Puritanism had effected various splits between action and intellect, the concrete and the abstract, real and ideal, the low and the high. In *The Wine of the Puritans,* Brooks phrased the idea metaphorically: "You put the old wine [European culture] into new bottles [the American setting],... and when the explosion results, one may say, the aroma passes into the air and the wine spills on the floor. The aroma, or the ideal, turns into Transcendentalism and the wine, or the real, becomes commercialism."[79] In modern times the vast, unbridgeable chasm was symbolized by the difference in attitude between "High Brow" and "Low Brow," each an unnatural extreme. What we need, said Brooks, echoing Arnold, James, and Brownell, is a "centre": "How much talent goes to waste every day, it seems, simply because there is no criticism, no standards, no authority to trip it up and shake it and make it think!"[80]

Brooks's central purpose was thus precisely what Arnold said was the purpose of criticism in "The Function of Criticism at the Present Time," namely "to create a situation." As Brooks said in *Letters and Leadership:*

In a famous essay Matthew Arnold said that it is "the business of the critical power to see the object as in itself it really is." If any of our critics had been able to act upon this principle, if they had been able to put aside their prepossessions and merely open their minds to the facts of American life, even without attempting any of the more heroic measures our life notoriously demands, I think the predicament of the younger generation would be far less grave than it is. For, as Arnold goes on to say, by seeing the object as in itself it really is, criticism "tends to make an intellectual situation of which the creative power can profitably avail itself." There, surely, is the very thing that Young America needs.[81]

For, "it has been the joyous prerogative of criticism to be on the spot when thoughts are being born."[82] This attitude, coupled to a political liberalism, made Brooks, even if unwittingly, remarkably similar to Arnold. Of course it needed no Arnold to show Brooks the way to the central humanistic position that he was occupying. Nevertheless Arnold was the greatest critic who had taken such a stand in relatively recent times. It is true that the beating of the bourgeoisie was likewise an ancient game—some of Chaucer's satiric targets are bourgeois—but again, Arnold had performed this service closest in time to the twentieth century, and he was dealing with conditions more similar to those of Brooks's day than were, say, those of Flaubert's. Furthermore, he had given a name that had stuck, "the Philistine."

That Arnold had, so to speak, got there first with the most was recognized explicitly by Ludwig Lewisohn, who was one of the leaders in the critical debate of the 'twenties. Lewisohn's personal debt to Arnold he tells in his autobiography:

My father discovered the volume containing Culture and Anarchy and Friendship's Garland and urged me to read it. I felt the impact of a kindred mind and the book became one of my deepest experiences, although its full import was revealed to me only years later. I read all of Arnold over and over again and I still think him the clearest-souled Englishman of his century.[83]

In *Cities and Men* (1927) Lewisohn asked the rhetorical question, "Why does nobody any more mention Arnold's name, when only recently every 'good liberal' was quoting him?" He replied that Arnold had become completely absorbed;[84] for

Arnold had already said everything that the critics of the 'twenties were saying:

> He discovered Main Street; he discovered Babbitt; he discovered Mr. Mencken's neo-Puritans, reformers, hundred-percenters.[85]

> How tonic it would be to have all our warm young liberals reread *Culture and Anarchy* ... and *Friendship's Garland* ...[86]

> He knew then what recent history has proved through blood and fire. Nothing can save the world except that "free play of the mind" for which he was always pleading ...[87]

And this was what American critics of the liberal persuasion were attempting to do in the first decade of the twentieth century:

> It is Arnold's perception that liberal American criticism shares; it is his task that we seek here to accomplish. The world has changed; the philosophical background of our effort is not quite his. But our aim is his own, the aim "of making human life, hampered by a past it has outgrown, natural and rational."[88]

Likewise, Robert Morss Lovett, at one time an editor of the liberal *New Republic,* stressed Arnold's influence as a liberal and even saw him as a progenitor of socialism. Because Arnold had seen that private property was the great obstacle to social wealth, he "is in line with the thought that is replacing the liberalism of the nineteenth century with the socialism through which alone democracy can survive."[89]

Beyond the explicit parallels and debts, such as have been evinced in the writings of Brooks, Lewisohn, and Lovett, two other general points in respect to Arnold's services were made by critics in the critical furor of the 'twenties. First, it was said, as it had been said so many times before, that he had elevated criticism by bringing it up to and close to the creative function. John Macy, in "The Critical Game," an essay presented along with many other essays in James Bowman's *Contemporary*

American Criticism, said: "Every man who plays with literature at all must be ambitious to succeed in some form of art that may be called 'creative,' as distinct from critical—a distinction which, since Arnold taught us our lesson, we know does not exist."[90]

The other Arnoldian precept in critics' minds was the idea that criticism "creates the situation." William Drake, in the introduction to his anthology *American Criticism, 1926,* claimed that contemporary American critics were putting this precept into practice: "Criticism, says Matthew Arnold, 'tends to make an intellectual situation of which the creative power can profitably avail itself.' It is precisely this that contemporary criticism, in its uncertain and prodigal way, is actually accomplishing."[91] Norman Foerster in his *American Critical Essays* made the same point: "... the critical movement is attracting more and more writers and readers to the effort to achieve an 'intellectual situation' capable of sustaining a new creative movement"[92]—and the New Humanists themselves, of whom Foerster counted himself one, were attempting to carry on "the premature effort of Arnold."[93]

That other famous dictum of Arnold's, that poetry would replace religion, did not concern many of the critics of the first decades of the twentieth century, except the Humanists, who rejected it. It did, however, engage the attention of one of America's great solitaries, George Santayana, who in his early days was an Arnoldian. Speaking of his undergraduate years at Harvard, Santayana tells how deeply *Gods of Greece* influenced him: "Perhaps Matthew Arnold moved in the background and inspired us,"[94] and, "as for English poets we admitted nobody less revolutionary than Swinburne or less pessimistic than Matthew Arnold."[95] In an earlier autobiographical sketch he said that he derived his concept of the historical spirit of the nineteenth century from reading the *Revue des Deux Mondes* and the works of Taine and Arnold.[96] According to his biographer George Howgate, "Santayana's attitude toward wealth, industry, athletics, in general, the whole machinery of life, is anticipated in Matthew Arnold, at times in very similar language."[97] Again, Howgate says, "Arnold is the nearest to Santayana because he exerted the most influence over Santayana's youth—this despite Santayana's recent derogatory remarks about Arnold."[98] Arnold's exaltation of poetry as prophecy, his scorn for Philistinism, his deference to the Greeks, his use of irony and lyricism in argument, even his disparagement of Shakespeare and his praise of Leopardi, are all found in Santayana's own work.[99] The thought of the two men met at the most profound level in an admiration for Spinoza, a distrust of formal metaphysics, and a respect for the poetry of Catholicism. But there were naturally great differences, too, between the detached Spanish-American philosopher and the committed English literary critic, as is evidenced by Santayana's attack upon Arnold's estimate of Shelley. To Santayana, the detached thinker, Arnold seemed much too much involved with *things*. "It is the soul of observant persons, like Matthew Arnold, that is apt not to be quite sane and whole inwardly, but somewhat warped by familiarity with the perversities of real things, and forced to misrepresent its true ideal, like a tree bent by too prevalent a wind."[100]

The two men most closely approximated each other in that area where poetry and religion are supposed to meet, and Santayana's *Interpretations of Poetry and Religion* (1900) carries on Arnold's argument into the twentieth century. In his preface Santayana announced his theme:

This idea is that religion and poetry are identical in essence, and differ merely in the way in which they are attached to practical affairs.[101]

The moral function of the imagination and the poetic nature of religion form, then, the theme of the following pages.[102]

The book itself is simultaneously an apotheosis of the Greek civilization, in which poetry and religion were actually one, and an indictment of the moderns, who have lapsed into "barbarism"—Santayana's word for Arnold's "Philistinism"—of which the minds of Browning and Whitman, inchoate, unintelligent, and tasteless, are good examples. For poetry has lost its religious function, that is, its interpretative power.

"The highest poetry, then, is not that of the versifiers, but that of the prophets, or of such poets as interpret verbally the visions which the prophets have rendered in action..."[103]

Santayana, however, pointed out the differences between the two activities, and certainly did not make so close an equivalence as did Arnold. He also severed poetry from conduct: "Religion is poetry become the guide of life, poetry substituted for science or supervening upon it as an approach to the highest reality. Poetry is religion allowed to drift, left without points of application in conduct..."[104]

But Santayana was a lone wolf, and has engendered no train of followers. Arnold's speculations on the interrelations between poetry and religion excited no great interest in the minds of American critics for at least the first three decades of the present century, which were largely given over to sociological considerations and quarrels about America's "destiny." Arnold was, however, to recruit one more direct and ardent disciple—Stuart P. Sherman.

CHAPTER V

STUART P. SHERMAN

STUART P. SHERMAN was the last Arnoldian in the direct nineteenth-century tradition of James and Brownell. He was the least distinguished of the three intellectually, and by his rather confused career he represents the passing of that tradition into moribundity. For Sherman's idea of Arnold was too simple and his reaction to him too direct. Indeed, his whole intellectual position was too shaky and insecure, and his relation to the realities of his own time too ambiguous, to enable him to maintain adequate vigor in his own career. If Arnold was a stimulating critic to James, and a provocative thinker for Brownell, he had become in the mind of Sherman a sacrosanct personality, one of those holy spirits out of the past, to be set up on a pedestal and uncritically worshiped. It is significant, too, that Sherman was an academician: thus Arnold had passed from a revolutionary creative writer, to a rather conservative critic, to, finally, a university professor. Arnold had become institutionalized and had suffered the fate that such a procedure at times entails. One aspect of this fate was Sherman's famous class in Matthew Arnold, which he gave for many years at the University of Illinois. Sherman's Arnoldianism was, of course, symptomatic, and illustrative of the fact that Arnold had captured the academic mind. Indeed, the fervor with which Sherman "preached" Arnoldian doctrines—there is no other adequate word to describe the process—would indicate that Arnold had become the Plato for the modern academy.

Sherman was engaged in a conscious and, in his own view, successful endeavor to carry on the critical tradition of James and Brownell, the latter being in Sherman's mind the most eminent of contemporary critics. Like Brownell, and like

Arnold himself, Sherman was trying to mediate between culture and democracy, between tradition and the present. His whole career, which involved various shifts, from Humanist to modernist, from university professor to book reviewer, falls into a pattern if it be kept in mind that the central preoccupations of his thought were "culture" and "democracy," and that his various changes in outlook are not so much a rejection of one for the other but rather involve a shift of emphasis between the two poles. The early Sherman seems to have been more alive to the claims of traditional culture; the later Sherman, more concerned with the progress of egalitarian democracy. But in all phases of his career Sherman kept Arnold, along with Brownell, as exemplar and guide.

Like Brownell before him, Sherman has provided us with his own sketch of American criticism and his own idea of the tradition that he was working in. Although he wrote no extended criticism of Poe, Sherman still would seem to have considered Poe no adequate predecessor, from his incidental remarks on the subject. Reviewing Brownell's *American Prose Masters,* Sherman expressed approval of Brownell's critical method, with its vigorous and thorough appraisal, each author being required to meet certain tests set up by Brownell himself: "... if [the writer] fails ... as Poe does, no seductions of style nor brilliance of ratiocinative power can save him; he leaves the court with only the rags of his honors."[1]

Sherman regarded Emerson as the first great apostle of culture. "In many respects he remains our greatest critic, our most fecundating and creative mind in the field of letters."[2] But, Sherman continued, Emerson established his point of view and developed his critical methods before the main results of the intellectual effort of the nineteenth century were fully accessible; consequently, Emerson "dated" rapidly as the century wore on. By 1870, Sherman pointed out, C. E. Norton was lamenting the fact that Emerson was declining and that no American critic was rising to take his place. With the increasing complexity of life and art, there was need for a reflective and rational intelligence, rather than the intuitive perceptions of Emerson. Norton had hoped that Lowell would satisfy this need, but in Norton's opinion Lowell had failed. Sherman himself summed up Lowell thus:

A genial and lovable man, Lowell was a fine example of American manhood; yet in the eyes of one of the friends who loved him best he was something too much of the flattered don, of the self-indulgent antiquarian, and of the plausible after-dinner speaker ever to feel the necessity of bringing himself and his culture thoroughly abreast of the modern world.[3]

Accordingly, the next generation of critics, men like Brownell, had to turn to Europe for guidance—to Arnold, to Sainte-Beuve, Taine, Ruskin, and Pater—for those "quickening catchwords" [and here Sherman lists all the familiar Arnoldian phrases], " 'conscience in intellectual matters,' 'study of perfection,' 'urbanity,' 'amenity,' 'sweet reasonableness,' 'grand style,' 'Hellenism,' 'curiosity,' 'free play of mind,' and 'the rest.' " Of Brownell's position in this evolving tradition Sherman concluded: "He does not begin where Lowell left off; his first book, *French Traits,* published in the year following Arnold's death, begins where Arnold left off."[5] Before Sherman arrived at this conception, he had gone to Harvard, had been exposed to Babbitt and later to More, and had become, for a time, an ardent Humanist. It was the doctrines and examples of Brownell and Arnold that lured him later from Humanism.

I

In the early works of Sherman one can find all the familiar Humanist doctrines—the distinction between "law for man" and "law for thing"; the preference for "representative man" over "individual man"; the necessity for an appeal to authority; the necessity for obedience to "the inner check"; and the deep distrust of Romanticism and its offspring, Naturalism. Sherman's first book, *Matthew Arnold: How to Know Him,* and his second, *On Contemporary Literature,* were both conceived on accepted Humanistic principles. In his review of Sherman's *Arnold,* Irving Babbitt, the master, set his seal of approval on the book: "Two or three good articles on Matthew Arnold have been written, notably that by Mr. W. C. Brownell in his *Victorian Prose Masters,* but Professor Sherman has the distinction of writing the first good book."[6]

The preface to *On Contemporary Literature* reads like a Humanist manifesto. In spite of Dewey and the relativists, said Sherman, one cannot abandon the notion of absolute values and the notion that humanity is now and will always be progressing toward them. But the world today is "the worst of all possible worlds" because "lust and law" are now alike. This confounding of dissimilar things is the logical outcome of the Naturalistic philosophy that has been subtly and slowly, but inexorably, encroaching upon all fields of knowledge and all human activities. The fruits of Naturalism are relativism and the repudiation of all standards. Nowadays, one makes one's truth as one needs it.[7] All this is ultimately the fault of Romanticism, the progenitor of Naturalism. The great revolutionary task of the nineteenth century was to put man into nature; the great task of twentieth-century thinkers is to get him out again, and this the Humanists propose to do.[8] Man is now living on the natural level, according to the "law for things"; he must be raised to the human level and must live by "the law for man." Quoting Babbitt, Sherman says that man must once more develop his "inner check," the will to refrain. Since this book was published in 1917 and since its author was at this time an unequivocal patriot, Sherman closes with an outburst of patriotism,

blaming the war upon the Germans, who, he argues, repudiate
the "law for man" and follow only "natural law."

The application of these principles to modern literature results
in a series of judgments eminently New Humanistic. In his
study of Dreiser's "barbaric naturalism" Sherman charged that
Dreiser portrays society as a jungle and man as an animal.
Dreiser's philosophy is a "crude and naïvely simple" naturalism.[9]
In another essay Sherman makes an extended comparison between H. G. Wells the Naturalist and Arnold the Humanist.
Wells's scientific approach is wrong, for, as Arnold shows,
humane letters alone lead to righteousness and wisdom, and, in
the sphere of conduct, which is three-fourths of life, the natural
sciences are impotent, conducive only to caprice and eccentricity.[10] In matters of sex Wells is crude, a "bomb-dropper"; Arnold
is a "Victorian reticent." In all endeavors Wells is an unprincipled liberator, urging onward the lawlessness of natural man.
If he had read and heeded his Arnold, he would have learned
that inner serenity springs from self-collection, self-control, and,
above all, from the Hebraic sense of personal righteousness,
which is the beginning of religious wisdom.[11]

Yet even at the time of the writing of Sherman's first two
books, it was apparent that there were chinks in his Humanist
armor, which Babbitt and More were quick to point out. For
them the most serious flaw in Sherman was his unqualified
allegiance to democracy. Babbitt noticed this in Sherman's book
on Arnold, particularly in the chapter on Arnold's political and
social beliefs. Sherman had contended that Arnold was essentially liberal and wished to uplift humanity as a whole. Babbitt's
own aristocratic sentiments balked at this, and he called the
chapter "ingenious but not always convincing," for Arnold is
not quite so "sanguine," although he "wished at least a society
in which the failure of any one to measure up to the best standards should be due to inner, not outer, hindrances."[12] In other

words, Arnold was an aristocrat who would set standards for humanity to reach for, rather than attempt to raise humanity as a whole. More also detected flaws in Sherman's creed. As early as 1912 he rejected an essay on Rousseau submitted by Sherman for publication in *The Nation*. Rousseau, according to Sherman, was not really attacking civilization, but was attempting to build a social system more in conformity to nature. Moreover, Rousseau was in accord with the master spirit of his time. More's rejection of these non-Humanist sentiments set off a debate in letters between the two men which was never settled decisively.[13]

Sherman, on his part, began early to forsee eventual estrangement from his mentors. In 1913 he reviewed books on Synge and George Moore for *The Nation* and attacked both authors as "aesthetic naturalists." For this he was congratulated by both More and Babbitt. But Sherman had begun to squirm, and when he was termed an "Anglo-Saxon ethicalist" by a University of Pennsylvania professor, he wrote, complainingly, to More:

... it is very essential to our purpose that [other critics] should think these essays have something to do with art. As Babbitt so admirably said in his Bergson essay, we should oppose enthusiasm to enthusiasm. Just at this moment I can not recall a really luminous opposition of enthusiasm to enthusiasm in the works of I. B....[14]

More, on his part, began to notice certain inconsistencies in Sherman's position. For one thing, the younger man was evincing much enthusiasm for state universities, which, according to More, were products of dangerous, democratic, and romantic fantasies.[15] Then at the same time Sherman could still castigate William Cobbett as a horrible embodiment of democracy and the vulgar rabble. More archly rebuked his palpably disappearing disciple: "Do you know that with all your genius (for you have a touch of that, my dear boy) you have not yet quite found yourself."[16]

The most significant critique by a Humanist on Sherman was

More's analysis of *On Contemporary Literature*. More, monolithic if not anything else, could see discrepancies in the book
which its more lightweight and volatile author probably did
not see himself. To More's mind there were two great ambiguities in Sherman's book: first, how could one reconcile Sherman's
two declarations that this was "the worst of all possible worlds"
and, antithetically, that humanity was inevitably progressing to
a higher civilization; second, how could one reconcile a rejection
of naturalism with a faith in democracy, both of which are
implicit in the book. Sherman would not agree that democracy
is naturalism, and he wrote to More, ". . . to defend democracy,
I shall have to write a book on that. Of course the thesis will
be that democracy is anti-naturalistic, and, possibly, that aristocracy is essentially naturalistic."[17] Fully conscious of the deep
differences of opinion between them now, Sherman continued,
"Then it will be seen clearly that disciple and Master, as the
Springfield *Republican* calls you, are drifting wide apart."[18]

After the war had summoned up his blood, Sherman became
positively Whitmanesque in his celebration of democracy and
the common man. In 1918, to More, he wrote: ". . . I meditate
a definition of democracy which will take the naturalistic curse
off. I haven't polished it up for production yet, but its general
shape glimmers in me something like this: Democracy is government by divine revelation to the people of the 'rights of
man.' "[19] By 1920 More was being taken to task for his lack of
faith in the common man, and in "An Imaginary Conversation
with Mr. P. E. More," published originally in *The Review,*
Sherman said that More was a Tory who felt that "the affairs
of men are really of small consequence—it vexes me to hear this
emotion [the satisfaction in being average] dismissed as fatuous
democratic self-complacency."[20] More was not disturbed by this,
and he replied, by letter: "What rather impresses me in your
dear average man is what impressed Sainte-Beuve, not his base-

ness or vileness so much as that which makes him average, his curious dullness and flatness of soul. The divine spark is in him, but there is some fatal flaccidity in him."[21] Again in 1921 More warned his wandering pupil and uttered a prophecy that was later realized: "My dear fellow, yours is but a sickly sort of democracy at bottom and needs a doctor. You had better go forward a little or turn back a little, or you will find yourself between two camps, pelted by both."[22]

But Sherman charged ahead into that form of fervid and specially qualified Americanism that was to mark his later years, and in the introduction to *Americans* (1922) he posted his new creed. He had once, he admitted, abhorred nationalism, but now: "On the contrary, the more deeply we loved the true constituent elements of [America's] loveliness, the more clearly we understood her inmost purposes and set ourselves to further them, the more perfectly we should find ourselves in accord with the 'friends of mankind' in all nations."[23] In *Americans,* Sherman honors various Americans: Whitman, whom Babbitt called a "cosmic loafer," is applauded as a "democrat with a thirst for distinction" and the poet laureate for America's "divine" constitution; Andrew Carnegie is presented as an American hero; and Joaquin Miller is upheld as representative of the vital spirit of the frontier. Sherman refers to a passage in Arnold's letters where Arnold had spoken with satisfaction of the unity that the 1865 *Essays in Criticism* possessed and the "admirable riches of human nature" that were brought to light by the figures he was discussing. "The 'admirable riches of human nature' are, I am sure," says Sherman, "also present in my group of Americans..."[24] Thus he is going to do for his generation what Arnold did for his, only in terms of the American tradition.

Babbitt, rather mildly for him, told Sherman that he was verging into an idealism that was Jeffersonian rather than Platonic, and that of this kind of idealism he (Babbitt) was far from representative.[25] But Sherman, after all, had to go his own way, added Babbitt, and it was not for him and More to demur. He only regretted that he and More and Sherman could not present a more united front to the enemy.[26] Sherman received letters in a similar vein from More and from Frank Jewett Mather.

By 1923 the break not only was complete but was becoming a hostility on the part of Sherman, who wrote to Mather: "I have agreed with More and Babbitt at a great many points. But I have never embraced with any completeness More's metaphysical doctrines: I don't understand them. As moral sages, I think them right at many vital points..."[27] Moreover, More and Babbitt were too Olympian, too far removed from the scene of action; their literary interests were too restricted; they were too "remorselessly negative"; and, finally, Babbitt was too dogmatic and More too mystical: "... Babbitt ends his *chevaux-de-frise* of arbitrary 'definitions' warranted to eviscerate every gizzard and break every neck born into this disastrous world since Aristotle; while More retreats into a blinding white mist of Platonism where God himself would think twice before pursuing."[28] Thus the Humanists lost their most energetic and promising pupil. Henceforth, although by degrees, Sherman was to drift farther and farther towards modernism. Before his death he was writing appreciatively of Dreiser. Meanwhile, he looked around for the father-image that he always seemed to need and found it in Brownell.

II

The relationship between Brownell and Sherman was a prolonged idyll of mutual admiration. As Sherman's biographers say, "Toward no men of letters of his time did Sherman's feeling have quite that shade of reverence which entered into his admiration for Mr. Brownell."[29] The two men were personal friends, and in 1922 Sherman wrote an introduction to a reprinting of Brownell's *American Prose Masters*. In 1923 Sherman was elected to the American Academy of Arts and Letters mainly through the efforts of Brownell and More; in 1924 Brownell proposed his membership in the Century Club. Brownell dedicated his last book, *Democratic Distinction in America,* published in 1927, the year after Sherman's sudden death, "to the memory of Stuart Pratt Sherman."

As early as 1909, while still in the Humanist fever, Sherman, in a review of *American Prose Masters,* claimed that Brownell was making American criticism, for the first time, a genuine profession and art: "The workmanship in general is so admirable, the principles so explicit, so sound, so classical, that the essay might well serve both as a model of criticism and as a brief manual of critical theory."[30] In 1914 Sherman reviewed Brownell's *Criticism* and again remarked on Brownell's unique place in American letters: "[Brownell's are] works of rare distinction in the field of American criticism—works in which singularly acute and unintermittent thinking is expressed with almost flawless precision."[31] And the reviewer wrote to the author: "... I say that these essays make the greater part of all the critical work in America, before and since their time, seem both slovenly and unintelligent."[32] Beyond this, Sherman considered himself to be in perfect agreement with the older critic. Not to be outdone, and gentleman of the old school that he was, Brownell replied in kind: "... to be championed, and assured that he is a champion, by the authority he considers the champion, is a rosy delight."[33]

Brownell's appeal for Sherman was many-sided. For one thing, Brownell was an Arnoldian. Sherman, in *Points of View,* noted this with approval: "Among the critics and apostles of culture, Arnold is easily the first in his estimation—the most frequently quoted and the most pervasively present as an invisible influence."[34] For another thing, Brownell's high seriousness connected him with the first American Arnoldian, Henry James, whom Sherman also considered a model of fastidiousness and taste. In a letter to Brownell he remarked: "I have been rather painfully impressed by the rareness of our really disciplinary books—I mean books which conduce to the habit of discrimination, using the word as you and Henry James use it."[35] In his essay on Hawthorne, in *Americans,* Sherman used as his authorities for Hawthorne's greatness—he is defending the "Puritan" against the attack of Mencken and others—James, "the most fastidious and the most sophisticated of critics," and Brownell, "an exacting critic."[36] In his essay on James, Sherman cited Brownell as an authority to support his judgment that some of James's criticism itself is the best ever written by an American.[37] In any event, there existed in Sherman's mind a connection between James and Brownell as the most fastidious and elegant of American critics, and whenever he thought of Brownell he saw the shadow of Arnold in the background. This succession was, in effect, an aristocracy: "Mr. Brownell is a critical representative of our literary aristocracy . . . , that small, highly civilized minority of writers who love perfection and seek it, who love truth and pursue it, who love beauty and create it."[38]

Gentility and aristocracy constituted only one part of the appeal. The other part consisted in the fact that Brownell, like Arnold but unlike More and Babbitt, was a political liberal concerned with American democracy and with the welfare of the people as a whole. In Sherman's mind, Brownell had endowed democracy and belief in it with "spiritual refinement"[39] and had, moreover, made any disdain for democracy a vulgarity:

If Mr. Brownell had struck out no other bold phrase than "plebeian antagonism to democratic feeling" he would deserve to be remembered. If he had developed no other thesis than this, that an instinct for equality is "a constituent of refinement" and sensitiveness a mark of true democracy, he would still be an important contributor to American culture.[40]

Back of this sentiment, in the minds of both Brownell and Sherman, is Arnold's statement in *Mixed Essays* that "our love of inequality is really the vulgarity in us, and the brutality, admiring and worshipping the splendid materiality."

It was in this fashion, as cultural aristocrat and as political liberal, that Sherman embarked upon his own major effort amid the general critical warfare of the 'twenties. Sherman thought that there was an unequivocal issue and that there were two parties directly opposed over this issue, the "Party of Culture" and the "Party of Nature." Sherman summed up his own function thus:

One party holds that we shall never achieve adequate national expression until we have received the inspiration and mastered the technic of traditional art. The other party holds that we shall never achieve any national expression unless we follow our instincts and fearlessly utilize our fresh experience.[41]

Both parties are right in their way, but they are mutually antagonistic and must be reconciled. Brownell, in Sherman's mind, had proposed a solution, giving the Party of Nature its due, without sacrificing the high standards of Arnoldian culture:

Neither an iconoclast nor a reactionary, he has been steadfastly and consistently a man of intensely contemporary sympathies and interests: he has stood unflinchingly for reason as our supreme instrument; eminent in culture, he has valued the past as it could be used in the present; a convinced democrat, he has criticized the brutality of our individualism and has commended the study of French equality and the French social instinct as a means to refine our own society and to make it more delectable . . .[42]

Brownell's solution, in fact, had made it unnecessary to turn to Europe, as he himself had had to do when Lowell failed to provide the needed link with Emerson. "Since the appearance of Mr. Brownell's books it is no longer necessary to turn to England and France for initiation into modern criticism."[43] Brownell had absorbed the past; he had gone to France, "as Arnold went, as 'a merchant of light' to discover its characteristic virtues and powers and superiorities and, so far as possible, to bring them home to his countrymen";[44] he had concerned himself at all times with the American present; and, above all, he had accepted and acted upon Arnold's pronouncement that all arts should be directed at "the humanization of man in society."[45]

In this way would Sherman carry on, wedding the American tradition of Emerson, Whitman, and Thoreau to the culture of Arnold. Like Brownell, he would, as the critic, uphold high cultural standards, conservative ethics, and a passion for democracy. But Sherman's concept of culture was very narrow, colored even by racial prejudice. And his Arnold was in great part the genteel Matthew who, along with Waldo, kept eternal vigilance over the proprieties from Boston walls. To Sherman, culture was Anglo-American and "gentlemanly." Hence he thought that many of the major critics of his day were repudiating the only cultural traditions that could produce great art in America. The Spingarns and the Menckens were spurning both our English and American heritages. They were tossing out the English tradition as "unserviceable lumber," and native American culture they stigmatized as "puritanical, effeminate, or over-intellectualized."[46] These "alien-minded" critics, said Sherman, were deliberately trying to deny American culture's deepest impulse, "its profound moral idealism." This "profound moral idealism" he called the Puritan spirit; it was this that had built America and would sustain its future greatness.

Sherman thus entered the battle of the 'twenties as the self-styled champion of his own conception of Puritanism. According to this champion, Puritanism was not intolerant, narrow, and fanatic, as Mencken and others said, but was, on the contrary, liberal, progressive, individualistic, and ethically sound. The eternal Puritan was characterized by "dissatisfaction with the past: courage to break sharply from it, a vision of a better life, readiness to accept discipline in order to attain that better life, and a serious desire to make that better life prevail ..."[47]

The Puritan spirit, then, is the spirit of all great American writers—Emerson, Whitman, Thoreau, and the rest. For Sherman, their spirit was by no means insular or narrowly American. They learned much, as we must learn much, from Europe. Franklin, for instance, is a prime example of the patriotic American who had acquired the high culture of Europe. As such, Franklin was no simple horse trader: "All Europe had wrought upon and metamorphosed the Yankee printer.... With no softening of his patriotic fibre or loss of his Yankee twang, he has acquired all the common culture and most of the master characteristics of the Age of Enlightenment..."[48] Whitman's plea for world brotherhood was interpreted by Sherman as yet another manifestation of the American Puritan spirit's reaching out to acquire the best that has been thought and said. Whitman was thus a true "cosmopolitan," and "no aspiration is ... more thoroughly American than cosmopolitanism."[49]

There were two elements in American culture that must be welded together: the cultured elevation of the Nortons, Emersons, and Brownells and the strength and the crude vigor of the Twains and Bret Hartes—the Western writers whom Sherman called, quoting Emerson, "the earthy, rough, Jacksonian element." Of this grandiose scheme, Sherman wrote to Brownell in 1922: "I want to get the Emersons and Jacksons together, and their offspring to intermarry. I believe the American breed will profit by the misalliance. On the one hand we tend to have a horse without a rider; on the other hand, a rider without a horse."[50] This drama of Sherman's is obviously Arnold's joining of Hebraism (vigor, roughness) with Hellenism (sweetness, light), rewritten in American terms.

The rider, then, must keep in contact with the European cultural developments in order to transmit new impulses to his countrymen and protect them from their own provinciality. Sherman wrote to William Ellery Sedgwick in 1920:

> All the great literatures tend to something at the center like a thoroughbred strain.... France and England both show the thoroughbred strain, that "solidarity"... More definitely, I suppose we mean a certain continuity, in the central writers, of a certain quantity and quality of culture, of a certain purity and distinction of style, and, above all, of a certain elevation of feeling and a clearness and breadth of vision and a serenity of tone.... American literature can exhibit these qualities only intermittently. The thoroughbred strain is thin and broken.[51]

And the finest example of that thoroughbred strain was, of course, Matthew Arnold.

III

Sherman's career was both curiously checkered and singularly monolithic. He began as a Humanist but ended as a kind of "professional American," described by Ernest Boyd in his essay "Ku Klux Kriticism" as "Nordic, Protestant, and blond";[52] he began as a university professor preoccupied with the past, but he ended as a journalist surveying the present. Yet his essential bias, even in his later "liberal" days, was always deeply conservative, and over his entire career there presided a bland spirit: that of Matthew Arnold, although Sherman's "Arnold" was far different from that of James and was only a distant cousin to Brownell's. Sherman was, in a sense, the end product of the direct Arnoldian tradition. Brownell had noticed Arnold's habit of characterizing the personality of the objects of his critical study, of reading the man through his works. Sherman carried this critical method to its logical conclusion, by concentrating almost exclusively upon the personality of the writer and by judging his subject according to whether he was ethically "uplifting." Arnold's idea that poetry should move into the vacuum created by the decay of orthodox religion was completely taken over by his twentieth-century disciple: "In an unfinished world, where religion has become so largely a matter of traditional sentiments and observances, poetry has work to do, poetry of any high seriousness."[53] And Sherman's own critical pronouncements are essentially exhortations to righteousness. On the basis of their general agreement, or supposed agreement, in outlook, Arnold affected Sherman in many ways—in his cultural, religious, educational, and political ideology; in the matter of style; and as an embodiment of an ideal personality, whom he urged his students and readers to emulate.

Sherman's intimate acquaintance with Arnold long antedates the influence of Babbitt and Humanism; in fact, it could successfully be argued, as his lifelong friend Homer Woodbridge suggests, that much of Babbitt's appeal for Sherman resulted from the resemblance of Babbitt to Arnold.[54] Of his own early reading Sherman said: "... I read through while in high school the works of Spenser, of Keats, of Shelley, of Byron, of Tennyson, the whole works of Matthew Arnold, politics and theology included, Plato, Milton's *Areopagitica,* and some of Hooker's *Ecclesiastical Polity*."[55] It was appropriate then that Sherman's first book should have been on Arnold. Babbitt noted in his review of this book: "Without being blindly partisan, Professor Sherman is himself a convinced Arnoldian ..."[56] The book, written for the "How to Know Him Series," is fairly elementary, as might be expected. It gives, nevertheless, a complete picture of Arnold, his character, his poetry, and all phases of his criticism. Sherman stressed the religious and moral elements in Arnold, and the over-all impression that the reader derives is not that Arnold was a literary artist and critic, but that he was a

great religious and moral teacher—a prophet, if you will. The
literary elements in Arnold that Sherman stressed are the so-
called virtues of restraint, decorum, and reverence for the established and the traditional. Arnold here is a Humanist, but,
although Sherman himself moved away from Humanism, he
took Arnold with him and kept him as a general guide and as
a personal inspiration.

First of all, in the realm of ideas, Sherman accepted Arnold's
dictum that culture consists in the knowing of the best that
has been thought and said. In 1908, in a famous letter to *The
Nation* in which he castigated the "medievalism" of the Harvard Graduate School, Sherman wrote, "Whether one likes it
or not, English literature is the main road to culture—the culture that Arnold meant: a knowledge of the best that has been
thought and said in the world."[57] Sherman's main contention was
that Arnold, despite the fact that his standards were unsound
according to the rules and regulations of modern scientific scholarship, was more truly a cultural leader than a medieval specialist
could be. In 1913 Sherman repeated the same criticism in a
protest against the renowned methods of Professor Kittredge.
Here again he used Arnold as the ideal teacher of culture, in
contrast to the scientific scholars who deadened literature:

The great field for the discovery of facts, memorable chiefly because
they have been forgotten, has long been the Middle Ages, and Professor Kittredge is a mediaevalist. To a mind in which the master
impulse is a wide-ranging curiosity this tract of literature is endlessly
fascinating, by virtue of just those qualities which, to a mind with
ulterior purposes like Matthew Arnold's, for example, made it seem
almost negligible—its prolixity, its formlessness, its naïve supersti-
tions, its lack of high seriousness, its insolidity of substance.[58]

Positively, it was Arnold who pointed the way to the proper
appreciation of literature: "Most of Arnold's essays ... remain

as sound, and vital, and interesting today as when they were written. By their virtues he probably exercises thirty years after his death a more constant and important influence upon current literary opinion than any other English critic living."[59] Arnold's success was due to three factors: first, he did not waste time with the transitory and ephemeral, but concerned himself only with the "abiding"; second, he had a certain gusto and zeal for his subject; and, finally and most important, he had a large number of sound and durable principles.[60] Above all, even in his purely literary criticism, Arnold was ethically "uplifting." For literary criticism, despite what modern sophisticates might say, should give good directions to our hearts and consciences, as Arnold's criticism did.[61] Indeed, Arnold had a magic touch in this respect and was like the Pied Piper of Hamlin![62]

Because of this ethical emphasis in Arnold, Sherman, whose admiration for Emerson was considerable, could see no conflict of allegiances in Arnold's Emerson lecture. According to Sherman, Arnold was actually paying Emerson the greatest tribute, despite the famous threefold negation:

These limitations of Emerson's power are commonly quoted as if detraction were the main burden of Arnold's message. As a matter of fact they are preliminary to his deliberate and remarkable declaration that in his judgment Emerson's essays are the most important work done in prose in our language during the nineteenth century.... Because, says Arnold in a phrase full of significance, "he is a friend and aider of those who live in the spirit."[63]

For Sherman there could be no higher praise. Furthermore, in all of Arnold's ethical activities there was a certain highly desirable but old-fashioned decorum. In *Points of View* Sherman lamented the absence of this Arnoldian and Victorian reticence in the "crude" productions of the naturalists: "When our literature passed from the hands of scholars and gentlemen into the hands of our barbarian artists of what Emerson called the 'Jacksonian rabble,' it lost much of the high seriousness, the decorum, and the impeccable decency characteristic of the New England school."[64]

In religion proper Sherman considered Arnold his teacher, for in Arnold's writings truth is identified not with beauty, as in the work of Keats, but with God, as in the Gospels and in the works of religious, as opposed to aesthetic, poets.[65] Thus, despite the fact that Arnold was a free thinker, his religious writings had given new life to the Bible.[66] Furthermore, Arnold had not entirely ruled out the divine element in human experience, as his critics had charged, for, according to Sherman: "The primary fact in his religious experience was his consciousness of his own *soul*."[67]

In fact it was Arnold's midway position, hinting at but not insisting upon the existence of some kind of power outside man, that attracted Sherman. When More wrote expressing some doubts about Arnold's religious position and its "restrictions," Sherman replied that Arnold's emphasis on morals rather than metaphysics was sound. He admitted that More had had greater religious experience than himself, but said that although he recognized his own limitations in this sphere with his intellect, he could not feel them with his heart. Arnold gave him just about as much religion as he could receive and never gave him anything that he could not accept.[68] Sherman explained that he could never achieve mystical insights of his own; for people who could achieve that level of religion Arnold was perhaps unnecessary, but for such men as himself, who were inclined to "worldliness," Arnold afforded exactly the stimulus necessary to sustain them in "keeping up appearances."[69]

In the matter of public education, Sherman conceived of Arnold as a liberal who foresaw and accepted the complete extension of the electorate, welcomed the prospect, and predicted correctly how education must be administered. Naturally, Sherman applauded Arnold's championship of humane studies against the scientific emphasis of Huxley and Spencer. Sherman agreed that only the discipline of the great classics could develop the necessary moral fiber in mankind: "To Arnold, who waives the question of man's ultimate origin, man is now *essentially* a moral being, who by certain discipline has fortified his instinct for righteousness, wisdom and beauty, and who by the continued use of these disciplines may expect to make progress in perfecting his essence."[70] At the same time Arnold was not one-sided; he gave the study of science its due, but merely pointed out its inadequacies. His special service as an educator was that of mediating between divergent extremes, "in showing how far literature and the natural sciences go together, and where they part."[71]

As an Eastern-bred, Harvard-educated man, Sherman was always well aware of the Eastern attitude toward large Midwestern state universities, and throughout most of his life, and against the assaults of people like More, he defended their function and efficacy. In his essay "Education by the People" Sherman defended the state university against English critics who had voiced the familiar objections to the education of the masses. Again Arnold was on his side. We are told, for instance, says Sherman, that if we are going to be governed by the people we must be ready to submit to their "collective folly." To this objection the advocate of the state university replies that if we are to be governed by the people, then the sensible course is to educate one's governors. Another critic may say that the only solution to the political problem is a wise paternal government which will protect the people from its own folly. On the contrary, Sherman answered, a really wise and paternal government forestalls any distress by showing people how to provide for themselves. To clinch his argument Sherman cites an "Oxford graduate," who

> tells us that the remedy for the "evils of democracy" is to strengthen the power of the State by making it the central organ for the dissemination of the best that has been said and thought in the world. These words the Faculty of a State university would probably recognize as fairly descriptive of their undertaking. They would dignify the entire range of human conduct by discovering for all the people, and by making prevail from the lowest to the loftiest, the right and excellent form of every activity.[72]

It follows, then, that the ideal critic and man of letters is one who is democratic and who will try to make his ideas prevail with the general public. Comparing More and Arnold in this respect, Sherman complained that More took so little pains to be comprehended that it looked as if he thought himself addressing the Athenian democracy rather than the modern American democracy.[73] Now, as similar as More and Arnold were, in point of view, More had never felt the Englishman's passion for diffusing his ideas and for making them prevail from one end of society to the other. In the last analysis, therefore, More was not one of the great men of culture.

> They are those who, in Arnold's famous words, "have labored to divest knowledge of all that was harsh, uncouth, difficult, abstract, professional, exclusive; to humanize it; to make it efficient, outside the clique of cultivated and learned, yet still remaining the *best* knowledge and thought of the time, and a true source, therefore, of sweetness and light."[74]

This missionary zeal, which Sherman admired in Arnold, is certainly crucial to an understanding of the twists and turns in his own career. It explains, in part, at least, the drift away from the Humanists, the increasing preoccupation with American democracy and contemporary literature, and the final decision to abandon his position as Professor of English at the

University of Illinois and to become head of the *New York Herald Tribune*'s book section, besides his long-time connection with *The Nation*. However ineffective Sherman may have been as the savior of the "Puritan spirit" or as a pleader for "edifying literature," it must be granted that he did possess the missionary zeal and that he preached with energy, enthusiasm, and wit. His ideas were simple and clearly expressed, aimed at the largest possible public. In his own mind the critic was prophet and in America it was his duty "to effect a redintegration of the national will on the basis of a genuinely democratic humanism, recognizing as its central principle the duty of bringing the whole body of the people to the fullest and fairest human life of which they are capable."[75]

Against an "apostle of culture," of course, two charges can be leveled, as they were at Arnold. Either, first, he is a snob, or, conversely, he is a vulgarizer. Sherman absolved Arnold, and inferentially himself, from both strictures. To the assumption that Arnold was a snob Sherman replied by bracketing him with Emerson. Neither was afraid of his world, and they did not think that what they prescribed for the superior class would entail the ruination of the multitude. They thought of culture not as a "thing" but as an enlightening and wide-ranging spirit, which was peculiarly adapted to the large-scale democratic societies of the future.[76]

On the other hand, Arnold was not unduly simplifying or lowering his ideals; in fact, he had felt that the middle classes were deserving of and would be appreciative of genuine "ideas." In 1927 Sherman said:

In turning over recently the letters of Matthew Arnold I was much struck by a passage, written in 1864, in which he declared that the "stock vulgar liberalism" of the old stagers "will not satisfy even the middle class, whose wants it was originally modeled to meet, much longer." If liberalism is to prosper, he suggests, it will have to be raised from the level of routine political cant to the level of ideas and humane emotions.[77]

For Sherman, true democratic liberalism was not a leveling tendency but an elevating tendency. Whitman's specimen of the average man was, according to Sherman, someone like Lincoln or Grant, and Whitman's ideal democracy was to be made up of millions of these superb aristocrats. For Whitman was a democrat with an "exorbitant thirst" for distinction.[78] By such reasoning was Sherman able to effect a marriage of Arnold and Whitman, a union which either of the principals, had they known, would have considered one to have been arranged only by the powers of darkness.

Yet with all his belief in democracy and his fervid hopes for the future, Sherman had to admit, as Brownell had not, that Arnold's *Civilization in the United States* was essentially correct: that America was "uninteresting" and that the United States had failed to solve the human problem. Sherman said that not only was Arnold right but contemporary American literature was proving him so. Mark Twain's late pessimism was an indication that American writers were beginning to see through the "romantic illusion" of the worship of the common man. This trend, first exemplified in Twain, is also apparent in the Haldemans' *Dust,* which, through its point of view and despite its dramatization of the American success story, has the over-all effect of demonstrating that our civilization has "failed to solve the human problem."[79] This type of criticism, apparent in Sinclair Lewis, Frank Norris, Edith Wharton, and others, was directed against the identical defect that Arnold had pointed out, namely that American civilization lacked elevation and beauty and was dull and uninteresting. As such, it could not appease the vague but "acutely painful hunger" for the good life that the average man carried in his breast.[80] And if all these speculations and adjurations on Arnold's part and on his own about democracy and culture were to be branded as either irrelevant to literary criticism or impossible to actualize, Sherman replied in *Critical Woodcuts:*

...I am not conscious of any alteration in my ancient conviction that all human activities have, up their sleeves, an ulterior object and ultimate justification in happier living; and that it is rather specially the "function" of critics to be engaged in an incessant untiring exploration in quest of "the good life."[81]

Arnold affected Sherman not only ideologically but in the more personal realm of method and style. Joseph Warren Beach, comparing the two in this respect, found manifest resemblances: the use of an imaginary character for dialogue: Arnold's "Thunder-ten-Tronckh" and Sherman's "dear Cornelia"; the pose of Socrates and the use of dialectics; the marshaling of the heads of discourse and the constructing of neat formulas; the repetition of key phrases; and the whimsical wit.[82] Sherman had been repelled by the coldness of the Humanists, and he said of More:

...when I observe how persistently he repels the advances of the vulgar by flinging a handful of political and social icicles in their faces, I wish from the bottom of my heart that he had loved the exclusive, metaphysical, aristocratic Plato less and the hobnobbing, inquisitive, realistic, democratic Socrates more.[83]

In Arnold, as contrasted with More, Sherman found a spirit of drollery and gaiety overlying the basic seriousness. Arnold was not coldly aloof, but had a "companionable" attitude.[84] In a letter to William Ellery Sedgwick, noting the fact that Arnold was still being quoted as often as any living critic, with the possible exception of Mencken, Sherman ascribed much of Arnold's efficacy to the fact that he was always ready to indulge in literary controversy, to allow personality to appear, and to employ gentlemanly yet "deadly" raillery in controversy.[85]

It was in this spirit that Sherman entered into combat with Mencken, seeking to rout the enemy with wit rather than with heavy utterances, as the Humanists sought to do. For example:

At this point enters at a hard gallop, spattered with mud, H. F. Mencken high in oath—thus justifying the Goethean maxim: *Aller Anfang ist schwer*. He leaps from the saddle with sabre flashing, stables his horse in the church, shoots the priest, hangs the professors, exiles the Academy, burns the library and the University, and, amid the smoking ashes, erects a new school of criticism on modern German principles...[86]

The concluding section of this same essay on Mencken is even more indicative of Arnold's deep influence stylistically. Here Sherman refers to Arnold explicitly, quotes from one of Arnold's favorites, Joubert, and borrows the famous Arnoldian device, used by Arnold against Newman, of verbalizing a proper name. The essay is cast in the form of the various experiences of a *jeune fille* [that is, a young American] on the modern American literary scene. At the end, the *jeune fille* comes upon a man, Philip Littell, smiling over something he has just read, and she asks him what has so pleased him. " 'A thought,' he replies gently, 'phrased by a subtle writer and set in a charming essay by a famous critic. Listen: 'Ou il n'y a point de délicatesse, il n'y a point de littérature.' 'That's a new one on me,' says the *jeune fille*." But Sherman provides a footnote for the Joubert quotation and a translation. "Translated: 'When one begins to Menckenize, the spirit of good literature flees in consternation.' "[87]

Arnold's ultimate appeal to Sherman went beyond the explicitness of ideas and method and into the more profound and intangible realms of personality and experience. Sherman was a complex and ambitious personality, and like all such he had his problems. His two biographers, Zeitlin and Woodbridge, who, between them, were at his side most of his life and who knew him perhaps as well as anyone did, have remarked on the great influence that Arnold, solely as a person and exemplar, had upon him:

In Matthew Arnold he found the same impulses, the same emotional crises and spiritual problems, the same conflicts of temperament and reason that he had experienced or was experiencing in his own breast, and he also found what seemed to him the triumph over difficulties through the exercise of control and character. The first chapter [of Sherman's *Arnold*] reads at many points like an avowal of personal troubles or personal aspirations.[88]

The result of this personal admiration and identification was Sherman's course on Matthew Arnold at the University of Illinois.

As the Humanists, Sherman told his students, were one-sided, Arnold was the ideal well-rounded man, a kind of Elizabethan gentleman flourishing in the nineteenth century. But although he strove all his life in many endeavors, he was no sunny optimist but had stoically disciplined himself to control all his emotional impulses. Sherman advises all young people to learn from Arnold:

There is an interesting and true passage in the letters of Matthew Arnold which spirited young fellows encounter with a chill. It is this: "The aimless and unsettled, but also open and liberal, state of our youth we *must* perhaps all leave and take refuge in morality and character."[89]

And this was the personality that Sherman's students were asked to emulate.

Of the course itself Sherman's colleague Professor Zeitlin says: "He made Matthew Arnold one of the most popular subjects in the English curriculum by offering him as a pattern for the life of the educated man."[90] According to Zeitlin, Sherman spent "endless pains" on this course, perfecting and polishing it from year to year. Sherman encouraged the students, in imitation of Arnold and as he did himself, to keep a notebook of thoughts and maxims, in order to develop in them the habits of reflection and meditation.[91] At the same time Sherman emphasized the aesthetic elements in Arnold, as evidenced by his "purity" and "delicacy." Sherman pointed out the lack of those qualities in most American writers, except—naming among others the two other major American Arnoldians—Hawthorne, Henry James, C. E. Norton, Santayana, W. C. Brownell.[92] Arnold's cosmopolitanism was stressed, and the students were told that what American culture needed most was an infusion of foreign cultures.[93] Throughout the course, Zeitlin says, Sherman emphasized what he called Arnold's "ulterior purposes" by telling his students:

> ... the highest aim which education could propose was to make good citizens of the world, to bring the entire body of humanity into a harmonious civil life, ... pointing out also how badly we in America stood in need of "fineness, elevation, distinction, high and intelligent seriousness, the grand style (less jazz and razz), the sense for exquisite workmanship, philosophical depth, the romantic note, glamour, the English sense for the delights of homes and gardens and flowers, permanence and solidity," and that these defects could be corrected by reaching out in spirit to the great writings of other lands and other apostles.[94]

Sherman himself summed up the purposes of the course in the final lecture, which was printed in the posthumous *Shaping Men and Women*. The over-all aim was simple:

> Now, I told you on the first day that we met for this course that, if the course was good for anything, you would not be the same when you came out of it as when you came in.... You have been asked to study a personality; and in many more or less subtle ways you have been asked to imitate a model. You have been asked to imitate the Arnoldian personality. Those to whom the course has been of the most value, I think, have become in some measure Arnoldians.[95]

Sherman goes on to say that he has admiration for many other literary personalities, such as Shakespeare, Goethe, and Emerson.

But Arnold has some points of superiority over most of them, and he has some traits that make him especially appropriate for university men and women of the present day. For Arnold represents "wholeness of self-development."

In matters of religion, Arnold holds that all men are basically religious: "And so the Arnoldian man respects religion under all its manifestations as an impulse which craves satisfaction."[96] Accordingly, the follower of Arnold strives to bring all civilization and culture under the protection of God, "to make Him the patron of truth and high seriousness; to admit freely that religion is a poetic interpretation of reality, is morality touched with emotion."[97]

In politics, the "Arnoldian person" "believes in the inevitability of democracy, and he accepts what may be called the religion of democracy; namely that the object of politics is to bring the entire body of the people to the fullest and most human life of which they are capable."[98] Sherman added that there is no place for snobbishness in the "true Arnoldian," although acceptance of democracy does not mean the relinquishing of standards.

The "Arnoldian" believes that the great need of society is a richer civilization. The way to that richer civilization is through culture, through

...more extensive knowledge of the best that has been said and thought in the world and more extensive diffusion of the temper of sweetness and light; more curiosity about intellectual matters, more eagerness to have intelligence hit the mark, more disinterested desire to have truth prevail, a more critical temper.[99]

No one, I am sure, would have been more amazed than Arnold, who took nothing, including himself, without some reservations, at the aura of holy awe that hung about this lecture, for Sherman progressed through the entire Arnoldian creed, literary, social, religious, political, and cultural, and accepted every utterance of the master as gospel. Sherman closed the lecture with a long list of phrases, such as "sweetness and light," "Philistinism," "urbanity," and the like, to which Arnold had given currency, and told his students that acquaintance with the phrases and their meaning was the true mark of culture and education. In Sherman's opinion, Arnold had set forth a complete pattern of thinking and a way of life, and his students were urged to adopt this way of life. From the mouth of the lecturer to the mind of the student is a long and intricate path, especially at a large state university, but it would seem that for many graduates of the University of Illinois the words "Arnold" and "culture" must have been synonymous.

IV

Sherman represents the last and fullest expression of the "cult" of Matthew Arnold. Remembering Whitman's distaste for Arnold one finds it difficult to envisage a critic who could hold both Whitman and Arnold in such high esteem without any perceptible friction. Sherman achieved this by tempering Arnold's aristocratic tendencies and by attributing to Whitman "a thirst for distinction"; thus the strange duet, Arnold and Whitman, is set up as a partnership of allies working in the same cause. It is interesting, too, to see Sherman, late in his career, attempting to appreciate Dreiser and Sherwood Anderson, both of whom were anathema to him in his Humanist days. Dreiser in *An American Tragedy* is a "sound moralist,"[100] and Sherwood Anderson's *Dark Laughter* has "high seriousness."[101] By the very terms he uses one can see that Sherman is still very much the Arnoldian, and is attempting, not very successfully, to make his old attitudes fit new circumstances. But he would or could only go so far in an appreciation of the moderns, and Joyce, for example, was not acceptable. Of *Ulysses* Sherman said: "It seems to have originated in fathomless disgust for almost every force of race, country, and time which made James Joyce what he is."[102]

Despite the fact that Sherman had written one of the first good books on Arnold, it is evident that his picture of Arnold was considerably more blurred, besides being much more inclusive, than that of either of his two predecessors, James and Brownell. First, of course, Sherman had inherited not the living human being, in full career, that James had met, nor even the just recently deceased eminent English critic of Brownell's imagination, but a great figure from the past, with the innumerable historical accretions that such an image picks up. The aura of controversy that clung to Arnold in James's day and, to a certain degree, in Brownell's day, had been completely dissipated in Sherman's time by the total absolution that history tends to grant. Moreover, history had bestowed upon Arnold certain attributes and had connected him with certain elements in America—conservative, New Englandish, Victorian—that had had the effect of taking him out of context, of resolving, simply, the complexity of his mind, and of making him a symbol of the *ubi sunt* feeling that sexagenarians were addicted to in the early decades of the twentieth century. Arnold the revolutionary had become the "Uncle Matthew" of Beerbohm, and almost inevitably became the patron saint of such a "young conservative" as Sherman. History not only had washed away the sins of Arnold, but had simplified him and given him a halo.

History had also, in the realm of literary criticism proper, been working another vein which was to condition Sherman in his response to Arnold. The very faculty that Brownell had praised in Arnold, and in Arnold's master Sainte-Beuve, that is, the re-creation of the "personality" of the author under study, the synthesis of the "spirit" of the author, became with Sherman a frank avowal of the adventures of his soul among the souls of the departed. Thus Arnold's own method, if Brownell's conception of that method is correct, was ultimately turned back upon its progenitor with an enthusiasm and awe that would have surprised no one more than Arnold himself. The distance that James kept between himself and Arnold and the irony that he allowed to play about his picture of Arnold, and the firm objectivity that Brownell always preserved toward Arnold, gave way finally to the effusions of Sherman and the personal identification.

History is not exclusively responsible for these transformations, however: Sherman himself was a weaker vessel than either James or Brownell, lacking both the incisive aesthetic intelligence of the former and the incisive rational intelligence of the latter. His career is a veritable paradigm for lack of strength and penetration of mind, and all his gifts, energy, quickness, even a kind of brilliance at times, were corroded by his fundamental lack of balance and his penchant for sentimentality. When excited he could turn ugly, and he often did in critical debate, as when, during World War I, he kept insisting on the Germanic affinities of Mencken, even to the point of saying that the name of Mencken's publisher was "Knopf."

These gifts and liabilities were placed at the disposal of an ambitious man who wished to play a great role in the national destiny. Randolph Bourne is reported to have said that Sherman was the most dangerous man in America and that one could not be too nice in the choice of weapons with which one fought him.[108] But Bourne himself was being sentimental in this judgment, for history has shown that Sherman had not the power and force to play the role he wished.

In his own historic role, Sherman seems to have seen himself as the Arnoldian figure: the cultivated man who was yet concerned with specific practical issues; the moral conservative; the diagnoser of the national conscience and the arbiter of her history; the serious man who went forth to do battle with wit and repartee. But twentieth-century America was not nineteenth-century England, nor was Sherman another Arnold. Whereas Arnold's accomplishment was real, it is difficult to see how Sherman finally affected anybody. For the direct Arnoldian tradition in America he signaled the death knell, for in Sherman's hands Arnold had become a platitude rather than a thought, a personality rather than an idea, a subject for hagiography rather than intellectual substance.

PART THREE

RESURGENCE

CHAPTER VI

T. S. ELIOT

IN A SUMMARIZING REVIEW of his critical career, F. O. Matthiessen spoke of his early admiration for Arnold and of his later
being propelled, along with others of his generation, toward
T. S. Eliot and I. A. Richards. It was a swing of the critical
sensibility from the "spirit" to the "letter" of literature.[1] This
generalization explains much of what has happened in literary
criticism in the last four decades, Eliot replacing Arnold. But
in the early part of the twentieth century, Arnold, besides being
an aid and comfort to Impressionism, Humanism, and liberalism, had become *the* prototypical English critic, especially in
academic circles. He was clothed with that nostalgia in which
the present envelops the past, and had become an astral symbol
for those engaged in the battles of the "hopeless" present.
Arnold's criticism, wrote Terence Connolly in 1934, was very
different from the "degenerate literary criticism of today that
bases its judgment upon literary craftsmanship alone, with no
regard for the suitableness of the writer's subject."[2] But Arnold
was also an authority for those who did *not* consider the present
absolutely "hopeless"; for them he was a permanent and never-
failing guide. In the academic world it seemed—to some, anyway—that Arnold had become the permanent English critic
and that to be a professor of English meant being, by definition,
an Arnoldian. T. H. Vail Motter, in the *AAUP Bulletin* in
1941, made just this claim. Woodrow Wilson had been, he said,
the American Arnold in the field of education,[3] and he concluded that "he who teaches in the American college is committed by his vocation to the way of Arnold and Wilson, which
is the liberal way..."[4] Writing in the *Sewanee Review* in 1936,
Everett Hunt declared: "... we shall see more and more clearly

that Arnold's critical method will remain one of the guides of life."[5]

It is obvious from these testimonies that Arnold was the pre-eminent critic writing in English. Eliot himself, in 1925, referred to "the academic estimate of Arnold as Literary Critic which prevailed some twenty years ago." "At one time," Eliot remarked, "it seemed that Arnold was assured for perpetuity, in literary manuals, the place of the ultimate English critic."[6] It is obvious also, from Eliot's assumption that Arnold was no longer the "ultimate English critic" and from the defensive tone of some of the encomiums mentioned above, that the throne upon which Arnold had been ensconced was not secure and that a Pretender, who was Eliot himself, was grasping for the Crown. Nor were the Arnoldians unaware or unapprehensive of what was happening. When Eliot criticized Arnold, in a lecture at Harvard in 1932, Carleton Stanley, Professor of English at the University of Toronto, replied: "The malice of a little soul is impotent against a great soul. *On His Own Blindness* is the proper title for the lecture of T. S. Eliot . . ."[7] But, the "malice of a little soul" aside, the defenders of Arnold were defending what was not completely and unqualifiedly defensible, for the world had moved on, and literature with it, and, for better or worse, T. S. Eliot has been the literary dictator of the earlier part of the twentieth century, as Arnold was for the latter part of the nineteenth. Eliot's influence, to put it mildly, has been enormous, although he himself, as late as 1933, remarked: "Examination of the criticism of our time leads me to believe that we are still in the Arnold period."[8] Moreover, no one was more conscious than Eliot himself that he was challenging Arnold's position and doctrine, that the Time-Spirit which Arnold had apotheosized had rung in its changes and that the age demanded new spokesmen. In *The Use of Poetry and the Use of Criticism* he made the demand very clear:

The majority of critics can be expected only to parrot the opinions of the last master of criticism; among more independent minds a period of destruction, of preposterous overestimation, and of successive fashions take place, until a new authority comes to introduce some order.... no generation is interested in Art in quite the same way as any other; ... Hence each new master of criticism performs a useful service merely by the fact that his errors are of a different kind from the last; and the longer sequence of critics we have, the greater amount of correction is possible.[9]

All this was only necessary and just: "So our criticism, from age to age, will reflect the things that the age demands; and the criticism of no one man and of no one age can be expected to embrace the whole nature of poetry or exhaust all of its uses."[10]

But the relationship between the two critics is not one of simple negation and rejection. It is, rather, threefold: On one level there are obvious resemblances. On another level, that is, in Eliot's explicit criticisms of Arnold, there are obvious differences. On a third, and more profound level, there is an intimate kinship by which Eliot assumed the same position as Arnold, but made radical and carried to an extremity his predecessor's thought. To put it another way, Eliot asked the same questions as Arnold, but asked them often at a deeper level and invariably provided a more extreme or radical answer.

I

Eliot's own critique of Arnold is complex, if not inconsistent. It has always been a mixture of admiration and distaste, from the very start. If there is any pattern, it resides in the fact that Eliot's own career as a critic follows in a general way the archetypal pattern of Arnold's: from literary criticism, to religious and social criticism, and, finally, to the problems of culture and education, in the widest sense. He was largely concerned with

Arnold's literary criticism in the early days of his own career, was more concerned with the religious side of Arnold in his mid-career, and more recently has been concerned with problems of general culture and education, in Arnold's way. But this pattern is by no means symmetrical, for Arnold as a literary critic always figures in Eliot's speculations, both favorably and, more often, unfavorably. If any trend is discernible, it is that Arnold was clearly the "enemy" in the early days, but gradually became an "ally," except in the sphere of religion, as Eliot's career went on. In any event, Eliot has consistently found himself dealing with the same problems that Arnold did, and indeed this is inevitable, for there is hardly any subject for a contemporary critic, literary, social, political, religious, or cultural, that can be taken up without first disposing of Arnold in one way or another.

There are, of course, many abstract resemblances between the two critics: the reverence for tradition and the Graeco-Roman heritage; the concern for the classics; the preoccupation with the relationships between religion and literature; the connection with twentieth-century Humanism (in Eliot's mind Humanism issued "very naturally from his [Arnold's] doctrine,"[11] and Eliot himself has always been sympathetic to Humanism); the conservative attitude toward morals; the distaste for eccentric individuality, coupled to an admiration for genuine originality; the habit of insisting upon the idea of European cultural unity, while at the same time upholding cultural pluralism and the necessity for knowing other cultures; the distaste for the Romantic's intellect and the distrust of the Elizabethan's sensibility; and, finally, the negative attitude toward the historical Renaissance. Even in the realm of general method there are similarities between the two. Both critics have been amazingly successful in impressing themselves upon their age, and not the least factor in these successes has been a facility in compressing an idea into a catchword; thus in our time "Sweetness and Light" has given way to the "objective correlative."

Again, both men are remarkable for the number of connections they have managed to maintain in a world which each thought was flying apart. First, there is the connection with economic reality; both men, unlike so many writers before and after, have been jobholders and salaried employees. At the same time, and at the other extreme, they have been poets and thus have had a genuine relation to the creative literature of their time. Yet both have maintained an academic status. Withal, they have concerned themselves with religion, politics, sociology, education, literary criticism, the drama, and, in the largest sense and perhaps encompassing all these things, the problems of culture in modern society. That Eliot is conscious of carrying on the work of Arnold in this sphere, we know from his own testimony. In the introduction to *The Sacred Wood,* Eliot, apologizing for his own earlier objections to Arnold, said, "on re-reading ... I can better appreciate his position. And what makes Arnold seem all the more remarkable is, that if he were our exact contemporary, he would find all his labor to perform again."[12] This would seem to imply that Arnold's efforts were necessary but in vain. But in reference to a summation by Arnold himself of his own career, in which he declared he had won no battles but had kept open the lines of communication, Eliot said in 1925:

This is the Arnold who is capable of being a perpetual inspiration. His "party" has no name, and is always, everywhere and inevitably in the minority. Were he alive today he would find Populace and Barbarians more philistinized, and Philistia more barbaric and proletarianized than in his times. The greatest, the only possible victory for Arnold and his disciples is to continue to "keep up the communications" with the future and with the past.[13]

By 1928, in *Lancelot Andrewes,* it was made explicit that Arnold's work was not in vain. Before the temple of Philistinism Arnold had "hacked at the ornaments and cast down the images, and his best phrases remain for ever gibing and scolding in our memory."[14] "It is not to say that Arnold's work was vain if we say that it is to be done again; for we must know in advance . . . that the combat may have truces but never a peace."[15] For there is no such thing as a "Lost Cause," because there is no such thing as a "Gained Cause." All one can do is to "keep things alive"; and this was what Arnold had done, and what Eliot was trying to do.

II

It would be all too easy to exaggerate the similarities between the two critics, for the differences are many and significant. In many ways, they seem to be direct opposites, even in physical presence. When Arnold came to America, some Americans were disappointed by his robust appearance and, their preconceptions shattered, declared that Arnold looked more like an English laborer than like an English aristocrat.[16] It is doubtful that these same critics would have said the same of Eliot, who is certainly an American's idea of what an Anglican divine should look like. Moreover, the tone and tenor of the respective careers of the two critics diverge diametrically. Hamilton Wright Mabie remarked in 1895 that Arnold was the "larkiest" of English critics, and that there is, in much of his controversial writing, a note of zest and joy, as if the contemporary arena were a carnival and he were charging into it dressed in motley. In contrast, there is in much of Eliot's work, especially the earlier, a certain primness that verges on the funereal. Nobody has described it better than the poet himself did in his short self-portrait:

> How unpleasant to meet Mr. Eliot!
> With his features of clerical cut,
> And his brow so grim
> And his mouth so prim

> And his conversation, so nicely
> Restricted to What Precisely
> And If and Perhaps and But.
> How unpleasant to meet Mr. Eliot!
> With a bobtail cur
> In a coat of fur
> And a porpentine cat
> And a wopsical hat:
> How unpleasant to meet Mr. Eliot!
>   (Whether his mouth be open or shut.)[17]

This same disparity, between flamboyance and reserve, is observable in the contrast between the prose styles of the two critics: Arnold, the supple and urbane, winding himself around his subject with mock retreats and apologetic flank attacks; Eliot, terse, epigrammatic, and precise, or endlessly qualifying.

What Arnold would have thought of Eliot, we shall, unfortunately, never know; but Eliot has described the cast of Arnold's mind and found it not profound. That Arnold was aware of the powers of darkness is evident from his own testimony, but, in the strenuous tradition of his father, and in response to his own stoicism, he refused to dwell upon them. To Eliot, living in the apocalyptic twentieth century, Arnold's refusal to look into the jaws of hell was a weakness and had cut Arnold off from the furthest reaches of human experience: "Arnold's notion of 'life,' in his account of poetry, does not perhaps go deep enough."[18] Eliot's attitude toward Arnold is like that of the tormented ascetic toward the well-fed liberal; it is like Dostoevski's saintly criminals expressing their disdain for Western "gentlemen." Arnold, said Eliot, speaks of "discipline," but it is the "discipline of culture, not the discipline of suffering."[19] Life is made up of "horror," "boredom," and "glory," and Arnold had known only the "boredom": "The vision of the horror and the glory was denied to Arnold, but he knew something of the boredom."[20] Arnold never went deep enough: he lacked the "auditory imagination" which sinks to "the most primitive and forgotten, returning to the origin and bringing something back, seeking the beginning and the end."[21] This comment is perhaps not one person talking about another, but is the twentieth century judging the nineteenth. In any event, the two critics, in their materials and in their methods, diverge sharply, and they are separated even more sharply by the very different characteristics of the respective historical periods in which they operated.

It is obvious, first of all, that Eliot is no part of the general Arnoldian tradition in America. He has had nothing to do with Sherman or Brownell, although certainly he is related to James, as an expatriate and as a seeker after "discrimination" and subtlety in criticism. Certainly, too, in Sherman the Arnoldian image had become both vague and provincial, and vagueness and provinciality were the two elements in English criticism against which Eliot was strongly protesting. As late as 1919 Eliot could still say, like James and Arnold before him: "We generally agree in conversation that the amount of good literary criticism in English is negligible."[22] The charge was evidently meant to apply to Arnold's work as well as to that of the present century, for in the same essay Eliot said, apropos of Arnold Bennett's statement about Arnold: "... and he says also that Matthew Arnold with study and discipline might have been a great critic, which is probably a superstition."[23] Not only was Eliot no part of the Arnoldian tradition in America; he took what can only be described as a monumentally "long" view of American culture itself. A self-styled member of the European community, he seems to regard America as an experiment the ultimate consequences of which can still not be foreseen. His main contention seems to be that the issues raised by the Civil War have not yet been reconciled, or the conflict concluded. In the lectures which were afterwards collected in *After Strange Gods,* Eliot told a Virginia audience in 1933 that the Southern culture was the last hope, since New England culture was being wiped out by the invasions of the "foreign-born" and by industrialism. "The Civil War was certainly the greatest disaster in the whole of American history":[24] the country had never recovered and perhaps never would. In 1936 Eliot said that the monster of industrialism and mass organization was still throttling the development of native culture: "I have little hope for the future of America until that country falls apart into its natural components, divisions which would not be simply those of the old North and South and still less those of forty-eight states."[25]

Shifting the ground of the argument from industrialism to religion, Eliot said in *The Idea of a Christian Society* in 1939 that if the United States and Canada "are to develop a positive culture of their own, and not remain merely derivatives of Europe, they can only proceed either in the direction of a pagan or of a Christian society."[26] For at present the society of the United States, like that of most of the West, Europe included, is merely "neutral." In *Notes Towards the Definition of Culture* he returned to the Civil War theme and once more, taking the longest possible view, suspended judgment:

The real revolution ... was not what is called the Revolution in the history books, but is a consequence of the Civil War; after which arose a plutocratic elite; after which the expansion and material development of the country was accelerated; after which was swollen that stream of mixed immigration, bringing (or rather multiplying) the danger of development into a *caste* system which has not yet been quite dispelled. For the sociologist, the evidence from America is not yet ripe.[27]

It was not that America was without her artists and writers. Poe is better than Shelley, Whitman than Browning. Indeed, the very isolation that the American writer endured worked in his favor, for the starved environment brought out, or almost forced out, the full mental capacity and the "originality" of these writers.[28] Still, and it is James's complaint all over again, the American world was thin and shadowy, lacking corruption and self-dependency.[29] Only Hawthorne, Poe, and Whitman had attained greatness within its confines.

An American tradition in criticism was practically nonexistent. Significantly, the only American critic that Eliot singled out for praise was the one who had been most derided by the American Arnoldians—Edgar Allan Poe. With all its flaws, his work, viewed as a whole, said Eliot, presents "a mass of unique shape and impressive size to which the eye constantly returns."[30] It would not be an exaggeration to say that Poe, the perennial outcast of American culture, had been the one American creative writer who had significantly influenced Eliot, although this influence was felt by way of Baudelaire, Mallarmé, and Valéry. As a critic, too, Poe "deserves the study of every English critic."[31] Emerson, once regarded as the central American critic, was already an "encumbrance" and not a "real observer of the moral life," as was Hawthorne.[32]

From the American movements in criticism which were a part of his intellectual environment in his undergraduate days, Eliot has remained equally detached, except, of course, from Humanism. In a review of *The Reinterpretation of American Literature,* edited by Norman Foerster, Eliot outlined his concept of the course of American criticism in the latter part of the nineteenth century and the early part of the twentieth century. During the latter part of the nineteenth century, under the aegis of President Eliot of Harvard, literature had been pursued according to the Teutonic methods of scholarship, as exemplified by Kittredge. But now—Eliot was writing in 1929—there is a tendency to fly in the other direction and place an exaggerated emphasis on contemporary literature. Babbitt was a good mean between these extremes, scholarly but not withdrawn from the problems of literature and life in the present; and of Babbitt's disciples, Foerster is "the most brilliant."[33]

Behind these developments was a larger progression, covering three generations of critics. The earliest generation had consisted of Babbitt and More, who were the first to attempt to deprovincialize America and to replace its dilettante criticism with the disciplined standards of Sainte-Beuve, Taine, and Renan.[34] The next generation, represented most clearly by Mencken and Brooks, was a regression, for Mencken was only destructive and negative, while Brooks was merely querulous.[35] But a third generation had come along. It was made up of disciples of the first generation;[36] among its members were Mumford, Munson, and Allen Tate, and its foremost representative in the universities was Foerster. This third generation was making the "sanest attempt" yet witnessed to criticize and control postwar America.[37]

Now it is obvious that, in Eliot's mind, the Humanist literature was the only solid body of critical opinion produced by America, and he even jammed Allen Tate into the category. Yet the position of the Humanists was vulnerable, he felt, and again, it was the fault of the culture: "But it is not the fault of Mr. More or Mr. Babbitt that the culture of ideas has only been able to survive in America in the unfavorable atmosphere of the university."[38] Welcoming Lawrence Hyde as a potential leader for Humanism, Eliot said in 1931 that there was needed a leader of "the second, or perhaps the third, generation of humanists; and in these days of dog-eat-dog in the criticism of literature and life, that is no small promise."[39]

Furthermore, Babbitt and More had their weaknesses, irrespective of circumstance. More had accepted Arnold's dictum that literature was a "criticism of life," which, in Eliot's eyes, was a "facile" phrase that did not do justice to the complexity of great literature.[40] Moreover, like his prototype Sainte-Beuve, More was primarily a moralist, a good thing to be but no guaranty of excellence in criticism.[41] Babbitt, in this respect, was saner and more balanced, but he lacked the religious insight, and in the last analysis his Humanism was merely a by-product of Protestant theology in its death agonies.[42] And the followers of Babbitt and More were too academic, literary, and fanatical; indeed, the American Humanists, in their refusal to embrace religion, were on their way to discrediting their own movement. "There is no opposition between the religious and the *pure* humanistic attitude: they are necessary to each other. It is because Mr. Foerster's brand of humanism seems to be *impure,* that I fear the ultimate discredit of all humanism."[43]

III

Arnold could not be dealt with so summarily, and, further, he had fastened his hold on the very public, literary England and America, that Eliot thought was provincial and incoherent. Like Arnold, James, and Brownell, Eliot turned to the French for the intellectual virtues of clarity, hardness, and precision and for the aesthetic virtues of seriousness and completeness. In the new preface to the 1928 edition of *The Sacred Wood* he acknowledged the debt: "... I was much stimulated and much helped by the critical writings of Remy de Gourmont. I acknowledge that influence and am grateful for it."[44] Just as Arnold and Brownell had preached these French traits at the nineteenth century Anglo-American world, Eliot preached them at its twentieth-century counterpart. But, in the revenges of time, Arnold, or the Arnoldian tradition, had become in a way the very embodiment of the defects that Arnold himself had once inveighed against: vagueness, oversimple moralism, and lack of intellectual vigor.

It is important to remember, however, that Eliot's primary

concern was with poetry and with effecting, along with Pound and others, a poetic revolution. In their eyes the poetry of Arnold and of the rest of the nineteenth-century poets was, by and large, a continuation of the Romantic tradition; the language of this poetry had abstracted itself into a diction and rhythm far removed from speech and was therefore on its way to, if not actually in, a state of petrifaction. Writing retrospectively in 1942, Eliot said:

Every revolution in poetry is apt to be, and sometimes to announce itself as, a return to common speech. . . . The followers of a revolution develop the new poetic idiom in one direction or another; they polish or perfect it; meanwhile the spoken language goes on changing, and the poetic idiom goes out of date.[45]

Thus the original role that Eliot adopted was not that of the critic, and particularly not the critic of society, but that of the poet-critic, the reformer of the language. He saw himself in the tradition of Wordsworth and, preëminently, Dryden. Since Dryden developed the "natural" style, equally beholding to the spoken language and to prose: "It is hardly too much to say that [he] found the English speechless, and he gave them speech."[46]

But creation needed criticism, and the revolution in poetry needed a revolution in criticism as well; and for the accomplishment of this, Arnold must be disposed of.

In Eliot's critique of Arnold there are three charges that are repeated without essential change: first, Arnold was a propagandist and moralist rather than a critic; second, Arnold was a vague and an inexact thinker; and third, he was completely wrong in thinking that poetry could be an adequate substitute for religion. The first charge, that Arnold was a propagandist rather than a critic, is actually equivocal, since it could turn either into an accusation or a lament, depending upon what perspective Eliot was adopting at the time. At times Eliot regrets the fact that Arnold necessarily had to engage in nonliterary polemics and thus waste his strength on what might well have been done by second-order minds, had there been any in England: "In a society in which the arts were seriously studied, in which the art of writing was respected, Arnold might have become a critic."[47] This same kind of charge, without the patronizing tone, is made in an essay on Benda:

Matthew Arnold was intelligent, and by so much difference as the presence of one intelligent man makes, our age is inferior to that of Arnold. But what an advantage a man like M. Benda has over Arnold. It is not simply that he has a critical tradition behind him, and that Arnold is using a language which constantly tempts the user away from dispassionate exposition into sarcasm and diatribe.... It is that the follies and stupidities of the French ... express themselves in the form of ideas.... A man of ideas needs ideas, or pseudo-ideas, to fight against. And Arnold lacked the active resistance which is necessary to keep the mind at its sharpest.[48]

Here, Arnold is seen as the talented victim of the circumstances which he had been the first to diagnose and fight against. But to understand is not to forgive, and, more often than not, Arnold is blamed, irrespective of circumstances, for not being a true critic. In "The Perfect Critic" Eliot said that Coleridge was the last genuine critic, that Arnold was a propagandist for literature, and that, since his time, all criticism has been either vague impressionism or empty verbalizing.

For Arnold was too vague and imprecise. In Eliot's essay "The Function of Criticism" Arnold is accused of being "blunt": "Matthew Arnold distinguishes far too bluntly, it seems to me, between the two activities [creation and criticism]: he overlooks the capital importance of criticism in the work of creation itself."[49] And in "The Return of Matthew Arnold" the charge of vagueness or imprecision is generalized:

We realize now that Arnold was neither thorough enough, nor comprehensive enough, to make any fundamental alterations of literary values: he failed to ascend to first principles; his thought lacks the logical vigor of his master Newman; his taste is biased by convictions and prejudices which he did not take the trouble to dissect to their elements. The best of Arnold's criticism is an illustration of his ethical views, and contributes to his discrimination of the values and relations of the components of the Good life ...[50]

Behind this general charge are two specific objections to Arnold: first, he was vague; second, he had a tendency to confuse different activities. To do away with the vagueness, Eliot was to propose a criticism that would work by "analysis and comparison methodically, with sensitiveness, intelligence, curiosity, intensity of passion and infinite knowledge..."[51] This meant, above all, an attention to technique: "The critic is interested in technique—technique in the widest sense."[52] For this, Arnold and Sainte-Beuve are useless:

The criticism which a poet can find of use to himself is first the advice and conversation of older poets, and second, the writings of Dryden, Campion, and half a dozen other poets, and third, his own criticism of better poets than he. He can learn more from Jespersen's English grammar than from Sainte-Beuve.[53]

Not only must there be precision and specificity in each area of activity; there must be no confusion between related but separate activities. The "confusion of genres" which Babbitt saw as one of the chief sins of Romanticism and of the modern world became also for his pupil Eliot a capital crime. With the founding of *Criterion* Eliot issued a pronouncement to those who had accused the new movement in poetry and criticism of being "divorced from life":

A literary review should maintain the application, in literature, of principles which have their consequences also in politics and in private conduct; and it should maintain them without tolerating any confusion of the purposes of pure literature with the purposes of politics or ethics.

To maintain the autonomy, and the disinterestedness, of every human activity, and to perceive it in relation to every other, require a considerable discipline.[54]

The new era of criticism, then, was to constitute a clean break and a clear start. The fuzzy catchwords and categories of the nineteenth century were to be replaced with intellectual vigor. "I believe," said Eliot in 1926, "that the modern tendency is toward something which, for want of a better name, we may call classicism."[55] Under this dispensation there will be a higher and clearer conception of reason, and a more severe and serene control over the emotions by reason. This suggests the Greeks, "but it must inevitably be very different."[56] Just as every revolution in poetry announces itself to be a clearing of the air and a getting back to fundamentals, every new movement in criticism does the same.

It was the *mélange de genres* in Arnold's speculations on poetry and religion that, for Eliot, a convert, constituted the most serious evidence of his predecessor's confusion; in a review of I. A. Richards' *Science and Poetry* he questioned all of Richards' theories and concluded, "It is a revised version of Literature and Dogma."[57] In an essay on Bradley in which he linked Bradley and Arnold as allies in the continuing fight against Philistinism, Eliot carefully separated Arnold's religious writings from his other work. "... *Literature and Dogma* is irrelevant to Arnold's main position as given in the *Essays* and in *Culture and Anarchy,* ... the greatest weakness of Arnold's culture was his weakness in philosophical training, ..."[58] He then quoted with approval Bradley's attack on *Literature and Dogma,* for Arnold, "with all his great virtues," was not patient enough, or was too anxious for immediate effect, to avoid inconsistencies. The burden of Eliot's objection to Arnold's religious writing is perhaps all implicit in this statement: "But *if* there is a 'will of

God,' as Arnold, in a hasty moment, admits, then some doctrine of Grace must be admitted . . ."[59]

By this time (1928), then, Eliot had made a separation, which Arnold would never have allowed, between the religious writings of his predecessor and his other efforts. The now familiar objections—the charges of inconsistency, indefiniteness, and lack of power for consecutive reasoning—were repeated in "Arnold and Pater," although Eliot said that *Culture and Anarchy* and *Friendship's Garland* still stand, and that Arnold still appeals more than Ruskin and Carlyle. Yet he had taught that religion is morals and that religion is art, thus divorcing thought from religion and, in the realm of literary criticism, playing right into the hands of the unprincipled sensationism of Pater. But Eliot's own interests had broadened; he had proclaimed in 1928, in the famous, perhaps notorious, statement introducing *For Lancelot Andrewes:* "The general point of view may be described as classicist in literature, royalist in politics, and anglo-catholic in religion."[60] Complementary and pendent to this was a less well known declaration, of the same year, prefacing a reëdition of *The Sacred Wood,* in which, after mentioning his critical debt to Gourmont, he said: ". . . I by no means disown it [Gourmont's influence] by having passed on to another problem not touched upon in this book: that of the relation of poetry to the spiritual and social life of its time and of other times."[61] In short, he was repeating the pattern of Arnold, but he still protested against the poetic theory of two of his greatest predecessors, for "Poetry is a superior amusement"[62] (and thus has nothing to do with morals or religion), and

It will not do to talk of "emotion recollected in tranquility," . . . or to call it "a criticism of life," than which no phrase can sound more frigid to anyone who has felt the full surprise and elevation of a new experience of poetry. And certainly poetry is not the inculcation of morals, or the direction of politics; and no more is it religion or an equivalent of religion . . .[63]

Poetry certainly does have something to do with morals, and
even perhaps with politics, but it is difficult to establish the clear
connections.[64]

Henceforth the criticism of Arnold in Eliot's critical writings
was to be principally concerned with religion. In a tribute to
Dryden as the "normal" critic, Eliot enumerated the great English critics and found each of them wanting: Johnson had a too
"particular method"; Coleridge was no model, for obvious
reasons, and, furthermore, strayed off into philosophy; Wordsworth was "defending his own practices"; and Arnold was "too
largely concerned with finding the moral lesson."[65] As for the
current "heresy" that poetry could substitute for religion:

> The germ, or something more developed than the germ, of this
> way of thinking is to be found in the criticism of Matthew Arnold,
> who is to that extent an heresiarch. Arnold dismisses altogether the
> intellectual element in religion, and leaves only art and morals; . . .
> and truly moral art is all that Arnold leaves us in the place of re-
> ligious faith.[66]

This constituted the "new confusion" and could be seen, in
different ways, in Babbitt, Richards, and John Middleton Murry.
Dryden, on the other hand, was "a very great defender of
sanity."[67]

The lecture on Arnold in *The Use of Poetry and the Use of
Criticism* is Eliot's last major appraisal of his predecessor. Again,
he allows Arnold many kinds of virtues, but, with the fervor of
a convert, comes down hard on Arnold's religious speculations.
Arnold was right about the Romantics; and he had "real taste";
"The Study of Poetry" is a "classic" in English criticism.[68] He
was "in some respects the most satisfactory man of letters of his
age."[69] And "however well-nourished we may be on previous
literature and previous culture, we cannot afford to neglect
Arnold."[70]

Nevertheless, Arnold represented a period of only apparent,

not real, stabilization, and his position was both "shallow and premature."[71] Arnold was an "undergraduate" in philosophy and a "Philistine" in religion.[72] As for the idea that poetry may substitute for religion, "nothing in this world or the next is a substitute for anything else."[73] Arnold had exaggerated the importance of morals, placed the critical emphasis on the poet's feelings rather than on his poetry, and misjudged poets, such as Chaucer, because of his preconceptions. Arnold had no real "serenity," but only an impeccable "demeanor."[74] More important, perhaps, was the fact that Arnold was not a revolutionary or reformer in the real sense, which for Eliot means reformer of the language; rather, he tried to continue a dying tradition: he had "the convervatism which springs from lack of faith, and the zeal for reform which springs from dislike of change."[75] Nevertheless, Arnold had set the critical tone for the century, and Pater, Symons, Symonds, Stephen, Myers, and Saintsbury all followed in his train. Everything, finally, is relative, however; Dryden, Johnson, and Arnold had each introduced a point of view for his own age, but none of these points of view will do for ours. For our day, "A more profound insight into poetry and a more exact use of language than Arnold's are required."[76] But as for the canons of criticism which Eliot proposed in the lecture, it is difficult to see how Arnold, or any other thoughtful critic, could object or find any deviation from his own procedure. Criticism is a "department of thought"[77] (which was precisely Arnold's point). It seeks to find out what poetry is, what its use is, why it is written or read or recited; and it seeks to assess actual poetry. At all times it moves between the two poles of "What is poetry?" and "Is this a good poem?"

With *After Strange Gods,* Eliot became more concerned with orthodoxy and the problems of culture and religion than with literature and criticism proper. Still, Arnold was the archheretic for confusing religion and art. In enumerating modern literary

heretics, Eliot mentioned the fact that at sixteen there was oper-
ative in Yeats "the doctrine of Arnold, that Poetry can replace
Religion."[78] Now, in Eliot's mind, everyone in the final analysis
must be brought to the bar of orthodoxy; and he announced in
Essays Ancient and Modern: "The 'greatness' of literature cannot be determined solely by literary standards; though we must
remember that whether it is literature or not can be determined
only by literary standards."[79] And in the notes to *The Idea of a
Christian Society* he sputtered at the fact that John Middleton
Murry had quoted, "with apparent approval," a statement by
Arnold that the Catholic Church should make its claims for
universality on grounds of its forms rather than of its dogma:

> Well! if eternity and universality is to be found, not in dogma, but
> in worship—that means, in a common form of worship which will
> mean to the worshipers anything that they like to fancy, then the
> result seems to me to be likely to be the most corrupt form of
> ritualism.[80]

Eliot's prose work in his later years has been largely concerned
with education and culture. Again, Arnold is invariably the first
critic to be dealt with, not because he was wrong, but because he
was right, except that he did not go far enough. Thus, at the
very beginning of *Notes Towards the Definition of Culture,*
after the initial definition of what constitutes culture, and after
emphasizing the fact that culture must be seen in social as well
as individual terms, he says:

> The most easily remembered example of this selection is Matthew
> Arnold's *Culture and Anarchy.* Arnold is concerned primarily with
> the individual and the "perfection" at which he should aim. It is
> true that in his famous classification of "Barbarians, Philistines,
> Populace" he concerns himself with a critique of classes; but his
> criticism is confined to an idictment of these classes for their short-
> comings, and does not proceed to consider what should be the
> proper function or "perfection" of each class. The effect, therefore,
> is to exhort the individual who would attain the peculiar kind of

"perfection" which Arnold calls "culture" to rise superior to the limitations of any class, rather than to realize its highest attainable ideals.[81]

The result of this failure, on Arnold's part, to take into consideration the whole of society in its class stratification, gives a certain "thinness" to Arnold's culture. Arnold also failed to take into account the many varied ways in which the word "cultured" can be used about an individual; so that finally "the wholly cultured individual is a phantasm; and we shall look for culture, not in any individual ... [but] ... in the pattern of society as a whole."[82] These, then, were failures of Arnold in not thinking through the problem thoroughly enough, but "the facile assumption of a relationship between culture and religion is perhaps the most fundamental weakness of Arnold's *Culture and Anarchy.*"[83] In "The Aims of Education," a series of lectures delivered at the University of Chicago, Arnold's educational ideal, the pursuit of perfection, is allowed, but with the disclaimer that it is too individualistic in itself and must be supplemented with other, more social, aims. Borrowing from Professor Joad, Eliot states that there are three interrelated aims of education: first, the professional, or the preparation for earning one's living; second, the social, or training for good citizenship; and third, the individual, "or, in Matthew Arnold's way of putting it, the pursuit of perfection."[84] None of the three aims in itself is sufficient, and indeed they may, on occasion, clash with one another; but all must be kept in mind in any adequate educational system.

From this review of Eliot's critique of Arnold it now becomes obvious that there are two main points of attack: the logical and the religious. Arnold was too vague in his definitions and in his judgments, and he mixed categories; the most serious mixing of categories consisted in substituting art for religion. How much effect this attack has had upon Arnold's reputation and influence in America it is difficult to say. Certainly the charge of vagueness and the allied objection that Arnoldian criticism did not concern itself with technique have borne the most fruit, some of it rather strange. One wonders whether anyone would say now what Eliot did at Harvard in 1932, in the same lecture in which he said that English and American criticism was still living in the Arnold period:

> I hold indeed that in an age in which the use of poetry is something agreed upon you are more likely to get that minute and scrupulous examination of felicity and blemish, line by line, which is conspicuously absent from the criticism of our time, a criticism which seems to demand of poetry, not that it shall be well written, but that it shall be "representative of its age."[85]

As for the relationship between literature and religion and that between art and morals, these questions are still open. But certainly Eliot's orthodoxy is a minority position, and it is difficult to see how his criticism in this area could have affected Arnold's reputation generally. If, in sum, Eliot's criticism does not seek to demolish Arnold absolutely, and if, in sum, it contains much praise as well as blame, the reason is that there are deep and powerful affinities between the two critics. They both asked the same kind of questions, and their answers differ in degree rather than in kind.

IV

In the history of the poet-critic in England which was published as *The Use of Poetry and the Use of Criticism,* Eliot pointed out that one development—he did not term it an "advance"—in the history of English criticism was an accelerating growth of self-consciousness and subtlety, as the comparison of Dryden and Coleridge would attest. Arnold was in this line: "In the criticism of Arnold we find a continuation of the work of the Romantic poets with a new appraisal of the poetry of the past by a method which, lacking the precision of Johnson's, gropes toward wider and deeper connexions."[86] In reference to this groping toward wider and deeper connections, Eliot thanked Arnold for bringing forward the issue over which he was to quarrel with him most: "To Matthew Arnold we owe the credit of bringing the religious issue explicitly into the discussion of literature and poetry...My contemporaries seem to me still to be occupied with it, whether they call themselves churchmen, or agnostics, or rationalists, or social revolutionists."[87] This would seem to imply that Arnold had asked the right question but given the wrong answer, in Eliot's mind. When the general cast of Eliot's thought is contrasted with that of Arnold's, the same thing proves to be true again and again: whether it be due to a difference in historical period or a difference in personality, or both, Eliot invariably supplies an extreme solution for a problem that Arnold answers with a moderate remedy.

Both critics are advocates of cosmopolitanism, concerned with the European community, and fond of repeating Goethe's dictum that one cannot know one's own culture well without knowing another well. Yet the differences between their concepts of Europe are radical. The great European figure for Arnold was Goethe, and the great philosopher Spinoza. In the Renaissance he was not much interested, and of the Middle Ages he said: "I have a strong sense of the irrationality of that period, and of the utter folly of those who take it seriously, and play at restoring it; still, it has poetically the greatest charm and refreshment possible for me."[88] In short, Arnold's European community was, relatively, modern. He was greatly interested in the "race" of the nations, and much of his energy was directed to seeing that England would not fall behind. It is doubtful, as James attests, whether a mere European can have quite the all-embracing feeling for Europe that some Americans have, and certainly Eliot's concept of the spirit of Europe encompasses much more time and space than does Arnold's. In Eliot's eyes, Goethe, Arnold's Cosmopolitan thinker, is a "little provincial," "like our own nineteenth century authors."[89] His poetry exhibits partiality, impermanence in some of its content, and Germanism of sensibility. Goethe, to Eliot, seems "limited by his age, by his language, and by his culture."[90] Hence the embodiment of Europe for Eliot is Dante—not the spokesman for northern Europe of the nineteenth century, but the poet of all Western Christendom. And in *What Is a Classic?* Eliot pushes back behind the Middle Ages and Dante to find his "centre" in Rome: "But [Aeneas] is the symbol of Rome; and as Aeneas is to Rome, so is ancient Rome to Europe. Thus Virgil acquires the centrality of the unique classic; he is at the centre of European civilization..."[91] And behind this lies the influence of Greece that we inherit through the Graeco-Roman world:

We need to remind ourselves that, as Europe is a whole (and still, in its progressive mutilation and disfigurement, the organism out of which any greater world harmony must develop), so European literature is a whole, . . . The blood stream of European literature is Latin and Greek—not as two systems of circulation, but one, for it is through Rome that our parentage in Greece must be traced.[92]

It is not, of course, that the prophet of Hellenism and the preserver of the Christian tradition was by any means unaware of the heritage from Greece and Rome, but rather that to his mind the central tradition of Europe tended to express itself in terms of the modern rather than of the ancient world, through Goethe rather than through Dante or Virgil. Again, Arnold did not have that sense of the persistent *consequences* of past events which Eliot appears to have in the extreme, and which tends to make past history more vivid for him. As, for example, Eliot believes that the American Civil War has never been concluded, he thinks the same of the English: "The fact is simply that the Civil War of the seventeenth century . . . has never been con-

cluded. The Civil War is not ended: I question whether any
serious civil war ever does end."[93] Thus the past is more immediate to him than it is to Arnold, and the central unity of Europe
is found further back in time and space, at a more extreme
remove.

If Eliot's attitude toward the European past consists in making radical Arnold's position, so does his attitude toward the
present and the future. It is, in fact, Arnold's argument with
another turn on the screw, sometimes up to such a pitch that it
passes into its opposite and becomes antithetical to Arnold.
Arnold's judgment on liberalism was, essentially, that it was
mindless: it was too exclusively allied to "the instinct for expansion" and did not minister enough to the human desires for
manners, beauty, and intellectual accomplishment; it pursued
the wrong objects, such as the Deceased Wife's Sister's Bill, to
the detriment of its true objective: the cause of eradicating the
extremes of inequality. As a "Liberal of the Future" Arnold
prophesied, "... so long as the Liberals do only as they have
done hitherto, they will not permanently satisfy the community."[94] But in Eliot's mind, Arnold's objection that liberalism
was too exclusively tied to the "instinct for expansion" and that
it did not know what it wanted, becomes full-scale and a total
rejection of liberalism:

... [liberalism] tends to release energy rather than accumulate it, to
relax, rather than to fortify. It is a movement not so much defined
by its end, as by its starting point; away from, rather than towards,
something definite. Our point of departure is more real to us than
our destination; and the destination is likely to present a very different picture when arrived at, from the vaguer image formed in
imagination.[95]

Arnold's contention that liberals and conservatives never really
meet head on over principles and his approval of Cobbett's contempt for the two-party system are, again, in Eliot, raised to an

absolute: "In the sense in which Liberalism is contrasted with Conservatism, both can be equally repellent: if the former means chaos, the latter can mean petrifaction."[96] But, whereas Arnold worried about the future of liberalism and tried to strengthen it by criticism, Eliot calmly announces: "The attitudes and beliefs of Liberalism are destined to disappear, are already disappearing."[97]

Similarly, Arnold's critique on individualism is carried all the way in Eliot. When John Middleton Murry referred to the "inner self" and to the necessity of reliance upon it, Eliot said: "The inner voice, in fact, sounds remarkably like an old principle which has been formulated by an elder critic in the now familiar phrase of 'doing as one likes.' "[98] And the world of this freewheeling individualist is, in fact, an unreal one: "It is not that this world of separate individuals of the liberal democrat is undesirable; it is simply that the world does not exist."[99]

Again, Arnold's feeling for the historic sway and the internationalism of the Catholic Church, and his distrust of the ugliness and provinciality of certain of the Protestant sects becomes in Eliot complete: a conversion to Anglo-Catholicism, which conversion, in its turn, intensified and made absolute the rejection of liberalism, individualism, and Protestantism, and led him to place the "centre" of Europe in its historic Christian home.

But it would be false to multiply resemblances, which are not very apparent, without pointing out real differences, which are. Arnold's vision of a society of equals gives way to Eliot's idea of a Christian society, with its classes and orders. Arnold's "natural truth of religion" gives way to Catholic dogma; Arnold's insistence on self-help gives way to "God's grace." For Eliot has taken the ultimate position which provides the ultimate answers, something that Arnold always refused to do. Arnold, no doubt, would have rejected both terms of the now familiar either/or proposition that Eliot presented to his readers in 1936: "There are two and only two finally tenable hypotheses about life: the Catholic and the materialistic."[100] And both alternatives have, in fact, been rejected by the most eminent modern Arnoldian, Lionel Trilling.

Chapter VII

LIONEL TRILLING

IF ELIOT took the poetic-religious side of Arnold for his starting point, Trilling has appropriated the socioliberal side. As Eliot was concerned with poetry and its future, Trilling has dealt with prose fiction and its future. If Eliot's influence on the course of criticism has been in the realm of technique, Trilling's emphasis and impression have been in the direction of content and ideas. As Eliot's concern has been historical Christian civilization, Trilling's starting point has been the chief divergence from the historic unity of Western Christendom, namely, the French Revolution. As Eliot has returned to Europe and the past, Trilling has remained in and of America. Between them, in sum, they share the heritage of Arnold, not directly in the sense that Brownell and Sherman held that same heritage, but methodologically, in that they have been concerned with the same problems as Arnold and have often adopted his techniques, if not always agreeing with his ideas. Arnold's influence on Trilling is manifest and admitted, and Trilling himself speaks of Eliot's "long if recalcitrant discipleship to Matthew Arnold."[1] If Eliot signifies what Arnold means to the religious intelligence of the twentieth century, Trilling shows us the image of Arnold as seen by the liberal. It would perhaps be oversimplifying matters, although it is in a sense true, to say that Trilling answers Eliot's objections to Arnold in Arnold's name. He is also equally concerned with accommodating Eliot to the Arnold tradition. And on the subjects of the Romantics and the nineteenth century he diverges from both Arnold and Eliot.

Trilling's discipleship to Arnold also indicates, as had Sherman's before him, the powerful and continuing hold that

Arnold has exercised over the academic mind. Thus it is fitting that if one English professor, Sherman, had seemed to have permanently fossilized Arnold, another English professor, Trilling, has shown him to be very much alive and, indeed, even in a book that was a doctoral dissertation.

I

Trilling's relation to Eliot is somewhat like Eliot's to Arnold: Eliot is the acknowledged master who invariably must be dealt with when an important question arises. When Trilling comes to speak of the relation between ideas and literature, it is Eliot who must be disposed of, for it is he who has expressed the "modern" feeling about this important matter: "The modern feeling about this relationship is defined by two texts, both provided by T. S. Eliot."[2] Trilling then quotes Eliot's pronouncement, from his essay on Shakespeare, that he could see no reason for thinking Shakespeare and Dante were independent in their thought, and he refers to the celebrated remark by Eliot on James, that the latter's mind was too fine "to be violated by an idea." Admitting that Eliot, in his comment on Shakespeare, had an ulterior purpose in mind, namely, to contravene the nineteenth-century concept of poetry as communication, Trilling still quotes back at Eliot a nineteenth-century description, Carlyle's, of Shakespeare's greatness, which attributes it to the power of his intellect. And the statement on James is explained as a misconception of the very nature of thought that Eliot shares in common with his age, which can only think of thinking as something purely abstract and which has invented monstrous vocabularies to express this bodiless "non-thought." "Mr. Eliot, if we take him literally, does indeed misinterpret the relationship [between art and thought] when he conceives of 'thinking' in such a way that it must be denied to Shakespeare and Dante. It must puzzle us to know what thinking is if Shake-

speare and Dante did not do it."³ And in "Art and Fortune," an
essay with the theme that the novel of the future must deal with
ideas, Trilling refers to Eliot's two statements once more and
concludes: "But I do not understand what Mr. Eliot means
when he makes a sharp distinction between ideas and emotions
in literature; I think Plato was right when in *The Symposium*
he represented ideas as continuous with emotions, both spring-
ing from the appetites."⁴

Again, in a defense of the quietism of Wordsworth, here jux-
taposed against the violence, "the tigers of wrath," of modern
literature and life, Trilling cites Eliot as having set the tone of
modern criticism with his statement that Wordsworth mumbled
"the still, sad music of infirmity" and that he lacked an "eagle."
In the same essay, *The Cocktail Party* is mentioned as having
presented two ways of life, the ordinary humdrum one and the
life of spiritual heroism. But while Eliot calls them equally
valid, yet in his description of them he sets too little store on
ordinary life, seeing its boredom but none of its anguish and
glory. Thus, as Eliot had found Arnold to be without the apocalyptic imagination, the vision of the horror and the glory, Trilling reasserts the claims of the ordinary and the everyday against
Eliot. Most important, Eliot's notion that a dogmatic religion
is necessary is explicitly rejected by Trilling. For if in the past
religion has been one of the conditions of literature, it is not
necessarily a *sine qua non* for the literature of the future. "What
is more," Trilling adds, "I consider it from many points of view
an impropriety to try to guarantee literature by religious belief."⁵
As Eliot took Arnold's middle position on religion and literature
and carried it to the conservative right, Trilling swings it toward
the liberal left. Also, as might be expected, Trilling quarrels with
Eliot's politics and sociology. In an essay on Kipling he comments on Eliot's "ingenuous" distinction between tory and
fascist, made in reference to Kipling: "A tory, to be sure, is not

a fascist, and Kipling is not properly to be called a fascist, but neither is his political temperament to be adequately described merely by reference to a tradition which is honored by Dr. Johnson, Burke, and Walter Scott."⁶ In a review of *The Idea of a Christian Society* Trilling speaks of

certain deficiencies of Mr. Eliot's temperament where it joins with certain aspects of strict and theological Anglicanism, giving us such things as the cold ignorance of what people are really like, or a confusion of morality with snobbery or conformity, or even with a rather fierce Puritanism.⁷

In the same review he mentions Eliot's blindness to the problems of the relations between social forms and power, and power and wealth, and he asks the question that might be asked of any pleader for a "Christian" society; that is, if it is indeed adequate, then why has it failed historically? In morality, politics, and religion, then, Trilling attempts to confront Eliot with the liberalism of Arnold.

But Eliot is not simply "the enemy," for his views are necessary, even indispensable. Trilling is fond of quoting John Stuart Mill's prayer for liberals, from his essay on Coleridge:

"Lord, enlighten thou our enemies . . ."; sharpen their wits, give acuteness to their perceptions and consecutiveness and clearness to their reasoning powers. We are in danger from their folly, not from their wisdom: their weakness is what fills us with apprehension, not their strength.

In other words, all parties, and the liberals in particular, need intelligent adversaries. In Trilling's eyes, Kipling was a major disaster for liberalism because he was stupidly antiliberal and therefore easily dismissed. Eliot, however, is the proper Coleridge of his time, the antiliberal of intellectual power. It is true that Trilling once denied him even this function: at the end of the angry essay on Kipling, Trilling said that although Eliot could at one time "challenge the liberal sensibility," he could do so no longer, since "his judgment is so without illumination..."[8] But this statement was made in the original article, published in *The Nation* in 1943 as a review of Eliot's edition of Kipling; it was excised from the reprint, the "Kipling" in *The Liberal Imagination.* In Trilling's discussion of *The Idea of a Christian Society,* Eliot is made the Coleridge for the modern Mills. Eliot assumes, first of all, a moral basis for everything: "He means something that is personal in a way we have forgotten, and which, in a way we have denied, connects personal action with the order of the universe."[9] Unlike modern radicals, Eliot does not confuse means and ends; and he challenges liberal-radical thought at its weakest places. Moreover, Eliot's dualism refuses to admit any simple monistic solutions to problems and rejects the notion, inherent in Marxism, of a "final" conflict, after which all problems will be solved and history will grind to a halt. We shall always have to struggle, says Eliot, and this, according to Trilling, is what the political left must learn. Still, in summation, Trilling adds: "If I have tried to say that the assumptions of materialism have largely failed us, it was surely not to conclude that the assumptions of supernaturalism can aid us."[10] Eliot's whole position is manifestly impractical; nevertheless, he should be listened to, as Mill listened to Coleridge.

Behind these explicit disagreements and the idea of Eliot as a Coleridge, there is a general feeling, on Trilling's part, that Eliot is in the same central tradition in which he sees himself, and he attempts to accommodate Eliot to Arnold, in a "reluctant" discipleship. It should be added that Trilling is not without influence from Eliot's profound historical sense. Eliot's repeated statements that the English Civil War has never been concluded reappear twice in Trilling's pronouncements on the novel, once in a review of Leavis' *The Great Tradition* and again in "Art and Fortune": "(It is possible to say that the Cromwellian revolution appears in every English novel.)"[11] Whenever the opportunity arises, he attaches Eliot to Arnold. Eliot's distinction between poetry and verse, in his introduction to Kipling, "does not really advance beyond the old inadequate one—I believe that Mr. Eliot himself has specifically rejected it—which Matthew Arnold put forward in writing about Dryden and Pope."[12] When Eliot, in *The Idea of a Christian Society,* defends the "intelligent believer" and validates both his intelligence and his belief by reference to human experience, Trilling says: "This sentence . . . indicates that Mr. Eliot is perhaps closer than he would admit to the pragmatic theology of Matthew Arnold which he so much disdains."[13] And, finally, the whole concept of *The Idea of a Christian Society* is in the great tradition, which for Trilling means that of the Romantics and the nineteenth century:

Yet for all his enmity to romanticism, his own true place in politics and religion is in the romantic line of the nineteenth century. He continues the tradition of Coleridge and, after Coleridge, of Newman, Carlyle, Ruskin and Matthew Arnold—the men who, in the days of Reform, stood out, on something better than reasons of interest, against the philosophical assumptions of materialistic Liberalism.[14]

II

A man is known by the tradition in which he sees himself, and Trilling's tradition is in the line of Arnold, the Romantics, and the ideology of the French Revolution. With the American Arnoldian tradition, James excepted, he has, like Eliot, no ties. In 1939 he said that although one could no longer make the complaint that James had in his *Hawthorne*—for American life did now have a superb "thickness"—still, "though I have great admiration and affection for the American classics and an increasing interest, I know that they have been far less important to me than the traditional body of European writers."[15]

On the question of whether James or Whitman is more helpful to the contemporary writer, Trilling has said that he prefers James. Throughout Trilling's criticism as a whole run the familiar laments about American writing: the writer does not develop and push on, but breaks down; although the general achievement has magnitude, the individual suffers; Americans have a peculiarly gross concept of the nature of "reality" and hence think Dreiser more relevant than James; Americans have a fear or suspicion of "intellect" or "mind"; at the same time, the American mind is peculiarly unanchored in the gross actuality of its "real": "For some vestige of the old striving after new worlds which cannot be gratified seems to spread a poison through the American soul, making it thin and unsubstantial, unable to find peace and solidity."[16] And "somewhere in our mental constitution is the demand for life as pure spirit";[17] we dislike the *"conditioned,"* and do not take, for example, to Howells' celebration of the routine and the ordinary.

Of the criticism and concept of writing during his own time, Trilling provided an outline in 1930. Reviewing the attitudes of American writers and critics toward the literature of the last twenty years, he said that there were four stages. First, there had been a declaration of the nonexistence of literature; second, there was a celebration of the so-called "new literature" (*circa* 1915); third, there was the "discovery, some five years ago [*circa* 1925], of an immaturity and insufficiency in the new writers";[18] fourth, there was "now current" a sociological explanation for the failure of American writing and a Spenglerian prophecy of inevitable doom for American art. But this defeatism was all wrong, and the American writer could survive and produce, if he kept his head. The criticism of the 'twenties, vigorous though it was, was still simple-minded, for it existed in a "heroic practical simplicity," the critics apparently believing that all life's battles could be summed up by simple opposition between truth and hypocrisy, idealism and Philistinism, and "romanticism" and "realism.''[19] Writing in 1946 he said:

It is now more than twenty years since a literary movement in this country has had what I have called power. The literary movement of social criticism of the 1920's is not finally satisfying, but it had more energy to advance our civilization than anything we can now see, and its effects were large and good.[20]

In the nineteenth century, in contrast, there had been a vital tradition. Speaking of Howells' boyhood, Trilling said that the culture of the little Ohio towns was then still essentially "humanistic.''[21] And in the nineteenth century, in America as well as in Europe, literature was connected with and even "underlay" all the activities of the mind.[22] Again: "Of two utterances of equal quality, one of the nineteenth and one of the twentieth, we can say that the one of the nineteenth century had the greater *power*.''[23]

The greatness of the nineteenth century emanated properly from the Romantics. For, along with Arnold, it is the Romantics who keep cropping up in Trilling's work for reference and authority. In addition to his incidental references, there are his two essays on Wordsworth—the poet of Arnold, of Mill, of George Eliot—of whom it might be said that he nourished the starved emotions of the best nineteenth-century minds. But it is not only Wordsworth. In the essay "Art and Neurosis," Lamb is cited as authoritative. The New Criticism, so called, was essentially an attack, to use De Quincey's definition, "in the name of literature as power." Our historical sense, new-found since the nineteenth century, derives from, among others, Sir Walter Scott. Shelley is praised ". . . for his having foreshadowed many of the essentials of Freud," and for pointing "to our future.''[24]

F. Scott Fitzgerald's close resemblance to the Romantics is noted with approval: "Fitzgerald was perhaps the last notable writer to affirm the Romantic fantasy, descended from the Renaissance, of personal ambition and heroism, of life committed to, or thrown away for, some ideal of self."[25] Fitzgerald is compared to Wordsworth, for both had ascribed a peculiar value to their childhood as defining the whole of their lives, and they had similar theories of "emotional bankruptcy."[26] Fitzgerald is also compared to Keats, for his greediness for pleasure and for the quality of his morality and intelligence. The constant reference to the Romantics in Fitzgerald's works is noted, and he is finally described as the last expression of the Romantic line.

Without the help of that phrase, "the capacity for wonder," no college text book could hope to deal with the romantic poets. What they wondered at was, above all, the self, and as our epoch more and more denies the value and even the possibility of the self, Fitzgerald seems to have ended what they began, to be as far off as they, and to shine with their light.[27]

And this was the American writer whose broken body was placed, in a shabby Los Angeles funeral parlor, in the "William Wordsworth Room."

Trilling's drama of Western history is, like Arnold's and unlike Eliot's, relatively modern. It consists in the interplay and conflict between the central consequences flowing from the French Revolution and those coming from Romantic literature, the one setting in motion a series of ideas about politics and society, the other inaugurating a momentous exploration of the self. Historically, the two sets of ideas have clashed, although logically they should modify each other.

In their origin, the ideas behind the French Revolution—rationalism, liberalism, Liberty, Equality, Fraternity—were pristine because they had behind them a genuine moral fervor and a personal, nonabstract animus. The Revolution had an "interest in what man should be. It was, that is, a moral interest, and the world had the sense of a future moral revolution."[28] Yet the liberalist concept of the human mind was thin and unsatisfactory; it tended to make an abstraction of human nature and to deny the complexity and multitudinousness of the mind. Wordsworth was one of the first of the superior minds of the time to discern this lack:

Wordsworth was one of the first to make the protest when he discarded the Godwinian view of the mind, advanced a psychology of his own and from it derived a politics. No doubt his politics was, in the end, reactionary enough; but it became reactionary for this reason as much as any other: that it was in protest against the view of man shared alike by Liberal manufacturing Whig and radical philosopher, the view that man was very simple and individually of small worth in the cosmic or political scheme. It was because of this view that Wordsworth deserted the Revolution; and it was to supply what the Revolution lacked, or, in some part, denied, that he wrote his best poetry.[29]

Thus the Romantic movement complicated the ideology of the French Revolution, but the social ideas of the one are bankrupt without the moral and psychological insights of the other. And, in a review, Waldo Frank is praised for seeing something "which is worth seeing":

He stands, if only philosophically, in the tradition of Blake, who, having accepted the social ideals of the French Revolution, grew frightened of the Revolution's rationalistic materialism, by which, as he believed, the full nature of man was split, denied, and atrophied.[30]

For the Romantic poets, and especially Wordsworth, performed an inestimable function: "Matthew Arnold's statement cannot be bettered. In a wintry clime, in an iron time, Wordsworth taught us to feel."[31]

Moreover, the ideology of the French Revolution tended to predicate an atomic rather than an organic concept of society.

The great conservatives, Wordsworth, Coleridge, Newman, and Carlyle, with their plea for an organism rather than a collocation of atoms, saw more clearly than the liberals the true nature of what the good society should be. At the same time, Trilling is careful to absolve the Romantics of any charge of being ineffectual or abstract in their own sometimes extravagant explorations. Of the wildest of the Romantics, Shelley, Trilling says, though agreeing that Arnold's phrase the "ineffectual angel" is "remarkably exact": "But if Shelley was ineffectual as an angel, he was far from ineffectual as a man."[32] Like most of the Romantics, Shelley was "passionately reverential of fact."[33] And far from being the enemy of Christianity, as orthodoxy holds, the Romantics, especially Wordsworth with his emphasis on the Christian virtues, were actually its friend, a fact that Anglo-Catholicism, which likes to be so "strict" with the Romantics, is liable to forget.[34] It was the Romantics who had seized on the insight that Arnold was later to develop, namely that if literature could not save mankind, it was still not a dilettante diversion, but a genuinely civilizing force: "It has been the chief effort of the romantics of the right, the left, and the center to create a literature of *function* and even of *conscious* function."[35]

Trilling has also defended the Romantics against Arnold's charge that they lacked discipline and a sense of form. Arnold "does not see that order is not only a Greek temple at the end of a clear path, but also finding one's path in the wilderness, or clearing the wilderness away. The aesthetic theory and practice of the romantic poets was just such a struggle . . ."[36] And of the familiar thesis that Romanticism "failed" or eventually got itself mixed up with Fascism, Trilling said, while disclaiming to know what is meant by a "failure" in such a discussion: "All movements fail, and perhaps the Romantic Movement failed more than most because it attempted more than most; possibly it attempted too much."[37] In any event, such a charge would seem to imply that a literary movement should settle things once and for all, something obviously impossible.

Finally, it is Romanticism that lies behind Trilling's more modern admiration and tragic philosopher, Freud, whose thought is one of the culminations of the Romanticist literature of the nineteenth century.[38] The common characteristic of Freud and the Romantics was the perception of the hidden elements in human nature and the discovery of the opposition between this hidden element and the visible.[39] In modern terms one must use Freudian doctrine, the descendant of Romanticism, as a criticism of liberalism, the descendant of the ideology of the French Revolution; and for this activity, the friendly but severe criticism of liberalism, Arnold is indispensable.

III

The best introduction to Trilling's relationship to Arnold is Trilling's own estimate, which is historical and critical, attempting to explain Arnold's work in the light of his times and to evaluate the results objectively. Trilling's *Matthew Arnold* is by no means without strictures on its subject; it makes many of the objections to Arnold that have been made before. Against Arnold's religion it brings the familiar charge of vagueness and inexact thinking. Like Eliot, Trilling quotes Bradley on Arnold and concludes that Arnold was "basically confused about the nature of fact and verification."[40] In matters of literature Arnold was wrong in his distinction between serious and nonserious poetry, for by "seriousness" he meant solemnity, and therefore his "rankings," especially in the case of Chaucer, were misguided. In politics, he failed to see the strength, the solidarity, and the "Europeanism" of the English workers; and, like most liberals, he never came to real grips with the problem of power in government: "The everlasting question of philosophical politics is how to place power and reason in the same agent, or how to make power reasonable, or how to endow reason with power."[41] Moreover, like his century, he was addicted to racialism, although it is true that he was more interested in bringing peoples together than in separating them. Withal, the human mind itself is more complex than Arnold allowed for, and, by the same token, the relationships between literature and life are more complicated than Arnold thought. So, too, Arnold could lose track, in his sometimes excessive concern with urbanity and amenity, of the animal, biological basis for life, and, in a sense, Whitman was right when he charged that Arnold failed to see that everything ultimately came out of the "dirt."

Yet with all these lacks Arnold was still a "culture hero":

. . . that is, a man who gives himself in full submission and sacrifice to his historical moment in order to comprehend and control the elements which that moment brings. (As in tragic literature, as in general life, so in the life of intellect the heroic status does not depend upon the hero's material and effective success.)[42]

For Arnold was in the great humanistic tradition, the tradition that values the personal virtues of intelligence, amenity, tolerance, courage, and modulation and flexibility. In society it sees justice and continuity as the desired ends, and "gradualism" as a social principle. For its heritage it takes to itself nothing less than the best elements of Western civilization and draws upon the East as well. Its instincts are social—although it well knows the power of loneliness and pain—and it has a passion for the betterment of society. Working in this tradition Arnold had established criticism as an "intellectual discipline" among the English-speaking peoples and had set its best "tone."[43] Moreover, he had "shaped the academic opinions"[44] of our time, and had established the teaching of English literature as an "academic profession."[45]

More specifically, Arnold was continuing the work of the French Revolution,[46] although, like Burke, Wordsworth, and

Coleridge, he asserted the notion of an "organic" society. He saw that "history must be considered neutrally—and dialectically"[47] (that is, that what may be good for one epoch may not be the same for another). Thus, as bourgeois individualism was necessary and just before the French Revolution, its excesses had to be corrected in the nineteenth century, when *it* had become the status quo. While recognizing that each age has its own needs, the critic must attempt that impossible task, "to conciliate epochs,"[48] in order to assure the continuity that society must have. One of Arnold's master insights, and one which Brownell of all the Arnoldians had insisted upon, was the social basis of everything: "The great truth that Arnold is now to keep ever before him ... is that all human values, all human emotions, are of social growth if not social origin."[49]

Arnold brought literature and life, culture and politics, into a necessary conjunction: "Behind every critical judgment of literature Arnold will henceforth make his a social and political judgment."[50] His theory of style was actually a theory of morality,[51] and he had introduced a new criterion of literature, its *adequacy;* it must be *fortifying,* and it must ultimately guide the "idea-moved" masses.[52] At the same time, Trilling defends the famous "criticism of life" as a definition of what literature *does* rather than of what it *is.* Yet with all this social fervor Arnold was no simple optimist; no one was more aware of man's tragic condition. In fact, Arnold had taken over Wordsworth's myth of childhood and had kept the form but changed the content: "... it is not man's joy but his misery that is the mark of his dignity ..."[53]

Arnold was always nondoctrinaire, nonphilosophical, non-abstract; and this was good. In a review of Leavis' *The Great Tradition* Trilling inferentially explained his preference in this respect:

Mr. Leavis is not a critic who works by elaborated theory. As between Coleridge, on the one hand, and Dr. Johnson and Matthew

Arnold, on the other, he has declared his strong preference for the two latter—for the critic, that is, who requires no formulated first principles for his judgment but only the sensibility that is the whole response of his whole being.[54]

Against Eliot's "either/or" of Catholicism and materialism, Trilling posits what Arnold would have posited (and in fact did)—the intellect itself. In his review of *The Idea of a Christian Society* Trilling said that we now have but one thing left, "our pledge to the critical intellect,"[55] and then quoted a sentence from Arnold on the necessity for studying that with which we may disagree and may even consider maleficent.

All in all, it is Arnold's "methods" that Trilling likes rather than his conclusions, as he says in the introduction to *Matthew Arnold*. At the heart of Arnold's doctrine is simply a desire for objectivity, in Arnold's words, a desire "to see the thing as in itself it really is"; and, as a critic, "he would rather harry his friends than destroy his enemies."[56] His friends, of course, were the liberals; and if modern liberalism fails it is not because it does follow Arnold's principles, but rather "because it does *not* follow Arnold's realism."[57] Trilling's function, therefore, is to play Arnold's role, to be the continuer of the work of the French Revolution and the critic of liberalism from the side of the Romantics, Freud, and the "critical intelligence."

IV

Trilling's critique of liberalism is similar to and influenced by the critical estimate by the other English writer on whom he has written a book and whose work he admires, E. M. Forster. Like Arnold, Forster is "able to speak of his love for his country with whose faults he has never ceased to quarrel . . ."[58] And again like Arnold, he is the friendly critic of liberalism. Forster is the master of "moral realism," which is not concerned with "good" and "evil" but with "good-and-evil," and which consists in the "awareness not of morality itself but of the contradictions, paradoxes and dangers of living the moral life."[59] Hence, Forster assumes the comic manner which tolerates no absolutes: " 'Wash ye, make yourselves clean,' says the plot [of a Forster novel], and the manner murmurs, 'If you can find the soap.' "[60] For Forster has imagination, and "Surely, if liberalism has a single desperate weakness, it is inadequacy of imagination . . ."[61] The liberals want absolutes and simple conclusions, and Forster keeps pulling the rug out from under these neat conclusions, providing "a kind of mithridate against our being surprised by life."[62] At the same time Forster is a naturalist, descended from Erasmus and Montaigne, and he is "clearly in the romantic line."[63] He is not "eschatological," as are modern radicals, but is content with the human possibility and with the human limitations. He can accept, what liberals cannot, the fact of death, as its frequent and unexpected occurrence in his novels attests. On all counts he is the liberal with a mind and an imagination.

But if criticism of liberalism is needed in England, how much more is it needed in America, where there is in fact no conservative tradition, ideologically speaking, at all—no Coleridges to exert intellectual pressure on the Mills. Hence the declarations prefacing Trilling's *The Liberal Imagination*:

In the United States at this time liberalism is not only the dominant but even the sole intellectual tradition.[64]

It has for some time seemed to me that a criticism which has at heart the interests of liberalism might find its most useful work not in confirming liberalism in its sense of general rightness but rather in putting under some degree of pressure the liberal ideas and assumptions of the present time.[65]

Furthermore, this pressure can be best exerted through literature, since the literature of our time is increasingly political.

And although it [the political orientation of modern literature] is often resisted by many very good literary critics, it has for some time been accepted with enthusiasm by the most interesting of our creative writers; the literature of the modern period, of the last century and a half, has been characteristically political.[66]

The central job of criticism is, then, to recall "liberalism to its first essential imagination of variousness and possibility..."[67] To this end, literature, by nature given to complexity and variety, is peculiarly relevant.

Trilling's critique of American liberalism is extended, long-standing, and various. It is fundamental, too, since it charges that liberalism has failed in the two essentials of the Arnoldian tradition: high intelligence and complex morality; liberalism can be stupid and blind, and, worse, dishonest and immoral. Like Arnold's Mr. Roebuck, it is addicted to "catchwords" and to refusing to see the object as in itself it really is. Trilling's critique, though not always concerned with the same aspects of liberalism and though sometimes accusing liberalism of contradictory tendencies, is consistent in that it is always aimed at mindlessness, moral or intellectual.

The liberalism of the 'thirties, especially as it was affected by and incorporated into Marxism, was given to irresponsibility and a slackening of moral grasp. Trilling said in an essay on Dos Passos:

Among members of a party the considerations of solidarity, discipline and expedience are claimed to replace all others and moral judgment is left to history; among liberals the idea of social determination, on no good grounds, appears tacitly to exclude the moral concern: witness the nearly complete conspiracy of silence or misinterpretation that greeted Silone's *Bread and Wine* ...[68]

But if liberalism was quite willing to absolve individuals from responsibility, it demanded the ultimate and the impossible of the writer: he was supposed not only to solve all problems but to be on the right side as well. It was the liberal critics, said Trilling, who were at least partially responsible for the failures of Hemingway. Taking Edmund Wilson's distinction that there were two Hemingways, a writer of seriousness and craft, and a man who was liable to be embarrassingly naïve, Trilling argues that when Hemingway was left to himself as a writer, he wrote seriously and honestly of life as he saw it. But the full tide of the "liberal-radical" intelligence was turned on the man to make him "socially conscious." And when Hemingway, of all American writers the most under scrutiny, responded to this criticism and became "socially conscious," in the liberal sense, he produced such things as *The Fifth Column* or *To Have and Have Not:* "We have conceived the artist to be a man perpetually on the spot, who must always report to us his precise moral and political latitude and longitude."[69] Actually, Hemingway's best work, and especially in his early period, was precisely the kind of criticism that liberalism needed. Between the lofty speeches of Wilson and its attendant humanitarianism and the bloated corpses on the field of battle, Hemingway had seen the connection; he had seen how humanitarianism, with all its emphasis on fine "feelings," could still issue finally in blood: "And it seems to me that what Hemingway wanted first to do was to get rid of 'feelings,' the comfortable liberal humanitarian feelings; and to replace them with the truth."[70] Hence the terseness and understatement of his style. So, as Hemingway's career demonstrates, the writer should be left alone, to recount things as he honestly sees them.

Moreover, the liberals not only make exorbitant claims on others, but are often themselves stupid and hypocritical; especially did this prove true as they became committed to Marxism. In answer to a series of questions on the state of American writing in 1939, Trilling said of the intellectual middle class:

What for me is so interesting in the intellectual middle class is the dramatic contradiction of its living with the greatest possibility (call it illusion) of conscious choice, its believing itself the inheritor of the great humanist and rationalist tradition, and the badness and stupidity of its action."[71]

With all its assumptions that it has inherited this great past, the intellectual middle class is yet essentially contemptuous of history, and is animated by an almost wholesale commitment to the idea of progress: "And from the notion of progress has grown that contempt for the past and that worship of the future which so characteristically marks the radical thought of our time."[72] (Liberal, liberal-radical, and radical are here used interchangeably.)

Another characteristic of the liberal intelligence, perhaps connected with the commitment to the future, is the fear of death. In a review of *For Whom the Bell Tolls,* Trilling remarked on the fact that Hemingway, unlike the typical liberal, could face death and use it honestly in the novel, although he was more concerned with its egoistic and isolating aspects than its general and binding effects, as was Donne, from whom he borrowed his title. And the liberal's refusal to face death is compounded by the refusal to face evil. For example, *Let Us Now Praise Famous Men,* by Agee and Evans, is in Trilling's mind a "great book," and yet is flawed by the fact that Agee, in his account of the poor whites, fails in "moral realism" by refusing to "see these people as anything but good."[73] Allied to this sentimentality is a sugary sentimentalizing of the "little man"; Trilling spoke of the O. Henry prize stories of 1942 as being bound together by a "concept which is at this moment dear to the hearts of the decent intellectual middle classes—the 'little man,' human nature seen under the aspect of *PM.'*[74]

With all these blinkers, liberalism, as might be expected, feels itself to be in great need of a facile optimism. American psychoanalytic thought, as expressed by Karen Horney, has accordingly watered down Freud's irony and tragic insight and has produced in its stead the "progressive psyche, a kind of New Deal agency which truly intends to do good but cannot always cope with certain reactionary forces."[75] Thus the liberals cannot face reality and are always looking for a vicarious escape, usually in some sad story of the downtrodden, over whom they can experience the twin feelings of superiority and solicitude. Hence the "vicarious" escape they find in such a document as Richard Wright's *Black Boy,* even though its author was given to no self-pity; and hence also the great success of Steinbeck's *The Grapes of Wrath.*

Trilling also claims that although liberalism overvalues the political and social function of the writer, it undervalues or even dislikes literature itself. In 1948 he said that a recent trend was the increasing hostility among intellectuals to the "traditional methods of art, the methods of imagination, of symbol and fantasy,"[76] and he mentioned the middle-class hostility to Proust or Joyce or Freud. But this is, to use Arnold's phrase, "simply Philistinism," or, to use a more modern phrase, "cultural Stalinism."[77] In short, liberalism wants of literature only a reflection of its own optimistic, progressive, simple-minded psyche. Most serious of all, this ideology, the so-called liberal ideology, has itself produced no literature worthy of the name; and the great modern European literature, to which we respond so deeply, was written by men who were either indifferent to or hostile to the tradition of democratic liberalism.[78]

Trilling's own novel, *The Middle of the Journey,* is written as a metaphorical exemplification of his, and Forster's and Arnold's, critical liberalism. It is, in fact, a modern morality play with ideologies acting out the modern political drama. Significantly, a copy of Dostoevski's *The Possessed* is given to the protagonist, John Laskell, at the beginning of the book, when he is in bed and recuperating from an almost fatal illness.

The Middle of the Journey is itself a smaller and less intense version of Dostoevski's wholesale onslaught against Western liberalism, and the similarities between the two novels are manifest. In Trilling's novel, as in Dostoevski's, the action occurs in the country, among civilized, ideologically-minded people; there is a conspiratorial element; there is a silly and ineffectual liberal, and there are some not so silly liberals; there is a dangerous archconspirator of intelligence and force; there is a public occasion where a shocking event occurs; finally, there is a sudden death which precipitates the denouement.

More precisely, it is a novel about "seeing the thing as in itself it really is." John Laskell, faced with and half in love with death, recovers to pierce the veils of illusion which envelop the various political myths of our time. He is confirmed in what he has always known, that Kermit Lanser, the wealthy owner of a liberal journal devoted to "free speech," is both silly and ineffectual; he learns that his handsome, progressive, professional, liberal friends, the Crooms, are afraid to face reality, in that they refuse to contemplate the fact of death and the reality of Communism; he learns that their hired man, Duck Caldwell, whom they romanticize as honest, strong "natural" man, is really what he appears to be: a drunken, irresponsible, thoroughly unlikable vulgarian; he learns that Gifford Maxim, the apostate Communist, now on his way to God and another absolute, is just as powerful and clever, although not so virtuous, as he had always appeared to be. He learns, of himself, that there is no such thing as a "pure," guiltless act, but that there is not such a thing as "total" guilt either. He learns that with people the only anchors are truth and love, as his brief love affair with the honest Emily Caldwell proves to him; and that with ideas there is only the naked critical intelligence to be relied upon. At the ideological climax of the novel, Gifford Maxim makes his final intellectual assault on Laskell's "anachronistic" humanism by retelling, in modern form, "The Legend of the Grand Inquisitor." He declares to the Crooms and Laskell:

You [the Crooms] will preach the law for the masses, I will preach the law for the leaders. For the masses, rights and freedom from blame. For the leaders, duties and nothing but blame, from without and from within. We will hate each other and we will make the new world. And when we've made it and it has done its work, then maybe we will resurrect John Laskell.[79]

The liberal, progressive, unreflective Crooms are merely bewildered by this bizarre prophecy and angry at being linked to Maxim, whom they now detest for his desertion of the Party and for his saying that it really is a "conspiracy," but Laskell sees the effectiveness of Maxim's argument and "nods"; at this Maxim turns and points dramatically at Laskell: "The supreme act of the humanistic critical intelligence—it perceives the cogency of the argument and acquiesces in the fact of its own extinction."[80] Laskell replies, in the name of the critical intellect, in the name of Arnold if you will, and against the apocalyptic absolutes that others are trying to force upon him, by saying, "I do not acquiesce";[81] he speaks of the "ferocity" with which he will hold only to what the mind gives, to the liberalism of moral realism and intelligence.

The ending of *The Middle of the Journey* would seem to imply that the future of liberalism is very dark indeed, although not utterly hopeless. What is needed, of course, is an infusion of imagination. In *The Liberal Imagination* Trilling speaks of organizing "a new union between our political ideas and our imagination—in all our cultural purview there is no work more necessary."[82] The liberal democratic ideas are not weak in themselves; rather, it is the liberal's relationship to them that is weak. It is a relationship too abstract and unconnected and too imperfectly conditioned by the realities of existence. *The Liberal Imagination* closes with the following admonition.

But if we are drawn to revise our habit of conceiving ideas in this way and learn instead to think of ideas as living things, inescapably connected with our wills and desires, as susceptible of growth and development by their very nature, as showing their life by their tendency to change, as being liable, by this very tendency, to deteriorate and become corrupt and to work harm, then we shall stand in a relation to ideas which makes an active literature possible.[83]

V

In matters of literary criticism Trilling, like Arnold, has been consistently middle-of-the-road, in the sense that he has reaffirmed Arnold's position in an era when criticism generally had become either specialized or almost exclusively concerned with certain aspects of literature such as problems of technique. First, this modern criticism, according to Trilling, has tended to alienate, even more, "High-brow" from "Middle-brow" culture. In a review of Sinclair Lewis' *Bethel Merriday* in 1940, he regretted the fact that while the educated middle class once read such major talents as Anderson, Dreiser, and the early Lewis, they no longer read the best literature of the present day. The modern emphasis, in both literature and criticism, on the intricacies of literary technique had reached a dead end. In literature itself it was doubtful, for example, that Joyce's famed and elaborate technique had served any good purpose for other writers, because nobody since Joyce had been able to use it to any good effect.[84] In any event, aesthetic forms are finally shaped by moral or philosophic assumptions and by the certitude with which these are held.[85] Trilling welcomed Leavis' *The Great Tradition* because it stated that "... it is upon the degree and quality of moral intensity that all aesthetic considerations of the novel depend."[86] This was salutary, especially in view of all the "nonsense" that had been written about the technique of the novel.[87] Thus a writer like Forster, who is not dominated by the dogma of "the point of view," is to be admired for his freedom and invention, granted that at times he becomes too playful.[88] Most of the modern writers, in their passion for objectivity, have lost that "light touch" by which the nineteenth-century writer let his reader know that he knew that the reader was there. Shaw was perhaps the last great writer who was able to laugh with his audience, and perhaps the neglect of Forster is caused by his "colloquial" relationship with his readers.[89]

As for style, its proper course is not toward elaboration and literary complexity, but toward colloquialism and ease. *Huckleberry Finn* is the classic American prose, as Hemingway had said, and the problem of the American writer is to find his way back to it. Echoing Eliot's prescription for poetry, Trilling said: "There is in English what might be called a permanent experiment, which is the effort to get the language of poetry back to a certain hard, immediate actuality, what we are likely to think of as the tone of good common speech."[90] Thus the present cultural schism may finally be bridged when literature once more develops a "highly charged plain speech."[91] Of the modern semanticist movement that raises words per se to an absolute efficacy, Trilling maintains that, to the contrary, our troubles are caused by our wills rather than by our words.[92] And against the New Criticism's concern with "indirection" and "symbolism," he declares that poetry is actually much closer to rhetoric than many modern critics will admit.[93] Rhetoric, in its turn, connects poetry to an intellectual discipline, and the poets who most greatly impress us do so by the intellectual content of their work.[94] As for "pure" criticism: "Sooner or later, of course, any critic of large mind will touch upon social matters, because what we call culture may be defined as the locus of the meeting of literature with social actions and attitudes and manners."[95] Nevertheless, literature must still not be put at the service of any other activity or institution; it must be taught as the "inde-

pendent, contemplative experience, as a pleasure, a 'gay knowledge' ..."[96]

As Arnold's criticism was largely concerned with poetry and
its civilizing function, Trilling's has been preoccupied with the
civilizing function of the novel, and the emphasis again has
been upon centrality, wholeness, and common sense.

Thus he blames *New Yorker* fiction for sacrificing the traditional novelistic virtue of representing action in favor of a static
quality, by which all the energy of the author has gone into his
technique and into the sensibility that "saw" the static subject.[97]
On the other hand, the author of advance-guard or experimental
literature is denigrated in favor of the writer who can play the
game within the established conventions and yet can circumvent
or transmute the conventions themselves.[98]

Lacking the historical materials that it once worked on—
classes, manners, and money considerations—the novel can still
pursue its immemorial course of dealing with reality and illusion
through the agency of ideas. The form then will take care of
itself: "The form ... is not the result of careful 'plotting'—the
form of a good novel never is—but is rather the result of the
necessities of the story's informing idea ..."[99] For the novel has
always had and still has a great moral function. It first took fire
from the French Revolution:

... in every nation touched by the Revolution, the novel ... [took] ...
on its intense life. For what so animated the novel of the nineteenth
century was the passionate—the "revolutionary"—interest in what
man should be. It was, that is, a moral interest, and the world had
the sense of a future moral revolution.[100]

This moral function still persists, because the novel, of all
human agencies, deals most completely and fully with the intricacies of the human mind:

The modern novel, with its devices for investigating the quality of
character, is the aesthetic form almost specifically called forth to

exercise this modern way of judgment. The novelist goes where the law cannot go; he tells the truth where the formulations of even the subtlest ethical theorist cannot. He turns the moral values inside out to question the worth of the deed by looking not at its actual outcome but at its tone and style. He is subversive of dominant morality and under his influence we learn to praise what dominant morality condemns; he reminds us that benevolence may be aggression, that the highest ideals may corrupt. Finally, he gives us the models of the examples by which, half-consciously, we make our own moral selves.[101]

The novel is thus the moral arbiter, and has been the most effective agent of the moral imagination for the last two hundred years.[102] It is, as well, a summary and paradigm for the culture from which it springs.[103] And since the modern world is dying of its own excesses of the will, the novel is the great teacher:

The novel has had a long dream of virtue in which the will, while never abating its strength and activity, learns to refuse to exercise itself upon the unworthy objects with which the social world tempts it, and either conceives its own right object or becomes content with its own sense of its potential force...."[104]

We must not "overvalue the novel" and ask that it "change the world," any more than we should expect this of other forms of literature.[105] Nevertheless, literature has been doing what Arnold said it would do and performing many of the functions of religion. In an essay on Wordsworth, who, in a sense, inaugurated the whole movement, Trilling said:

There never was, I believe, a secular literature which so massively and explicitly as ours directed itself to the spiritual life, for good or bad carrying the problems of life and death into the market place. Alexandria was nothing to us when it comes to a theological population.[106]

For literature had always been and still was a "criticism of life."

CHAPTER VIII

MATTHEW ARNOLD AND
AMERICAN CULTURE

ARNOLD'S SUCCESS in America was immediate, far-reaching, and lasting. In the academic world in particular he has become a fixed star. It would not be an overstatement to say, as several nineteenth-century admirers of Arnold did say, that he had perhaps more readers in America than he had in England itself. For although a great deal of Arnold's impact as a critic in the English-speaking countries can be accounted for by the fact that he had offered the age precisely what it wanted and needed, there were also certain elements in his thought that made his writings permanently congenial to Americans in particular.

The age Emerson had diagnosed as "an age of criticism," and it was Arnold's distinction, like Sainte-Beuve's, to elevate the critical function itself. Nineteenth-century writers noted what the critics of the 1920's were later to give Arnold credit for: first, he had diminished the imagined gap or disparity between criticism and creation; and, second, he had connected criticism with ideas and with the total human situation. Thus he seemed to give criticism a range and flexibility which hitherto it had lacked. Arthur Benson, who fell under the Arnoldian influence at Oxford, said that before Arnold there had been two types of critics, the classifiers and the pronouncers of "right" and "wrong," but that Arnold was a critic "in the larger sense—in that he had his eye on life and his finger on the pulse of humanity—and thus he set himself to criticize the strange fruit of human utterance."[1] In the words of a modern scholar, Northrop Frye, Arnold is the only English critic "who suggests that criticism can be like history and philosophy, a total attitude toward experience."[2]

Moreover, Arnold had come upon the scene when the Western world was threatened with an overabundance of intellectual emanations from Germany, of two kinds, her ever-recurrent transcendental romanticism and her recently discovered scholarly methodology. German scholarship, with its enormous erudition and exhaustive precision and over-all passion for method, threatened to turn all literary studies into a species of pedantry. E. M. Chapman, writing in 1910, warned that Anglo-Saxons in general and Americans in particular were "in danger of exalting German clumsiness and ineptitude into a sort of fetish."[8] But Arnold's felicities—his keenness, swiftness, aptness, and lucidity—had served as a salutary reminder that criticism was an art rather than a science.

More important, Arnold's explicitly nonmetaphysical, common-sense approach to literature was an antidote to the spell of transcendentalism, and especially of Coleridge, which still lay like a thick mist over vast reaches of nineteenth-century criticism. It was one of Arnold's services, as one of his nineteenth-century admirers put it, to have "un-Coleridged criticism." For it seems to be a periodic effort of literary criticism to make itself respectable by becoming philosophical in the technical sense, and in modern times the philosophical rationale has generally arisen in and been imported from Germany. Thus, as Coleridge turned to German thought for a rationale for his intuitions and drew literary criticism, which had hitherto been a function of common sense or "taste," into the regions of metaphysics, so at the present time, through Cassirer, especially as he is interpreted by Suzanne Langer, literary criticism again seeks a philosophical basis, this time in modern symbolism. In between these two movements of philosophical aspiration lies the work of Arnold, deprecating technical philosophy, although not ideas, and resting finally on the dictates of common sense and the perceptions of sensibility. As such, the efforts of Arnold seem to be part of and an expression of a larger movement, a late nineteenth-century reaction away from transcendentalism and toward pragmatism and, in literature, toward a kind of classicism. Hence the admiration of Arnold and of the American Arnoldians for French culture, with its Cartesian emphasis on "clearness and distinctness" of ideas.

This pragmatic approach was and is especially appealing to American culture, which has had the distinction of translating this attitude into an official metaphysic. And there are other and more general aspects of Arnold's thought which, by the same token, have made it inherently congenial to Americans in any age.

First, if it can be said that America is preëminently, of all nations, a middle-class nation, Arnold knew the middle class as few other intellectuals have known it before or since. H. V. Routh has remarked that Arnold came to understand, as hardly any cultured men then could, all the prejudices and aspirations of the middle class, simply because of his duties as an inspector of schools. Normally his headquarters was London, "but his temporary abode was anywhere, and he might be meeting any type of humanity, from girl-pupil teachers to Cousin and Sainte-Beuve."⁴ At the same time, Arnold remained closer to his adversary than most middle-class rebels have been able to do, or wished to do. It is ironic when one compares Arnold's situation in "anarchic" England with Flaubert's in "orderly" France; for Arnold's relationship with his class was infinitely more congenial and remarkably solid; he managed, no matter what his opinions, to stay at the center of the national life of his country and to exercise always a public function. And Arnold therefore always knew that the middle class, with all its absorption in money-making, had yet ever cherished, if not actualized, a great vaporous dream—and nowhere more so than in America—the ideal of "cultural" self-improvement. (Flaubert, of course, was aware of the dream and thought it patently ridiculous, but Arnold, as he was the first to admit, shared it himself.) Hence it is appropriate that an American journal, *The Citizen,* the publication of the American Society for the Extension of University Teaching, should have urged its readers, extension students, to study Arnold. No other country, said *The Citizen,* has such a large class whose need for Arnold's doctrines is so great and who are "more able in certain respects to apply" them.[5] It should be observed, too, that Arnold's doctrines were used in support of the more ludicrous aspects of this individual pursuit of culture by the comfortable bourgeoisie. When Arnold was visiting America, *The Chautauquan* quoted some irreverent doggerel to this effect from *Punch:*

> To Matthew Arnold hark
> With both ears all avidity
> That Matthew—a man of mark—
> Says "Cultivate Lucidity."[6]

Since American culture has been conditioned to, perhaps predicated on, the idea of change, it is natural that Arnold, the celebrator of the Time-Spirit and the advocate of bending with, but not surrendering to, the implacable forces of history, should have proved especially adaptable. William Dawson said that Arnold's veneration for the Time-Spirit bordered on "awe," and that Arnold ascribed to this deity a power and authority almost beyond human comprehension.[7] And to a nation that had raised "practicality" virtually to the status of a religion, Arnold came as the devotee of the efficacy of practice. Samuel Parkes Cadman said that Arnold's literary genius was rooted in his intense practicality, and that in this respect "he was more American than English, and more French than either."[8] Allied to this attitude toward experience, in Arnold and in Americans generally, is a tendency to distrust technical metaphysics, and this inclination was only exacerbated by the intellectual tendencies in an age which was rapidly becoming more and more specialized and was removing all branches of thought further and further from the judgment of common sense and the check of experience. Arnold, in a sense, tried to fill the gap. As Dickinson Miller phrased it in 1906, admiring Arnold's "non-scientific" attitude, Arnold was the "philosopher of middle principles, the seer of the naked eye. . . . He gives us the sublimation of a rule of thumb."[9] For Arnold was a subscriber to a dictum uttered most succinctly by Santayana: "I think that common sense, in a rough dogged way, is technically sounder than the special schools of philosophy . . .";[10] and he probably would have said of himself what Santayana did say of himself: "For good or ill, I am an ignorant man, almost a poet, and I can only spread a feast of what everybody knows."[11]

Arnold had no very profound sense of history, as his commentators have always pointed out, and American culture generally has not been marked by a preoccupation with the past. It is significant that the two Americans who have been directly concerned with Arnold and who have had a grandiose historical sense, James and Eliot, became expatriates and, of all the American Arnoldians, were the least concerned with the diffusion of culture to the general electorate. But Arnold's thesis that one must harness the future rather than celebrate the past expressed the attitude that became embedded in the American Arnoldian tradition.

Thus the mutual congenialities between Arnold and America can be multiplied: the idea that the "races" must be conciliated to enrich one another; the ultimate belief that morality and conduct *are* more important than intelligence or knowledge; the indifference to the fine arts; and the love of nature, coupled to a sense of its vastness and indifference.

Finally, there was a paradox at the heart of Arnold's work, and it is the same paradox that lies at the heart of American culture: its twin and opposed impulses to joy and cheer and action on the one hand, and toward melancholy, loneliness, and despair on the other. Arnold managed to embody and to reconcile these contradictions in his own person, and no one was more surprised than his own friends that their nonserious, even flamboyant, companion had produced the melancholy lyrics of his early poetry. Even his sister, "K," to whom he was perhaps closest, confessed her surprise. It is significant that in America Arnold should have earned the admiration of such men as Emerson, at one extreme, and such as Melville and Lafcadio Hearn, at the other. Melville had in his library, generally marked and annotated, copies of *Culture and Anarchy, Friendship's Garland, Essays in Criticism* (1865), *Literature and Dogma, Mixed Essays, Irish Essays and Others, Poems* (1856), and *New Poems* (1867).[12] It was invariably Arnold's reflections on the melancholy or on the contradictions of experience that caught Melville's eye or impelled him to comment. Some of Melville's commentators assert that his description of Arnold in a letter written to James Billson, an English admirer, in 1885, qualifies considerably his admiration, as it certainly does. Melville was speaking of James Thomson, a neglected figure like himself:

...it would have been wonderful indeed had they [Thomson's essays] hit the popular taste. They would have to be painstakingly diluted for that—diluted with that prudential worldly element wherewithal Mr. Arnold has conciliated the conventionalists, while at the same time sharing the absurdity of Bumble. But for your admirable friend this would have been too much like trimming...[13]

But it is not always remembered that Melville added, characteristically, an "if" clause that undercuts his whole previous statement, for he concluded, "...if trimming, in fact, it be."[14]

That other eminent solitary of American letters, Lafcadio Hearn, likewise felt a kinship to Arnold. It is true that Hearn exploded when he heard that Arnold had expressed surprise to a New York reporter at being taken for a relative of Edwin Arnold, the author of *The Light of Asia,* which Arnold said was "unintelligible." "There was something petty," said Hearn, "in this observation;—betraying a peculiar vanity..."[15] Edwin Arnold, according to Hearn, had written verse "richer and stronger than anything poetical Matthew Arnold has ever written or could write."[16] None the less, in his Tokyo lectures, Hearn, though making reservations about Arnold, acclaimed him as a critic and as an embodiment of the sad wisdom of life, with its recognition of human limitation. Arnold was, said Hearn, "... a classical spirit in the middle of the romantic movement."[17] "Cold Matthew Arnold's poetry certainly is, but it makes us think."[18] In the chapter on "Pessimists," in his *Interpretations of Literature,* Hearn said: "As a critic he was certainly during his lifetime the first of his period."[19] And Oliver Wendell Holmes, who was *supposed* to be always lighthearted, found that his own melancholy, when it came upon him, was assuaged by Arnold's verse. According to his latest biographer:

His readers might want "The Broomstick Train"; he himself wanted to read Matthew Arnold's "Obermann" and "Obermann Once More," which had for him, then, a "melancholy charm ... hardly any verse possessed." He could find his own thoughts and feelings in some of Arnold's stanzas.[20]

Yet Arnold could appeal just as strongly to such fundamentally optimistic spirits as Emerson, because, despite the melancholy in his outlook, there was a vein of cheer and purpose as well. Arnold never gave way to the ultimate despair, and when inclined to do so he took refuge in that last infirmity of the noble mind, the feeling that somehow the common sense of mankind would "muddle through." It was perhaps this element that led Melville to make his reservations. In any event, to a nation that has been all bustle and cheer and yet has produced a

literature marked by a devastating sense of loneliness and isolation, Arnold, who with his prose answered to the one sense and
with his poetry to the other, was peculiarly congenial.

II

Like all lengthy historical evolutions, the direct American tradition of Matthew Arnold is not without its ironies, those strange
anomalies in the courses of events by which history defies logic.
As a person, as a literary critic, as a political thinker, and as a
religious controversialist, Arnold was turned inside out by time,
and some of his dearest friends became, unwittingly, his dead-
liest enemies.

It is ironic, first, that the "harsh" and "savage" controversialist
of the nineteenth century should have become a representative of
Victorian unction and blandness for the twentieth. Again, in
matters of literary criticism, whereas the nineteenth century was
inclined to think Arnold too much concerned with form and
style—this was Whitman's objection—the twentieth, in the
name of Eliot and those influenced by him, has rejected Arnold
for precisely the reason that he, and the critical tradition that he
inaugurated, was not concerned enough with technique and
precise analysis.

It is ironic too that Arnold should be attacked by many modern critics as the embodiment or an encourager of the very
dangers in literary studies that he himself had warned against.
For it was Arnold who said that too much history, in the study
of literature, was a dangerous thing and that it could lead to
stultification of the literary joy. He likewise warned against the
purely personal reaction, Richards' "mnemonic irrelevance."
Arnold anticipated modern criticism in other ways as well. It
was Arnold who first pointed out the evil spell which Milton's
mighty verse has cast over subsequent English poetry, which,
since his time, must always be "elevated" and "sonorous." It was

Arnold too who reached out into other disciplines and studies, as modern criticism does, to bring new and "fresh" ideas into the realm of literary criticism. And finally it was Arnold who, by calling into question the meaning of words—what, for example, the word "God," etymologically and historically considered, actually *meant*—anticipated the whole semanticist movement of modern culture.

One of the chief anomalies in Arnold's more recent reputation as a literary critic is the cloudy repute in which he has been held by many modern critics, whose motto and whose method is the "seeing of the thing as in itself it really is," but who, following T. S. Eliot, are given to characterizing Arnold as "vague." Granted that Arnold's own critical methods provided no such verbal apparatus for the analysis of poetry as do those of some modern critics, yet essentially his aim was theirs. Arnold would have considered their efforts fanatically minute, but his attitude, in both his poetry and his prose, was simply: to face the facts and grasp the essentials. Arnold has had his defenders in this respect; Leonard Brown, in 1934, made the extravagant claim that "The sole attitude which made it possible for Mr. Eliot to write his very fine poem *The Wasteland* rather than another sheaf of lyrics on trees, was Arnold's. For the business of poetry, from Arnold to Eliot, has remained constantly the sceptical representation of life."[21] According to Brown, there had been three alternatives for nineteenth-century writers. They could perpetuate a dying Romanticism; they could invent a synthetic one; or they could face things unequivocally, which Arnold did. The identifying mark of Arnold's "succession" is "an attitude.... The best minds subsequent to Arnold's have been like his. That is Arnold's glory, and he must not be confused for us."[22]

In politics, the "Liberal tempered by reflection" who thought that the future belonged to the masses became one of the patron saints of certain branches of American conservatism: the Anglophilia of Sherman, the moralism of Babbitt and More, and the ancestor-worshiping, "foreigner"-fearing Brahminism of New England.

The destiny of Arnold the religious critic has undergone a dual ironic metamorphosis. The "radical" theologian of the nineteenth century has become transubstantiated into a bulwark for traditional Christianity in the twentieth; but, at the same time, resurgent orthodoxy, especially in the person of Eliot, has renewed the original attack on Arnold's "compromise." Moreover, the whole religious side of Arnold's writings is involved in the more general irony residing in the fact that whereas the religious issue was generally considered to be dead around the turn of the century, it has reasserted itself with great force in the last two or three decades. I. A. Richards' early work, directly in Arnold's tradition, as Eliot recognized, set off a train of speculation which still continues in the present. Indeed, Allen Tate can hardly let a half year go by without discussing Arnold in connection with religion or poetry or both. In the *New Republic* of January 5, 1953, in an essay on the state of Catholic letters, he proclaimed:

What Catholic literature in America needs today is a Catholic Matthew Arnold. His critical dialectic would come to something like this: *Always ask questions.* Is this novel, is this poem good? As a novel, does this Catholic work compete with Proust or Henry James; or are we taking it because it was written by a Catholic with the right views?[23]

But he then goes on, as he has done so many times before, to criticize Arnold's "touchstone" theory, especially as it is illustrated by Dante's *"In la sua volontade è nostra pace,"* because Arnold was taking this line out of context and using it for its thought content rather than its poetic force and imagery. On August 31, 1953, Tate returns in the *New Republic,* again stressing the harmfulness of the "touchstone" theory, but his reservations decrease:

For years I had been puzzled by Arnold's use, as one of his touch-stones, of the famous line by Dante: *"E la sua voluntade [sic] è nostra pace."* I not only didn't agree that the will of God is our peace; I didn't think that the line was poetry. Now that I do agree that our peace is in the will of God, I still don't think that the line *taken alone* is poetry.[24]

The supreme irony, however, in the posthumous career of Arnold in America lies in the complex of interrelations between himself, Babbitt and More, and T. S. Eliot. Despite their objections to certain aspects of Arnold's thought, the New Humanists were, in a sense, Arnoldians. Arnold was the one English critic of the nineteenth century whom they praised with little reservation, and they considered Arnold's work to be a precursor of their own. Yet it has been their objections to Arnold, and not their praise, that Eliot has been able to impose so thoroughly on his age. For the major points of difference between Eliot and Arnold turn out to be exactly the cavils of Eliot's one-time teachers, Babbitt and More: Arnold was deficient in religious insight (More); he led to Pater (More); he lacked a binding philosophy and avoided first principles (More); he was a fuzzy thinker who shied away from precise analysis (Babbitt); he tended to confuse genres (Babbitt). Thus have Babbitt and More, without in their own persons having exercised any pervasive influence, unwittingly served to deflate the reputation of the one critic of the Anglo-American world whom they considered sound and healthy.

Finally, Arnold enjoyed the ironic fate of being praised both by the critics who considered him a representative Victorian and regretted the passing of his era and by the critics who considered him an atypical Victorian and thus, in actuality, a representative "modern." In an essay entitled "The Victorians, God Bless

Them!" (1932), Douglas Bush lauded Arnold, among others, for possessing a solid sense of values which the twentieth century might well try to recapture.[25] But Edmund Wilson, reviewing Trilling's *Matthew Arnold,* made the opposite point: "Matthew Arnold has stood up remarkably well; he has managed to sail on into our own time when many ships that seemed once to draw more water have gone down with the Victorian age."[26]

Irony is not, however, the keynote of the century-long Arnold tradition in America, for the image of Arnold remained steady in the eyes of his avowed followers, and if the issues with which they were concerned differed from those that Arnold dealt with, still his methods and his general attitude have survived.

In what is perhaps the central issue of American culture, the relationship to Europe, the Arnoldian tradition has played a dual role. If it may be said that there have been three alternative courses for American culture itself to take—independence from Europe, a reciprocal relationship to Europe, dependence upon Europe—then it may be said that the Arnoldian tradition has functioned in the latter two alternatives, and it has been the two great American writers most completely committed to the first alternative who came down most heavily on Arnold, namely Whitman and Twain.

As for the third alternative, the Arnoldian tradition has played a part in inspiring two great expatriates, James and Eliot, each of whom has been inclined to think that the America of his time was not yet ripe and that it must still be thought of as a province of Europe; its final promise was not yet to be seen or reckoned.

But while Arnold was a spokesman for cosmopolitanism, he was also an advocate of cultural pluralism, and it has been this side of his doctrine that has reinforced the second alternative, the reciprocal relation to Europe, and constitutes the central

Arnoldian tradition in America. It can be seen, in various ways, in Brownell, Sherman, and Trilling, and even, in certain respects, in James and Eliot. If there is anything that all the American Arnoldians have in common, and share with Arnold himself, it is a tendency to regard France as a cultural and intellectual beacon and to advocate, without abdicating nationality or individuality, learning from French sweetness and light. It is France that appears, again and again, as the disseminator of the stock of "fresh ideas" which Arnold said was the very life of criticism; and from James to Eliot and Trilling there is a common preoccupation among Arnoldians with the intellectual, artistic, and political legacy of France. It is perhaps not without significance that the weakest and the most provincial of the American Arnoldians, Stuart P. Sherman, was the least concerned with France and looked rather to England itself for the necessary cosmopolitan relationship. Thus the Arnoldian tradition almost invariably involves, expatriation or not, a preoccupation with French culture; and for those who have not become expatriates, it advocates a moderate rather than a radical Americanism and is liable to think James more useful than Whitman.

The Arnoldian tradition has also been continually relevant to what is perhaps the other chief paradox of American culture, the anomalies of the political traditions. As Trilling has pointed out, there is in America no genuinely conservative tradition, in the sense that an imaginative ideology embodying conservative principles has been *shared* by generations of Americans. It is true that there have been conservative instincts, but they have usually found expression either in chauvinism or in a blanket defense of property. There has been, on the other hand, a liberal ideology, but it has been inclined, at least in modern times, to be pragmatic and cultureless, and its vitality has generally emanated from the grass roots of practical distress—the plight of the nineteenth-century farmer or the general financial debacle of the 'thirties. Its masters, such as Roosevelt, have likewise been pragmatic and nonideological. The closest approach, in recent times, to a national leader who has been both liberally inclined and intellectually conversant was Woodrow Wilson (who has been called an "Arnoldian"), but his melancholy destiny would not seem to augur well for successors. Lacking, then, an infusion from thought or culture, the liberal ideology has tended to be not only simple-minded but anti-intellectual, and only sporadically has it produced reverberating literary or intellectual documents (Jefferson's work and that of his latter-day disciple, Parrington, are notable examples). Trilling is inclined to attribute this failing to a kind of every-recurrent simple-mindedness that follows in the train of liberal ideas, but the real problem lies deeper than this. For liberals have been telling liberals that they are simple-minded for almost a century now; John Stuart Mill, George Eliot, and Herman Melville come to mind, as well as Arnold. It is more to the point to ask why certain liberals are actually conservative in everything except their politics.

Conservatism in America has, in contrast, produced respectable philosophers, and in modern times, anyway, they must be awarded the palm. To take the latest instances, Babbitt, More, and Santayana: it is doubtful that for breadth and depth of knowledge and for intellectual power, there has been a liberal critic who can match More; or a philosopher and rhetorician to equal Santayana; or more than a very few minds as vigorous and as purposeful as Babbitt's. And yet America, lacking the age-old conservative tradition that all European cultures inherit and indeed committed in theory to a culture of utter classlessness and constant change that would make conservatism anomalous anyway, has not provided its conservative spokesmen with a following or even an audience, one of the reasons being perhaps that the real conservatives have been as critical of American

big business and American imperialistic ventures as have their
opposites, the liberals. In any event, a certain type of modern
liberal is generally in the position of being distrustful of the
panaceas of his fellow liberals, and, like Arnold, would give
everything—heart, mind, instincts—everything, that is, except
his vote—to the Burkes rather than to the Cobbetts of this world.
To this type of person—who is usually literary or intellectual in
interests and is thus committed to the preservation of the past,
and who is liable to possess a tragic rather than optimistic view
of experience and thus to have the conservative rather than the
liberal instincts, but who is yet in his politics liberally inclined,
is convinced that the classless society will and must come into
being in fact, and is determined that that society shall still pre-
serve and cherish "the best that has been thought and said"—
Arnold is indeed a culture hero and a prototype, as he was to
Brownell and Sherman and still is to Trilling, and, in great
part, to Eliot.

Such a position, it is true, is liable to be regarded as no position
at all by the world at large, especially by those who live on
slogans. It will be remembered (see p. 55, above) that as far
back as 1877 *The Nation* carped at Arnold's "inconsistent,"
"conservative radicalism." Yet the stance that Arnold took was
not completely original with him; it has a tradition at least as
old and venerable as that of the orthodox liberals and conservatives which it opposes. For the modern political situation of
the West (less, of course, Marxism) had hardly been adum-
brated, after the French Revolution, when John Stuart Mill
noticed that there were not merely two parties involved, but
three:

...the Coleridgeans...[were]...a second Liberal and even Radical
party, on totally different grounds from Benthamism and vehemently
opposed to it; bringing into these discussions [debates between Utili-
tarians and Tories] the general doctrines and modes of thought of

the European reaction against the philosophy of the eighteenth century; and adding a third and very important belligerent party to our contests.[27]

And there always has been, since Mill's time, a third party which, sharing nothing with the orthodox Tories, has tried either to overthrow the liberal ideology inherited from the eighteenth century in the name of a known past, as in the case of Coleridge, or complicate it, for the sake of an unknown future, as in the case of Arnold.

Arnold is the proper exemplar for the modern liberal in another respect, that is, as thought bears on or is related to action. In such pragramic cultures as those of England and America, the critic from the side lines, he who speaks but does not act, is often regarded with suspicion by his fellow citizens and with a feeling of guilt by himself. But on the question of action, Arnold answered that thought was a kind of action and that it was the business of a critic to be a critic and nothing else. To the objections from practical English politicians that he was always complaining and never doing, he replied:

But with the increasing number of those who awake to the intellectual life, the number of those also increases, who having awoke to it, go on with it, follow where it leads them. And it leads them to see that it is their business to learn the real truth about important men, and things, and books, which interest the human mind. For thus is gradually to be acquired a stock of sound ideas, in which the mind will habitually move and which alone can give our judgments security and solidity.[28]

This, he believed, is a rare good: "The critic who rightly appreciates a great man or a great work, and can tell us faithfully—life being short, and art long, and false information very plentiful—what we may expect from their study and what they can do for us; he is the critic we want..."[29] It was in this role that Arnold has exercised his deepest appeal, and established a tradition that insists upon cultural pluralism, political liberalism, and a literary criticism connected to ideas, on the one hand, and to experience, on the other. It conceives of the critic as prophet, one whose sole mission is "the humanization of man and society." To say that this tradition has persisted and still persists is perhaps but to say that the world today is still in the situation that Arnold first diagnosed so candidly—"Wandering between two worlds, one dead / The other powerless to be born"—and hence that, just as philosophy after the Greeks is a series of footnotes, modern criticism, after Arnold, until the new world is in fact finally born, is a continual reworking of the issues he first posed.

For he asked some of the more important questions which the world is still asking and has not yet successfully answered. What is to take the place of or fill the gap left by the demise of religion, in both its emotional and moral ministrations? How are individuality and excellence to be provided for and allowed expression in a completely democratic electorate? His answer, to both questions, was "culture," and he laid on the critic the enormous burden of making a sound connection between culture and society. Perhaps Arnold was completely wrong, as he was in other things—in the hope, for example, that the state would play the role that the aristocracy once had—and perhaps one of his masters, Newman, was both wiser and more realistic when he maintained that culture could most emphatically *not* guarantee morals: "Quarry the granite rock with razors, or moor the vessel with a thread of silk; then may you hope with such keen and delicate instruments as human knowledge and human reason to contend against those giants, the passion and the pride of man."[30]

Yet, for those who will not accept Eliot's dictum that we must finally bow to either the Priest or the Commissar, culture, especially in its literary manifestations, *has* become a substitute for religion and a social panacea. We have only to trace out the history of criticism from Dryden and Johnson, to the Romantics, especially Wordsworth and Coleridge, to Arnold, and to that of the twentieth century, to see the continual intensification and aggrandizement of the critical function and of the claims made for literature.

It is not only that literary criticism today has all the marks of religion: moral fervor, a conscious or unconscious concern with an absolute (the meaning of meaning), Alexandrianism, Church Fathers (Melville, Kafka, Joyce, Proust, Rilke, among others) endlessly glossed and interpreted, and an explicitly religious vocabulary. Even more significant is the fact that, beginning in the nineteenth century, literature itself began unmistakably to play the role that religion once had. The annals of nineteenth-century autobiography—Mill, George Eliot, Emerson, and Arnold are major instances—are filled with the tributes of agnostics, mystics, and sceptics to the religious and moral power of Wordsworth's poetry, and it would not be an overstatement to say that Wordsworth played the role of "savior" to some of the best nineteenth-century minds. Arnold, in making his claims for the religious functions of literature, was only stating a phenomenon that had become, in many instances, a *fait accompli*. It is true that in the twentieth century the same type of mind that in the nineteenth century came to rest in Wordsworth's poetry will now, the same problems having become more intensified, and even institutionalized into an international war that has been going on intermittently since 1914, take the ultimate step into an organized religion. For the steep and thorny path to heaven in the twentieth century is paved with the typewriters of literary critics. Nevertheless, religion is often a goal arrived at by the way of literature; and in the last two centuries, in agnostic or convert alike, literature and religion unmistakably overlap. It was in this way that Babbitt, a moralist, and More, a theologian, became literary critics.

But if literature must serve a quasi-religious function, it must be the social savior as well, as Arnold prophesied. For at least two centuries, serious literature—and Arnold is but one integer in a long tradition—has been counterattacking the future in the name of the past. John Stuart Mill in his essay on Coleridge said, in a great summation, that modern civilization has had the effect of dividing the human mind in two. One observer can see only the great advantages of progress: the multiplication of physical comforts, the advance and spread of knowledge, and the decay of superstition and tyranny. He becomes, like Arnold's Mr. Roebuck, a worshiper of the "enlightened" age in which he lives. But the other observer can only see the losses that progress has entailed: the relaxation of personal energy and courage; the slavery to artificial want; and the dull, mechanical character of man's life. "No two thinkers," concluded Mill, "can be more at variance than the two we have supposed,—the worshippers of civilization and independence, of the present and of the remote past."[31]

Literature, from the late eighteenth century onward, has been decidedly of the second party, the worshipers of the past and its departed virtues, and has assaulted urbanization, science, collectivism, materialism, and empiricism in the name of ruralism, emotion, individuality, spirit, and intuition. Nor has it been only the professed nature-lovers, from Wordsworth through the Brontës to Hardy and Lawrence in England, or the whole Emersonian and Thoreau tradition in America, that have carried on the attack. It likewise appears in such radically different writers as the urban liberal, Dickens, and the solitary metaphysician, Melville.

Arnold verbalized this entire tradition and, in an ideological form, injected it into politics, sociology, education, and the whole question of the future of culture. Thus the recent eruption of the professors of literature against the professors of education in America represents this literary counterattack in the field of education.

So Arnold cannot die, for we will not let him. Someone is always knocking on his grave either to admonish him for his errors or to congratulate him on his prescience. His name is evoked by almost everyone: by "young" conservatives such as the ubiquitous Peter Viereck, old conservatives, critical liberals, uncritical liberals, agnostics, believers, pure critics, impure critics, linguists, academic historians—in short, by anyone who is interested in literature, or ideas, or culture. Breathes there a thinking man so dead that he cannot be roused by the Arnoldian battle cry—in Edmund Wilson's enthusiastic misquotation: "So back, I say, to the Renaissance, with its hunger and thirst for books! Back to Matthew Arnold and the 'best that has been thought and felt [*sic*] in the world'!"[32] But, of course, although we know that Arnold asked the right questions, we cannot be sure he supplied the right answers. History, despite some portentous negative rumblings, has not finally spoken, and we still do not know whether Arnold's work and that of his followers is an augury of the future or a monument to the past.

NOTES

NOTES TO INTRODUCTION

[1] James Russell Lowell, *The Complete Writings of* ... (Boston and New York, Houghton, Mifflin & Co., 1904), XV, 116–117.

[2] *Ibid.,* pp. 204–205.

[3] *Ibid.,* II, 19.

[4] Ralph Waldo Emerson, *The Complete Works of* . . . (Boston and New York, Houghton, Mifflin & Co., 1904), I, 296.

[5] Walt Whitman, *The Complete Prose Works of* ... : Vol. II of *The Complete Poetry and Prose of Walt Whitman,* ed. by Malcolm Cowley (The American Classics Series; New York, Pellegrini & Cudahy, 1948), p. 225.

[6] Lowell, *Complete Writings,* I, 298.

[7] *Ibid.,* p. 316.

[8] John Burroughs, "Walt Whitman and His Recent Critics," in *In Re Walt Whitman,* ed. by Horace Traubel *et al.* (Philadelphia, published by the editors through D. McKay, 1893), p. 95.

[9] *Ibid.,* p. 96.

[10] *In Re Walt Whitman,* p. 386.

[11] Mark Twain, *Europe and Elsewhere* (New York and London, Harper & Bros., 1923), p. 13.

[12] Edgar Allan Poe, *The Complete Works of* . . . , ed. by James A. Harrison (New York, Thomas Y. Crowell & Co., 1902), VIII, 276.

[13] *Ibid.,* p. 277.

[14] *Ibid.,* XI, 2.

[15] *Ibid.,* p. 148.

[16] Lowell, *Complete Writings,* II, 118.

[17] *Ibid.,* p. 116.

[18] *Ibid.,* pp. 10–11.

[19] Emerson, *Complete Works,* VIII, 67.

[20] *Mark Twain's Speeches,* ed. by A. B. Paine (New York and London, Harper & Bros., 1923), p. 34.

[21] *In Re Walt Whitman,* p. 326.

[22] Lowell, *Complete Writings,* II, 117.

[23] Poe, *Complete Works,* XI, 6.

[24] *Ibid.,* XVI, 25.

[25] *Ibid.,* p. 196.

[26] Emerson, *Complete Works,* X, 255.

[27] *Ibid.*

[28] *Ibid.,* I, 228.

[29] *Ibid.,* p. 109.

[30] *Ibid.,* X, 89.

[31] *Ibid.,* p. 92.

[32] *Ibid.,* p. 163.

[33] *Ibid.,* VIII, 183.

[34] *Ibid.,* X, 152.

[35] Ralph Waldo Emerson, *Journals of* . . . , ed. by E. W. Emerson and W. E. Forbes (Boston and New York, Houghton, Mifflin & Co.), IX (1914), 480.

[36] Emerson, *Complete Works,* III, 164.

[37] *Ibid.,* VI, 196.

[38] *Ibid.,* VIII, 83.

[39] *Ibid.,* p. 176.

[40] *Ibid.,* X, 34.

[41] *Ibid.,* p. 36.

[42] *Ibid.,* p. 51.

[43] *Ibid.,* I, 91.

[44] *Ibid.,* p. 307.

[45] Edgar Allan Poe, *The Works of the Late* . . . , with a Notice by James Russell Lowell (New York, Redfield, 1857), I, vii.

[46] Lowell, *Complete Writings,* II, 3.

[47] *Ibid.,* p. 7.

[48] *Ibid.,* XIV, 143–144.

[49] *Ibid.,* VII, 274–275.

NOTES TO CHAPTER I

HENRY JAMES

[1] Henry James, *Hawthorne* (London, 1879), p. 42.

[2] *Ibid.,* p. 3.

[3] Henry James, "Matthew Arnold," *English Illustrated Magazine,* 1 (Jan., 1884), 242.

[4] *Hawthorne,* p. 62.

[5] Henry James, *French Poets and Novelists* (London, 1884), p. 60.

[6] Henry James, *Partial Portraits* (London, 1894), p. 9.

[7] *Ibid.,* p. 19.

[8] *Ibid.,* p. 30.

[9] Henry James, *Essays in London and Elsewhere* (London, 1891), p. 80.

[10] *Ibid.,* p. 79.

[11] Matthew Arnold, *Essays in Criticism* (Boston, Ticknor and Fields, 1865). The 1865 edition (First Series) included, among other things, "The Function of Criticism at the Present Time" and "The Literary Influence of Academies."

[12] Henry James, *Views and Reviews,* ed. by Le Roy Phillips (Boston, Ball Publishing Co., 1908), p. 83.

[13] Henry James, *Notes of a Son and Brother* (New York, C. Scribner's Sons, 1914), p. 458.

[14] *Views and Reviews,* p. 85.

[15] *Ibid.,* p. 87.

[16] *Ibid.*

[17] *Ibid.,* p. 88.

[18] *Ibid.,* p. 89.

[19] *Ibid.,* p. 92.

[20] *Ibid.,* pp. 93–94.

[21] *Ibid.,* p. 94.

[22] *Ibid.,* p. 96.

[23] *Ibid.,* p. 97.

[24] Henry James, *William Wetmore Story and His Friends* (Boston, Houghton, Mifflin & Co., 1903), II, 208.

[25] Henry James, *The Middle Years* (London, W. Collins Sons & Co., Ltd., 1917), p. 36.

[26] Ralph Waldo Emerson, *The Complete Works of* . . . (Boston and New York, Houghton, Mifflin & Co., 1904), VIII, 144–145.

[27] Henry James, *English Hours* (Boston and New York, Houghton Mifflin Co., 1905), p. 191.

[28] Henry James, *A Small Boy and Others* (New York, C. Scribner's Sons, 1913), p. 268.

[29] *Ibid.*, p. 281.

[30] *Ibid.*, p. 338.

[31] *Ibid.*, p. 415.

[32] *Notes of a Son and Brother*, p. 258.

[33] Henry James, *The Letters of . . .* , ed. by Percy Lubbock (New York, C. Scribner's Sons, 1920), I, 22.

[34] *Ibid.*, p. 228.

[35] Matthew Arnold, *The Works of . . .* (London, Macmillan & Co., Ltd., 1903–1904), XV (*Letters*, III), 105.

[36] *Views and Reviews*, p. 85.

[37] Frederic E. Faverty, *Matthew Arnold the Ethnologist* (Evanston, Ill., Northwestern University Press, 1951), p. 76.

[38] Arnold, *Works*, XIV (*Letters*, II), 320.

[39] Matthew Arnold, *Discourses in America* (London, 1885), p. 40.

[40] Henry James, " 'The Manners of the Day' in Paris," *The Nation*, 6 (Jan. 23, 1868), 73.

[41] *Ibid.*

[42] *Ibid.*, p. 74.

[43] Henry James, "The Parisian Stage," *The Nation*, 16 (Jan. 9, 1873), 24.

[44] *French Poets and Novelists*, p. 65.

[45] James, *Letters*, I, 51.

[46] *Ibid.*, II, 99.

[47] *Ibid.*, I, 104–105.

[48] Jerome H. Buckley, *The Victorian Temper* (Cambridge, Mass., Harvard University Press, 1951), p. 26.

[49] *French Poets and Novelists*, pp. 64–65.

[50] James, "Matthew Arnold" (in *English Illustrated Magazine*, cited in n. 3, above), p. 246.

[51] This evolution has been pointed out by Morris Roberts in his excellent book *Henry James's Criticism* (Cambridge, Mass., Harvard University Press, 1929), p. 5; and by the late F. O. Matthiessen in *The James Family* (New York, A. A. Knopf, 1949), p. 245. My exposition, then, to follow, is the third time around. Neither Roberts nor Matthiessen allows as much importance to the Arnoldian influence as do I.

[52] *A Small Boy and Others*, pp. 162–163.

[53] On Trollope's *Miss MacKenzie*, James wrote: "Mr. Trollope's offence is, after all, deliberate. He has deliberately selected vulgar illustrations." (Henry James, *Notes and Reviews*, ed. by Pierre de Chaignon La Rose [Cambridge, Mass., Dunster House, 1921], p. 72; article originally published in *The Nation* in 1865.) But: "His [Trollope's] great, his inestimable merit was a complete appreciation of the usual." (*Partial Portraits*, pp. 100–101.)

On George Eliot, in a review of *Felix Holt*: "Her plots have always been artificial— clumsily artificial—the conduct of her story slow, and her style diffuse. Her conclusions are signally weak . . . the works of a secondary thinker and an incomplete artist." (*Notes and Reviews*, p. 200; article originally published in 1866, in *The Nation*.)

But: "I have found myself, my life long, attaching value to every noted thing in respect to a great person—and George Eliot struck me on the spot as somehow *illustratively* great." (*The Middle Years*, p. 65.)

[54] *Notes and Reviews*, p. 103.

[55] Henry James, "Sainte-Beuve," *North American Review*, 130 (Jan., 1880), 52–53.

[56] *Ibid.*, pp. 62–63.

[57] Henry James, *The Art of the Novel* (New York, C. Scribner's Sons, 1934), pp. 53–54.

[58] *A Small Boy and Others*, p. 164.

[59] *The Art of the Novel*, p. 156.

[60] *Notes of a Son and Brother*, p. 78.

[61] *Ibid.*, p. 38.

[62] *Ibid.*, p. 106.

[63] Matthew Arnold, *Essays in Criticism*, Third Series (Boston, Ball Publishing Co., 1910), p. 138.

[64] James, "Matthew Arnold" (in *English Illustrated Magazine*, cited in n. 3, above), p. 242.

[65] *Ibid.*, p. 243.

[66] Virginia Harlow, *Thomas Sargeant Perry* (Durham, N.C., Duke University Press, 1950), p. 89.

[67] *Ibid.*, p. 314.

[68] James, "Matthew Arnold" (cited in n. 3, above), p. 244.

[69] *Ibid.*, p. 245.

[70] *Ibid.*

[71] *Ibid.*

[72] *Ibid.*, p. 246.

[73] *Ibid.*

[74] *Ibid.*, p. 241.

[75] *English Hours*, p. 24.

[76] *Ibid.*, pp. 29–30.

[77] Henry James, *The Scenic Art*, ed. by Allan Wade (New Brunswick, N.J., Rutgers University Press, 1948), p. 119.

[78] Arnold, *Works*, XIII (*Letters*, I), pp. 324–325.

[79] *Ibid.*, p. 257.

[80] *English Hours*, p. 170.

[81] Henry James, *Stories of Writers and Artists* (New York, New Directions, n.d.), p. 137.

[82] *English Hours*, p. 137.

[83] James, *Letters*, I, 124.

[84] *Ibid.*, p. 138.

[85] *Ibid.*, p. 188.

[86] Arnold, *Works*, III, 26.

[87] *English Hours*, pp. 73–74.

[88] Henry James, *The American Scene* (London, Harper & Bros., 1907), p. 366.

[89] *Ibid.*, pp. 321–322.

[90] *Ibid.*, p. 357.

[91] *Ibid.*, pp. 246–247.

[92] *Ibid.*, p. 267.

[93] *Ibid.*, p. 427.

[94] *Ibid.*, p. 452.

[95] *Ibid.*, p. 442.

[96] *Ibid.*, p. 10.

[97] *Ibid.*, p. 11.

[98] *Ibid.*, p 159.

[99] *Ibid.*, p. 315.

[100] *Ibid.*, p. 53.

[101] *Ibid.*, p. 262.

[102] *Ibid.*, p. 256.

[103] *Ibid.*, p. 264.

[104] *Ibid.*, p. 232.

[105] *Ibid.*, p. 364.

[106] *Ibid.*, p. 338.

[107] James Russell Lowell, *The Complete Writings of* . . . (Boston and New York, Houghton, Mifflin & Co., 1904), II, 134.

NOTES TO CHAPTER II

Arnold in America: 1865–1895

[1] Robert M. Lovett, "William Crary Brownell," *New Republic*, 56 (Oct. 10, 1928), 204.

[2] Arthur Hugh Clough, *North American Review*, 77 (July, 1853), 22.

[3] *North American Review*, 93 (Oct., 1861), 581–582.

[4] C. C. Felton, *North American Review*, 94 (Jan., 1862), 113.

[5] *Ibid.*, p. 120.

[6] William R. Alger, *North American Review*, 96 (Jan., 1863), 126.

[7] *Atlantic Monthly*, 16 (Aug., 1865), 255–256. E. W. Gurney, *The Nation*, 1 (July 6, 1865), 24–25. *The New Englander*, 24 (July, 1865), 600. *Hours at Home*, 2 (Nov., 1865), 5–8. *American Presbyterian Review*, n.s., 3 (Oct., 1865), 644–645. *Boston Review*, 5 (Sept., 1865), 511–513.

[8] "Lord Derby and Professor Arnold on Homer," *The New Englander*, 25 (Jan., 1866), 47–64.

[9] *The Nation*, 2 (May 18, 1866), 627.

[10] *Lippincott's Magazine*, 2 (Aug., 1868), 228–230.

[11] R. H. Stoddard, "Matthew Arnold," *Appleton's Journal*, 3 (Jan. 8, 1870), 48.

[12] Letter, "A Plea for the Uncultivated," *The Nation*, 5 (Sept. 12, 1867), 215; and leading article in the same issue, "Sweetness and Light," pp. 212–213.

[13] H. Hartshone, "American Culture," *Lippincott's Magazine*, 1 (June, 1868), 645.

[14] George Percy, "The Prose of Poets," *Hours at Home*, 7 (May, 1868), 20–28.

[15] *The Nation*, 9 (Nov. 11, 1869), 411.

[16] Theodore Clarke Smith, *The Life and Letters of James Abram Garfield* (New Haven, Yale University Press, 1925), II, 787.

[17] *Overland Monthly*, 11 (Aug., 1873), 185–188.

[18] *The New Englander*, 32 (July, 1873), 590–592.

[19] "Literary Scepticism," *American Church Review*, 25 (Oct., 1873), 534–567. Noah Porter, "Matthew Arnold: Literature and Dogma," *Christian Union*, 7 (June 25, 1873), 501–502; *ibid.* (July 23, 1873), pp. 61–62. *The Independent*, 25 (June 5, 1873), 714. *Baptist Quarterly*, 9 (1875), 412–421.

[20] *Lippincott's Magazine*, 12 (July, 1873), 126–128. *The Nation*, 17 (Aug. 21, 1873), 131–132. *Atlantic Monthly*, 32 (July, 1873), 108–111. *Scribner's Monthly*, 6 (Oct., 1873), 755. T. S. Perry, "Literature and Dogma," *North American Review*, 117 (July, 1873), 240–247. *The Galaxy*, 16 (Sept., 1873), 428–430. *Old and New*, 8 (Oct., 1873), 497–501.

[21] Charles A. Aiken, "Matthew Arnold's Literature and Dogma," *Presbyterian Quarterly Review*, 3 (Jan., 1874), 86–100.

[22] *The Nation*, 25 (July 12, 1877), 30.

[23] Matthew Arnold, *The Works of* . . . (London, Macmillan & Co., Ltd., 1903–1904), X (*Mixed Essays*), 22.

[24] T. W. Higginson, *North American Review*, 129 (July, 1879), 100.

[25] Arthur Verner, "Matthew Arnold's Mixed Essays," *Literary World*, 10 (May 10, 1879), 147.

[26] *International Review*, 6 (June, 1879), 699.

[27] William C. Brownell, *The Nation*, 29 (Oct. 23, 1879), 276.

[28] "Matthew Arnold on Equality," *Scribner's Monthly*, 18 (July, 1879), 466–467.

[29] "Recent Literature," *Atlantic Monthly*, 44 (Nov., 1879), 677.

[30] *Ibid.*, p. 678.

[31] Samuel McCall, "English Views of America," *International Review*, 13 (Nov., 1882), 426–436.

[32] E. S. Nadal, "Matthew Arnold," *The Critic*, 2 (May 20, 1882), 135.

[33] *Ibid.*, p. 136.

[34] A thorough and competent account of Arnold's tour has already been given by Chilson Leonard, in his "Arnold in America: A Study of Matthew Arnold's Literary Relations with America and of His Visits to This Country in 1883 and 1886," an unpublished Yale University dissertation, New Haven, 1932. The greater part of this thesis is concerned with Arnold's tour and the newspaper accounts of it. Leonard maintains, wrongly I think, that there was not any extensive Arnoldian influence in this country.

Arnold's tour, which started in New York, and then took him through New England, the middle Atlantic states, the upper South, and as far west as Chicago and St. Louis, covered the period from October, 1883, to March, 1884. The New York newspapers alone were kind to Arnold, but then their approval seems to have been dictated by sectionalism rather than admiration. As E. P. Lawrence says, "The rivalry between large cities in part accounts for the fact that New York alone defended Arnold and when newspaper attacks became more annoying, the journalists of that city never lost any opportunity to patronize their brothers in Boston and Chicago" (E. P. Lawrence, "An Apostle's Progress: Matthew Arnold in America," *Philological Quarterly*, 10 [Jan., 1931], 62–79). Boston of course became indignant at Arnold's deflation of Emerson. In the Middle West the attacks on Arnold became more raucous. Arnold's manner as a lecturer was described by a Detroit newspaper as that of "an elderly bird pecking at grapes on a trellis." Chicago said he had "harsh features, supercilious manners . . . and ill-fitting clothes." The Middle Western newspapers were fond of describing the lecture tour as a quest for "filthy lucre." The final opinion on Arnold of Joseph Medill, the powerful Chicago publisher, was that the Englishman was a "cur." On the other hand, the Chicago *Dial*, dedicated it seems to holding the torch of culture high aloft over the stockyards, was perhaps the most enthusiastic Arnoldian of all the American periodicals.

Practically all books on Arnold mention or describe the tour of 1883–1884. Special articles on the subject, in addition to that by Lawrence, are: J. D. McCallum, "Apostle of Culture Meets America," *New England Quarterly Review*, 2 (July, 1929), 357–381; and Howard M. Jones, "Arnold, Aristocracy and America," *American Historical Review*, 49 (Apr., 1944), 393–409.

[35] Walt Whitman, *The Complete Prose Works of* . . . : Vol. II of *The Complete Poetry and Prose of Walt Whitman*, ed. by Malcolm Cowley (The American Classics Series; New York, Pellegrini & Cudahy, 1948), 392.

[36] Horace Traubel, *With Walt Whitman in Camden*, Mar.–July, 1888, [I] (Boston, Small, Maynard & Co., 1906), 47.

[37] *Ibid.*, July–Oct., 1888, [II] (New York, Mitchell Kennerly, 1915), 4.

[38] *Ibid.*, Mar.–July, 1888; Nov., 1888–Jan., 1889, [III] (New York, Mitchell Kennerly, 1914), 189.

[39] *Ibid.*, p. 400.

[40] *Ibid.*, [II], 5.

[41] *Ibid.*, p. 204.

[42] *Ibid.*, p. 391.

[43] *Ibid.*, [III], 532.

[44] *Ibid.*, [II], 204.

[45] *Ibid.*, [III], 400.

[46] *Ibid.*, [II], 112.

[47] *Ibid.*, [I], 45.

[48] *Ibid.*

[49] *Ibid.*, [II], 497.

[50] *Ibid.*, [I], 232.

[51] *Ibid.*, pp. 22–23.

[52] James Russell Lowell, *The Letters of . . .*, ed. by C. E. Norton (New York, 1894), II, 347.

[53] James Russell Lowell, *The Complete Writings of . . .* (Boston, Houghton, Mifflin & Co., 1904), III, 256.

[54] *Ibid.*, VII, 322.

[55] *Ibid.*, II, 173.

[56] *Ibid.*, VII, 204.

[57] Lowell, *Letters*, II, 276.

[58] Laura Stedman and George M. Gould, *Life and Letters of Edmund Clarence Stedman* (New York, Moffat, Yard & Co., 1910), II, 63–64.

[59] Edmund C. Stedman, *Victorian Poets* (London, 1876), pp. 90–100.

[60] Stedman and Gould, *op. cit.*, II, 82.

[61] *Ibid.*, p. 81.

[62] *Ibid.*, p. 221.

[63] *Ibid.*, p. 64.

[64] *Ibid.*, p. 354.

[65] Edwin P. Whipple, *Recollections of Eminent Men* (Boston, 1887), p. 281.

[66] *Ibid.*, p. 283.

[67] *Ibid.*, p. 248.

[68] *Ibid.*, p. 285.

[69] Mark Twain, *The American Claimant* (New York, 1892), p. 79.

[70] *Ibid.*, p. 81.

[71] *Mark Twain's Speeches*, ed. by A. B. Paine (New York and London, Harper & Bros., 1923), p. 136.

[72] *Ibid.*, p. 131.

[73] William D. Howells, *Harper's Monthly Magazine*, 77 (July, 1888), 314.

[74] *Ibid.*

[75] *Ibid.*

[76] *Ibid.*, p. 315.

[77] William D. Howells, *ibid.*, 72 (Jan., 1886), 324–325.

[78] William D. Howells, *ibid.*, 75 (June, 1887), 156.

[79] *Ibid.*

[80] Editorial, "Matthew Arnold," *Literary World*, 14 (Nov. 3, 1883), 366.

[81] Horatio N. Powers, "Matthew Arnold," *The Dial*, 4 (Oct., 1883), 122.

[82] "Matthew Arnold's Influence," *The American*, 7 (Oct. 27, 1883), 37–38.

[83] James H. Morse, "Matthew Arnold," *The Critic*, 3 (Nov. 3, 1883), 437–438.

[84] Henry A. Beers, "Matthew Arnold in America," *The Century*, 27 (Nov., 1883), 155–157.

[85] A. H. Stoddard, "The Advent of Mr. Arnold," *Harper's Weekly*, 27 (Oct. 27, 1883), 675.

[86] H. W. Mabie, "Matthew Arnold," *Christian Union*, 28 (Nov. 1, 1883), 358–359.

[87] "Mr. Matthew Arnold's Visit," *The Nation*, 37 (Nov. 1, 1883), 366–367.

[88] Editorial, "Matthew Arnold's Visit," *Literary World*, 14 (Dec. 15, 1883), 446.

[89] *The Critic*, n.s., 1 (Feb. 2, 1884), 57.

[90] "Arnold on Emerson," *The Critic*, n.s., 1 (Jan. 12, 1884), 13.

[91] *Ibid*.

[92] Emma Lazarus, "Critic and Poet," in *The Critic*, n.s., 1 (Apr. 26, 1884), 198, poem reprinted from issue of Jan. 6.

[93] *The Nation*, 37 (Dec. 6, 1883), 460.

[94] "Literary Tact," *The Critic*, n.s., 1 (June 21, 1884), 289.

[95] *The Critic*, n.s., 2 (July 26, 1884), 43.

[96] Joel Benton, "Matthew Arnold," *Appleton's Journal*, 15 (Mar. 11, 1876), 341.

[97] *The Critic*, n.s., 1 (Jan. 12, 1884), 21.

[98] Ralph Waldo Emerson, *The Letters of* . . . , ed. by Ralph L. Rusk (New York, Columbia University Press, 1939), V, 421.

[99] Ralph Waldo Emerson, *Journals of* . . . , ed. by E. W. Emerson and W. E. Forbes (Boston and New York, Houghton, Mifflin & Co.), X (1914), 275.

[100] Editorial, "America's Impressions of Matthew Arnold," *Andover Review*, 1 (Jan., 1884), 86.

[101] A. B. Hyde, "Matthew Arnold," *Methodist Review*, 75 (Nov., 1893), 867–877.

[102] I am indebted for this anecdote to the late Mr. George McLean Harper, Professor of English, Emeritus, of Princeton University.

[103] The *Daily Princetonian*, 8 (Nov. 27, 1883), 227.

[104] *Ibid*.

[105] *Ibid*.

[106] *Ibid*., p. 226.

[107] "Scepticism and Literature," the *Nassau Literary Magazine*, 39 (Dec., 1883), 276.

[108] Bliss Perry, *And Gladly Teach* (Boston and New York, Houghton Mifflin Co., 1935), p. 123.

[109] Rufus M. Jones, *The Trail of Life in College* (New York, Macmillan Co., 1929), p. 59.

[110] William P. Trent, review, *The Forum*, 34 (Oct., 1902), 319.

[111] See editorial in the *Andover Review* cited in note 100, above, pp. 84–89. See also *Unitarian Review*, 12 (Oct., 1884), 120–129; and "A Theologian's Estimate of Matthew Arnold," *The Critic*, n.s., 1 (Jan. 5, 1884), 6.

[112] Mrs. Florence Coates, "Matthew Arnold," *The Century*, 47 (Apr., 1894), 936.

[113] Arnold, *Works*, XV (*Letters*, III), 148.

[114] *Ibid*., p. 182.

[115] William P. Trent, review in *The Forum* cited in note 110, above, p. 319.

[116] *Ibid*.

[117] Louis J. Swinburne, "Matthew Arnold in America," *Lippincott's Magazine*, 33 (Jan., 1884), 94–95.

[118] *The Dial,* 5 (Mar., 1885), 306.

[119] Matthew Arnold, "General Grant," *Murray's Magazine,* 1 (Jan., 1887), 130–144; and *ibid.* (Feb., 1887), pp. 150–166. Reviews: *The Critic,* n.s., 7 (May 14, 1887), 243; and James B. Fry, "Grant and Matthew Arnold. 'An Estimate,'" *North American Review,* 144 (Apr., 1887), 349–357.

[120] James B. Fry, "Mr. Matthew Arnold on America," *North American Review,* 146 (May, 1888), 515–519. The two "Word" essays and "Civilization in the United States," from the *Nineteenth Century,* and the estimate of Grant's *Personal Memoirs,* from *Murray's Magazine,* make up Arnold's *Civilization in the United States: First and Last Impressions of America* (Boston, 1888).

[121] T. W. Higginson, "Expert Opinion of Matthew Arnold's Article on American Civilization," *Our Day,* 1 (June, 1888), 478–499, reprinted from Cambridge *Independent.* Editorial, "Matthew Arnold's Last Criticism," *Andover Review,* 9 (May, 1888), 512–518. Editorial, *The Critic,* n.s., 9 (Apr. 21, 1888), 189. Anon., "Current Criticism," *The Critic,* n.s., 10 (Sept. 8, 1888), 177, reprinted from the *Philadelphia Daily News.* Horatio N. Powers, letter, "Mr. Arnold's Right to Criticize," *The Critic,* n.s., 9 (Apr. 21, 1888), 194. "Mr. Arnold's Discomfort," *The Nation,* 46 (Apr. 12, 1888), 294–295. Obituary, *The Independent,* 40 (Apr. 19, 1888), 490. Joel Benton, "Matthew Arnold on America," *Christian Union,* 37 (Apr. 26, 1888), 521–522.

[122] *Literary World,* 19 (May 26, 1888), 169.

[123] Melville B. Anderson, "Arnold and His Work," *The Dial,* 9 (May, 1888), 6.

[124] Charles E. Norton, obituary, *Proceedings of the American Academy of Arts and Sciences,* n.s., 15 (1888), 349–353.

[125] Horatio N. Powers, "Memorial Verses," *Literary World,* 19 (May 12, 1888), p. 152.

[126] Francis F. Browne, sonnet on Matthew Arnold, *The Dial,* 9 (May, 1888), 5. Helen Gray Cone, sonnet on Matthew Arnold, *The Critic,* n.s., 10 (Dec. 8, 1888), 290. See also William P. Andrews, obituary poem, "Matthew Arnold," *The Century,* 36 (July, 1888), 417.

[127] "Matthew Arnold," *The Nation,* 46 (Apr. 19, 1888), 316.

[128] T. W. Hunt, *New Princeton Review,* 6 (Nov., 1888), 355–369.

[129] F. H. Stoddard, "Tolstoi and Matthew Arnold," *Andover Review,* 10 (Oct., 1888), 359–369.

[130] I. T. Hecker, "Two Prophets of This Age," *Catholic World,* 47 (Aug., 1888), 684–693.

[131] George Woodberry, *Makers of Literature* (New York, Macmillan Co., 1900), pp. 6–7.

[132] *Ibid.,* p. 8.

[133] *Ibid.,* p. 11.

[134] John Burroughs, *Indoor Studies* (Boston and New York, Houghton, Mifflin & Co., 1902), p. 90.

[135] *Ibid.,* p. 136.

[136] John Burroughs, *The Heart of Burroughs's Journals,* ed. by Clara Barrus (Boston and New York, Houghton Mifflin Co., 1928), p. 148.

[137] Sara Orne Jewett, *Letters of . . . ,* ed. by Annie Fields (Boston and New York, Houghton Mifflin Co., 1911), p. 54.

[138] *Ibid.,* p. 24.

[139] Philip Littell, *New Republic,* 1 (Jan. 2, 1915), 26.

[140] *Ibid.*

[141] Brander Matthews, "Matthew Arnold and the Drama," *The Bookman,* 44 (Sept., 1916), 1.

[142] Charles C. Starbank, "Religious Thought in England," *Andover Review,* 10 (Nov., 1888), 473–491.

[143] Stephen H. Thayer, "Matthew Arnold's Influence on Literature," *Andover Review,* 12 (Sept., 1889), 262–275.

[144] Charles A. L. Morse, "Matthew Arnold's Letters," *Catholic World,* 63 (July, 1896), 486–496.

[145] Mrs. G. Van Rensslaer, "Mr. Arnold and American Art," *The Century,* 36 (June, 1888), 314.

[146] Louise S. Houghton, "Matthew Arnold and Orthodoxy," *New World,* 6 (Dec., 1897), 629–638.

[147] John Fiske, *The Unseen World, and Other Essays* (Boston, Houghton, Mifflin & Co., 1900), p. 108.

[148] John Fiske, *Excursions of an Evolutionist* (Boston, 1899), p. 298.

[149] Melville B. Anderson, "Matthew Arnold's Later Criticism," *The Dial,* 9 (Mar., 1889), 284.

[150] "Matthew Arnold's Latest Essays," *The Critic,* n.s., 12 (Oct. 12, 1889), 173.

[151] George Woodberry, *The Bookman,* 2 (Feb., 1896), 508.

[152] "The Arnold Aftermath," leading article in *The Dial,* 20 (Apr. 1, 1896), 193–194.

NOTES TO CHAPTER III

William Brownell

[1] W. C. Brownell, *Tributes and Appreciations* (New York, Privately printed, 1929), p. 3.

[2] William C. Brownell, *American Prose Masters* (New York, C. Scribner's Sons, 1909), p. 262.

[3] *Ibid.,* p. 163.

[4] *Ibid.,* p. 167.

[5] *Ibid.,* pp. 168–169.

[6] *Ibid.,* p. 168.

[7] *Ibid.,* p. 296.

[8] *Ibid.,* p. 349.

[9] William C. Brownell, *Democratic Distinction in America* (New York and London, C. Scribner's Sons, 1927), p. 151.

[10] *American Prose Masters,* pp. 351–352.

[11] Gertrude Hall Brownell, *William Crary Brownell* (New York and London, C. Scribner's Sons, 1933), p. 366.

[12] William C. Brownell, *Victorian Prose Masters* (New York, C. Scribner's Sons, 1901), p. 157.

[13] Gertrude H. Brownell, *op. cit.,* pp. 360–361.

[14] *Victorian Prose Masters,* p. 149.

[15] *Ibid.,* pp. 150–151.

[16] *Ibid.,* p. 152.

[17] *Ibid.*

[18] *Ibid.,* pp. 152–153.

[19] *Ibid.,* p. 155.

[20] *Ibid.,* pp. 156–157.

[21] *Ibid.,* p. 156.

[22] *Ibid.,* p. 160.

[23] *Ibid.,* p. 162.

[24] *Ibid.*, p. 167.

[25] *Ibid.*, p. 167–168.

[26] *Ibid.*, p. 169.

[27] *Ibid.*, p. 176.

[28] *Ibid.*, p. 169.

[29] *Ibid.*, p. 171.

[30] *Ibid.*

[31] *Ibid.*, p. 172.

[32] *Ibid.*, p. 176.

[33] *Ibid.*, p. 185.

[34] William C. Brownell, *The Genius of Style* (New York and London, C. Scribner's Sons, 1924), pp. 84–85.

[35] Edith Wharton: "One need but open 'French Traits,' that masterpiece of forty years ago which is a masterpiece still, to understand why the art of criticism has been called creative." In *W. C. Brownell, Tributes and Appreciations,* pp. 3–4; "an astonishingly penetrating estimate of the national character," *ibid.*, p. 5. In the same book (p. 52), M. Chevrillon commented, "Son livre *French Traits* est l'étude la plus délicate et pénétrante que je connais de l'esprit social français."

[36] William C. Brownell, *French Traits* (New York, 1890), p. 65.

[37] Matthew Arnold, *The Works of* . . . (London, Macmillan & Co., Ltd., 1903–1904), III, 54.

[28] *French Traits,* p. 411.

[39] *Ibid.*, p. 380.

[40] *Ibid.*

[41] Arnold, *Works,* VI, 50.

[42] *Ibid.*, p. 48.

[43] *French Traits,* p. 384.

[44] *Ibid.*, p. 167.

[45] *Ibid.*, pp. 197–198.

[46] *Ibid.*, p. 161.

[47] *Ibid.*, p. 365.

[48] *Ibid.*, p. 372.

[49] Robert Morss Lovett, "William Crary Brownell," *New Republic,* 56 (Oct. 10, 1928), 204.

[50] Matthew Arnold, *Essays in Criticism,* Third Series, ed. by E. J. O'Brien (Boston, Ball Publishing Co., 1910), p. 143.

[51] William C. Brownell, *Criticism* (New York, C. Scribner's Sons, 1914), p. 1.

[52] *Ibid.*

[53] *Ibid.*, p. 16.

[54] *Ibid.*, p. 18.

[55] *Ibid.*, p. 70.

[56] *Ibid.*, p. 71.

[57] Arnold, *Works,* III, 41.

[58] *Criticism,* p. 20.

[59] *Victorian Prose Masters,* p. 165.

[60] *Ibid.*, pp. 165–166.

[61] *Criticism,* p. 11.

[62] *Ibid.*, p. 41

[63] *Victorian Prose Masters,* p. 166.

[64] *Criticism,* p. 80.

[65] *Ibid.*, p. 82.

[66] Gertrude H. Brownell, *op. cit.* (in n. 11, above), p. 381.

[67] *Victorian Prose Masters,* p. 177.

[68] *Democratic Distinction in America,* p. 113.

[69] Matthew Arnold, *The Popular Education of France* (London, 1861), p. xxxii.

[70] William C. Brownell, *Standards* (New York, C. Scribner's Sons, 1917), p. 21.

[71] *Ibid.,* p. 38.

[72] *Ibid.,* p. 70.

[73] *Ibid.,* p. 72.

[74] *Ibid.,* p. 111.

[75] *Ibid.,* p. 149.

[76] Arnold, *Works,* X (Mixed Essays), ix.

[77] *French Traits,* p. 335.

[78] *Democratic Distinction in America,* p. 64.

[79] *Ibid.,* p. 71.

[80] *Ibid.,* p. 63.

[81] *Ibid.,* p. 194.

[82] *Ibid.,* p. 22.

[83] *Ibid.,* p. 23.

[84] *Ibid.,* p. 64.

[85] *Ibid.,* p. 49.

[86] *Ibid.,* p. 147.

[87] *Ibid.,* pp. 28–29.

[88] *Ibid.,* p. 24.

[89] *Ibid.,* p. 33.

[90] *Ibid.,* p. 32.

[91] *Ibid.,* p. 38.

[92] *Ibid.,* p. 33.

[93] *Ibid.,* p. 169.

[94] *Ibid.,* p. 167.

[95] *Ibid.,* p. 48.

[96] *Ibid.,* p. 41.

[97] *Ibid.*

[98] *Ibid.,* p. 45.

[99] *Ibid.,* p. 42.

[100] *Ibid.,* p. 43.

[101] *Ibid.,* pp. 152–153.

[102] *Ibid.,* p. 25.

[103] *Ibid.,* p. 27.

[104] *Ibid.,* p. 57.

[105] *Ibid.,* p. 89.

[106] *Ibid.,* p. 67.

[107] *Ibid.*

[108] *Ibid.,* p. 56.

[109] *Ibid.,* p. 60.

[110] *Ibid.,* p. 90.

[111] *Ibid.*

[112] *Ibid.,* p. 93.

[113] *Ibid.,* p. 109.

[114] *Ibid.,* p. 119.

[115] *Ibid.,* pp. 159–160.

[116] *Ibid.,* pp. 164–165.

[117] *Ibid.*, p. 166.
[118] *Ibid.*
[119] *Ibid.*, p. 197.
[120] *Ibid.*, p. 217
[121] *Ibid.*, p. 222.
[122] *Ibid.*
[123] *Ibid.*, p. 246.
[124] *Ibid.*, pp. 259–260.

NOTES TO CHAPTER IV

ARNOLD IN AMERICA: 1895–1930

[1] Hamilton W. Mabie, *Book Reviews*, 3 (Dec., 1895), 217–220.

[2] "Personalia: Coleridge, Arnold, Stevenson," *Poet Lore*, 8 (Feb., 1896), 100–105.

[3] Florence Earle Coates, "Matthew Arnold," *The Century*, 47 (Apr., 1894), 937.

[4] Minnie E. Hadley, "Matthew Arnold: Man of Letters," *Education*, 23 (Sept., 1902), 47.

[5] Joseph H. Crocker, "Matthew Arnold," *New England Magazine*, 9 Jan., 1894), 632, 638.

[6] John Burroughs, "On the Re-Reading of Books," *The Century*, n.s., 33 (Nov., 1897), 149.

[7] *Matthew Arnold and the Spirit of the Age*, ed. by Greenough White (New York and London, G. P. Putnam's Sons, 1898). White gives the history of the club in his introduction. The collection is made up of papers originally written for and read to the club.

[8] *Ibid.*, p. 3.

[9] *Ibid.*

[10] *Ibid.*

[11] *Ibid.*, p. 95.

[12] *Ibid.*, p. 103.

[13] *Ibid.*, p. 93.

[14] *Sewanee Review*, 7 (Oct., 1899), 508.

[15] *The Outlook*, 59 (May 7, 1898), 90.

[16] Charles Forster Smith, "Matthew Arnold," *Sewanee Review*, 7 (Apr., 1899), 189.

[17] *Ibid.*, p. 204.

[18] Vida Scudder, *Social Ideals in English Letters* (Boston and New York, Houghton Mifflin Co., 1923), pp. 235, 239, 242. (This is a new and enlarged edition of the 1898 edition.)

[19] W. H. Johnson, "The 'Passing' of Matthew Arnold," *The Dial*, 27 (Nov. 16, 1899), 351–353.

[20] Vida Scudder, "Arnold as an Abiding Force," *The Dial*, 27 (Dec. 16, 1899), 481–482.

[21] *The Nation*, 69 (Nov. 23, 1899), 396–397.

[22] *The Critic*, 40 (May, 1902), 409–413.

[23] "A Group of Biographies," *The Outlook*, 72 (Dec. 6, 1902), 852–853.

[24] W. P. Trent, *The Forum*, 34 (Oct., 1902), 311–319.

[25] H. W. Boynton, *Atlantic Monthly*, 90 (Nov., 1902), 706–707.

[26] William C. Brownell, "Arnold and Ruskin," *The Bookbuyer*, 25 (Nov., 1902), 318.

[27] Edith Wharton, *The Lamp*, 26 (Feb., 1903), 51.

[28] George Saintsbury, *Matthew Arnold* (London, Blackwood, 1899), p. 72.

[29] *Ibid.*, p. 88.

[30] *Ibid.*, p. 169.

[31] Herbert W. Paul, *Matthew Arnold* (London, Macmillan & Co., 1902), p. 4.

[32] *Ibid.*

[33] *Ibid.*

[34] *Ibid.*, p. 173.

[35] William H. Dawson, *Matthew Arnold and His Relation to the Thought of Our Time* (New York and London, G. P. Putnam's Sons, 1904), p. iii.

[36] *The Nation*, 78 (Apr. 23, 1904), 318–319.

[37] Edith J. Rich, "The Cult of Matthew Arnold," *The Dial*, 37 (Oct. 1, 1904), 200–203.

[38] "Some Recent Books," *Contemporary Review*, 85 (June, 1904), 904–905. *The Arena*, 31 (June, 1904), 658–660. *Current Literature*, 37 (Nov., 1904), 433–436. *The Outlook*, 76 (Apr. 16, 1904), 946–947. H. W. Boynton, "Books New and Old," *Atlantic Monthly*, 93 (May, 1904), 707–708. *The Critic*, 45 (Sept., 1904), 273–276.

[39] Horatio S. Krans, "Two New Books on Matthew Arnold," *The Outlook*, 78 (Nov. 12, 1904), 680–682. Robert T. Kerlin, "Matthew Arnold: 'A Healing and Reconciling Influence'?" *The Arena*, 32 (Oct., 1904), 362–369.

[40] Peter A. Sillard, "Matthew Arnold Intime," *Atlantic Monthly*, 95 (Feb., 1905), 269.

[41] "Modern Poets and Christian Teaching," *The Nation*, 84 (Mar. 21, 1907), 268–269.

[42] "Matthew Arnold Twenty Years After," *The Nation*, 86 (May 7, 1908), 416–417.

[43] Charles Leonard Moore, "Arnold and Lowell," *The Dial*, 45 (Sept. 16, 1908), 157–158.

[44] Stuart P. Sherman in *The Nation*, 91 (Oct. 20, 1910), 371.

[45] Logan Pearsall Smith, *Unforgotten Years* (Boston, Little, Brown & Co., 1939), pp. 124–125.

[46] Ellery Sedgwick, *The Happy Profession* (Boston, Little, Brown & Co., 1946), pp. 67–68.

[47] Christopher Morley, *The Powder of Sympathy* (Garden City, N.Y., Doubleday, Page & Co., 1923), p. 100.

[48] G. L. Strachey, *Literary Essays* (London, Chatto & Windus, 1948), p. 210.

[49] Florence Moynihan, "Arnold the Humanist," *Catholic World*, 116 (Dec., 1922), 330–337. Brother Leo, "Matthew Arnold, Poet and Essayist," *ibid.*, pp. 320–330.

[50] H. L. Mencken, *Prejudices: Fourth Series* (New York, A. A. Knopf, 1924), p. 9.

[51] *Civilization in the United States*, ed. by Harold Stearns (New York, Harcourt, Brace & Co., 1922), p. 101.

[52] Randolph Bourne, *History of a Literary Radical* (New York, B. W. Huebsch, Inc., 1920), p. 108.

[53] Malcolm Cowley, *Exile's Return* (New York, W. W. Norton & Co., Inc., 1934), p. 55.

[54] V. F. Calverton, *Sex Expression in Literature* (New York, Boni & Liveright, 1926), p. 239.

[55] Matthew Arnold, *The Works of . . .* (London, Macmillan & Co., Ltd., 1903–1904), XIII (*Letters*, I), 329.

[56] James Huneker, *Promenades of an Impressionist* (New York, C. Scribner's Sons, 1910), pp. 228–229.

[57] *Ibid.*, p. 390.

[58] Edmund Wilson, *The Shores of Light* (New York, Farrar, Straus & Young, 1952), p. 383.

[59] Morley, *op. cit.* (in n. 47, above), p. 100.

[60] *Ibid.*, p. 108.

[61] Ludwig Lewisohn, "Matthew Arnold: 1888–1922," *The Nation,* 115 (Dec. 24, 1922), 708.

[62] Paul Elmer More, *Shelburne Essays, Seventh Series* (New York, G. P. Putnam's Sons, 1910), p. 233.

[63] Matthew Arnold, *Selections from the Prose Works of* ..., ed. by Lewis E. Gates (New York, 1897), p. 171.

[64] Lewis E. Gates, *Studies and Appreciations* (New York, Macmillan Co., 1900), p. 205.

[65] Joel E. Spingarn, *The New Criticism* (New York, Columbia University Press, 1911), pp. 34–35.

[66] *Ibid.*, p. 34.

[67] More, *op. cit.* (in n. 62, above), p. 218.

[68] Paul Elmer More, *New Shelburne Essays,* III (Princeton, Princeton University Press, 1936), pp. 31–35.

[69] Irving Babbitt, "Matthew Arnold," in *Spanish Character and Other Essays,* ed. by Frederick Manchester and others (Boston and New York, Houghton Mifflin Co., 1940), pp. 48–65. This was originally a review of Sherman's book on Arnold in *The Nation,* 105 (Aug. 2, 1917), 118.

[70] More, *Shelburne Essays, Seventh Series,* pp. 230–234.

[71] Norman Foerster, "Matthew Arnold and American Letters Today," *Sewanee Review,* 30 (July, 1922), p. 306.

[72] Robert Shafer, *Christianity and Naturalism* (New Haven, Yale University Press, 1926), p. 195.

[73] Bourne, *op. cit.* (in n. 52, above), p. 31.

[74] Van Wyck Brooks, *New England: Indian Summer* (New York, E. P. Dutton & Co., 1940), p. 143.

[75] Van Wyck Brooks, *The Confident Years: 1885–1915* (New York, E. P. Dutton & Co., 1952), p. 600.

[76] Bourne, *op. cit.,* p. xxxii.

[77] Van Wyck Brooks, *America's Coming-of-Age* (New York, B. W. Huebsch, 1915), p. 63.

[78] *Ibid.*, pp. 171–172.

[79] Van Wyck Brooks, *The Wine of the Puritans* (New York, M. Kennerly, 1909), pp. 17–18.

[80] Brooks, *America's Coming-of-Age,* p. 153.

[81] Van Wyck Brooks, *Letters and Leadership* (New York, B. W. Huebsch, 1918), p. 62.

[82] *Ibid.*, p. 65.

[83] Ludwig Lewisohn, *Up Stream* (New York, Boni & Liveright, 1922), p. 94.

[84] Ludwig Lewisohn, *Cities and Men* (New York, Harper & Bros., 1927), p. 32. This chapter is a reprint of the *Nation* article already referred to in note 61, above.

[85] *Ibid.*, p. 32.

[86] *Ibid.*, pp. 32–33.

[87] *Ibid.*, p. 33.

[88] Ludwig Lewisohn, *The Creative Life* (New York, Boni & Liveright, 1924), p. 89.

[89] Robert Morss Lovett, "The Mind of Matthew," *The Nation,* 148 (Mar. 11, 1939), 298. This is a review of Lionel Trilling's book, *Matthew Arnold.*

[90] John Macy, "The Critical Game," in James Bowman, ed., *Contemporary American Criticism* (New York, Henry Holt & Co., 1926), pp. 257–265.

⁹¹ William A. Drake, ed., *American Criticism, 1926* (New York, Harcourt, Brace & Co., 1926), p. viii.

⁹² Norman Foerster, ed., *American Critical Essays, XIXth and XXth Centuries* (London, Oxford University Press, 1930), p. vii.

⁹³ *Ibid.*, p. xi.

⁹⁴ George Santayana, *Persons and Places* (New York, C. Scribner's Sons, 1944), p. 240.

⁹⁵ George Santayana, *The Middle Span* (New York, C. Scribner's Sons, 1945), p. 19.

⁹⁶ George P. Adams and William P. Montague, eds., *Contemporary American Philosophy* (London, G. Allen & Unwin, Ltd., 1930), II, 244.

⁹⁷ George W. Howgate, *George Santayana* (Philadelphia, University of Pennsylvania Press, 1938), p. 52.

⁹⁸ *Ibid.*, p. 207.

⁹⁹ *Ibid.*

¹⁰⁰ George Santayana, *Winds of Doctrine* (New York, C. Scribner's Sons, 1913), p. 175.

¹⁰¹ George Santayana, *Interpretations of Poetry and Religion* (New York, C. Scribner's Sons, 1900), p. v.

¹⁰² *Ibid.*, p. x.

¹⁰³ *Ibid.*, pp. 284–285.

¹⁰⁴ *Ibid.*, p. 289.

NOTES TO CHAPTER V

STUART P. SHERMAN

¹ Stuart Sherman, *Points of View* (New York and London, C. Scribner's Sons, 1924), p. 109.

² *Ibid.*, p. 91.

³ *Ibid.*, p. 93.

⁴ *Ibid.*, p. 94.

⁵ *Ibid.*, p. 95.

⁶ Irving Babbitt, "Matthew Arnold," *The Nation*, 105 (Aug. 2, 1917), 117.

⁷ Stuart Sherman, *On Contemporary Literature* (New York, Henry Holt & Co., 1917), p. 9.

⁸ *Ibid.*, p. 10.

⁹ *Ibid.*, p. 91.

¹⁰ *Ibid.*, p. 56.

¹¹ *Ibid.*, p. 65.

¹² Babbitt, "Matthew Arnold," p. 120.

¹³ Jacob Zeitlin and Homer Woodbridge, *Life and Letters of Stuart P. Sherman*, I (New York, Farrar & Rinehart, Inc., 1929), 220 ff.

¹⁴ *Ibid.*, pp. 234–235.

¹⁵ *Ibid.*, pp. 237–238.

¹⁶ *Ibid.*, p. 238.

¹⁷ *Ibid.*, p. 342.

¹⁸ *Ibid.*, p. 343.

¹⁹ *Ibid.*, p. 348.

²⁰ Stuart Sherman, *Americans* (New York, C. Scribner's Sons, 1923), p. 336.

²¹ Zeitlin and Woodbridge, *op. cit.*, I, 376.

²² *Ibid.*, II, 497.

²³ *Americans*, p. x.

[24] *Ibid.*, p. xii.

[25] Zeitlin and Woodbridge, *op. cit.*, II, 545.

[26] *Ibid*, p. 546.

[27] *Ibid.*, p. 548.

[28] *Ibid.*, p. 549.

[29] *Ibid.*, p. 517.

[30] Stuart Sherman, *The Nation*, 89 (Dec. 30, 1909), 650.

[31] Stuart Sherman, *ibid.*, 99 (Dec. 31, 1914), 777.

[32] Zeitlin and Woodbridge, *op. cit.*, II, 524.

[33] *Ibid.*, p. 529.

[34] *Points of View*, p. 112.

[35] Zeitlin and Woodbridge, *op. cit.*, II, 562.

[36] *Americans*, p. 125.

[37] *On Contemporary Literature*, p. 232.

[38] "Mr. Brownell and Mr. Mencken," *The Bookman*, 60 (Jan., 1925), 632.

[39] *Points of View*, p. 113.

[40] *Ibid.*, p. 115.

[41] *Ibid.*, p. 89.

[42] *Ibid.*, p. 125.

[43] *Ibid.*, p. 95.

[44] *Ibid.*, p. 96.

[45] *Ibid.*, p. 95.

[46] *Americans*, pp. 19–20.

[47] Stuart Sherman, *The Genius of America* (New York and London, C. Scribner's Sons, 1923), p. 55.

[48] *Americans*, p. 32.

[49] *Ibid.*, p. 160.

[50] Zeitlin and Woodbridge, *op. cit.*, II, 522.

[51] *Ibid.*, pp. 498–499.

[52] Ernest Boyd, "Ku Klux Kriticism," in *Criticism in America* (New York, Harcourt, Brace & Co., 1924), pp. 309–320.

[53] *The Genius of America*, p. 26.

[54] Mr. Homer Woodbridge, Professor of English, Emeritus, of Wesleyan University, said this to the writer in conversation.

[55] Stuart Sherman, *Shaping Men and Women* (Garden City, N.Y., Doubleday, Doran & Co., Inc., 1928), p. 13.

[56] Babbitt, "Matthew Arnold" (cited in n. 6, above), p. 117.

[57] Stuart P. Sherman, *The Nation*, 86 (May 14, 1908), 442.

[58] Stuart P. Sherman, "Professor Kittredge and the Teaching of English," *The Nation*, 97 (Sept. 11, 1913), 230.

[59] Stuart P. Sherman, *Matthew Arnold, How to Know Him* (Indianapolis, Bobbs-Merrill Co., 1917), p. 132.

[60] *Ibid.*, pp. 132–133.

[61] *Ibid.*, p. 185.

[62] *Ibid.*, p. 143.

[63] *Americans*, pp. 73–74.

[64] *Points of View*, p. 61.

[65] *Matthew Arnold, How to Know Him*, p. 19.

[66] *Ibid.*, p. 314.

[67] *Ibid.*, pp. 59–60.

[68] Zeitlin and Woodbridge, *op. cit.*, I, 300.

[69] *Ibid.*

[70] *Matthew Arnold, How to Know Him*, p. 211.

[71] *Ibid.*, p. 212.

[72] *The Genius of America*, p. 153.

[73] *Americans*, p. 330.

[74] *Ibid.*, p. 332.

[75] *The Genius of America*, p. 230.

[76] *Ibid.*, p. 141.

[77] Stuart Sherman, *The Main Stream* (New York and London, C. Scribner's Sons, 1927), p. 125.

[78] *Americans*, p. 179.

[79] *The Genius of America*, p. 217.

[80] *Ibid.*, p. 219.

[81] Stuart Sherman, *Critical Woodcuts* (New York and London, C. Scribner's Sons, 1926), p. xiii.

[82] Joseph Warren Beach, *The Outlook for American Prose* (Chicago, University of Chicago Press, 1926), pp. 92 ff.

[83] *Americans*, p. 333.

[84] *Critical Woodcuts*, p. 231.

[85] Zeitlin and Woodbridge, *op. cit.*, II, 492.

[86] *Americans*, p. 5.

[87] *Ibid.*, p. 12.

[88] Zeitlin and Woodbridge, *op. cit.*, I, 297.

[89] *Points of View*, p. 31.

[90] *Shaping Men and Women*, p. xxxv.

[91] Zeitlin and Woodbridge, *op. cit.*, II, 414. According to Zeitlin, Sherman's faith in the educational process was not dimmed by the disillusioning discovery that many of the undergraduates were buying their "maxims" in bookstores.

[92] *Ibid.*, p. 415.

[93] *Ibid.*

[94] *Ibid.*, p. 416.

[95] *Shaping Men and Women*, p. 269.

[96] *Ibid.*, p. 272.

[97] *Ibid.*, p. 273.

[98] *Ibid.*, p. 274.

[99] *Ibid.*, p. 275.

[100] *The Main Stream*, p. 143.

[101] *Critical Woodcuts*, p. 13.

[102] Theodore Spicer-Simson, *Men of Letters of the British Isles* (New York, W. E. Rudge, 1924), p. 96.

[103] Zeitlin and Woodbridge, *op. cit.*, I, 336.

NOTES TO CHAPTER VI

T. S. ELIOT

[1] F. O. Matthiessen, *The Responsibilities of the Critic* (New York, Oxford University Press, 1952), p. 3.

[2] Terence Connolly, "Matthew Arnold: Critic," *Thought*, 9 (1934), 194

[3] T. H. Vail Motter, "Culture and the New Anarchy," *AAUP Bulletin*, 27 (June, 1941), 298.

⁴ *Ibid.,* p. 303.

⁵ Everett Hunt, "Matthew Arnold and His Critics," *Sewanee Review,* 44 (Oct., 1936), 467.

⁶ Article signed "Crites," "The Return of Matthew Arnold," *Criterion,* 3 (Jan., 1925), 162.

⁷ Carleton W. Stanley, *Matthew Arnold* (Toronto, University of Toronto Press, 1938), p. 91.

⁸ T. S. Eliot, *The Use of Poetry and the Use of Criticism* (Cambridge, Mass., Harvard University Press, 1933), p. 121.

⁹ *Ibid.,* pp. 101–102.

¹⁰ *Ibid.,* p. 134.

¹¹ T. S. Eliot, *Selected Essays, 1917–1932* (New York, Harcourt, Brace & Co., 1932), p. 348.

¹² T. S. Eliot, *The Sacred Wood* (London, Methuen & Co., 1950), p. xi. This book, originally published in England in 1920, was reprinted in 1928 with some revisions and a new preface. All pages given in the notes below refer to the 1950 edition.

¹³ "The Return of Matthew Arnold" (cited in n. 6, above), p. 162.

¹⁴ T. S. Eliot, *For Lancelot Andrewes* (London, Faber & Gwyer, 1928), p. 74.

¹⁵ *Ibid.,* p. 75.

¹⁶ Arnold was always disturbing both his admirers and his detractors by his robust appearance and his social aplomb. Arnold had been a culture hero for Logan Pearsall Smith in the latter's undergraduate days at Harvard, but Smith later suffered the misfortune of meeting his early idol in Germany: ". . . a tall figure in a suit of large checks, with a broad face and black whiskers, marched in with the jaunty air of an English school master . . ." Arnold then slapped his brown gloves down on a table and proceeded to amuse some Russian ladies with an account of the favorable reception he had received at a Saxon court from certain "dear princesses." Was this, thought Smith, the "exquisite apostle"? "I looked at this large, cheerful figure, I listened to this boastful conversation, with dismay." *Unforgotten Years* (Boston, Little, Brown & Co., 1939), pp. 134–135. Julian Hawthorne said Arnold looked as if he should have been the head of a great business firm or a country gentleman. *Shapes that Pass* (Boston and New York, Houghton Mifflin Co., 1928), p. 229.

¹⁷ T. S. Eliot, "Lines for Cuscuscaraway and Mirza Ali Beg," Part V of "Five-Finger Exercises," *The Complete Poems and Plays of T. S. Eliot* (New York, Harcourt, Brace & Co., 1952), p. 93.

¹⁸ *The Use of Poetry and the Use of Criticism,* pp. 111–112.

¹⁹ *Ibid.,* p. 95.

²⁰ *Ibid.,* pp. 98–99.

²¹ *Ibid.,* p. 111.

²² T. S. Eliot, "Criticism in England," *The Athenaeum,* 4650 (June 13, 1919), 456.

²³ *Ibid.*

²⁴ T. S. Eliot, *After Strange Gods* (London, Faber & Faber, Ltd., 1934), p. 16.

²⁵ T. S. Eliot, *Essays, Ancient and Modern* (London, Faber & Faber, Ltd., 1936), p. 127.

²⁶ T S. Eliot, *The Idea of a Christian Society* (London, Faber & Faber, Ltd., 1939), p. 45.

²⁷ T. S. Eliot, *Notes Towards the Definition of Culture* (London, Faber & Faber, Ltd., 1948), pp. 45–46.

²⁸ T. S. Eliot, "American Literature," *The Athenaeum,* 4643 (Apr. 25, 1919), 237.

²⁹ *Ibid.*

³⁰ T. S. Eliot, *From Poe to Valéry,* lecture delivered to Library of Congress (Washington, 1949), p. 1.

[31] T. S. Eliot, "American Critics," *T.L.S.*, 1405 (Jan. 10, 1929), 24.

[32] "American Literature" (cited in n. 28, above), p. 237.

[33] "American Critics" (cited in n. 31, above), p. 24.

[34] *Ibid.*

[35] *Ibid.*

[36] *Ibid.*

[37] *Ibid.*

[38] *The Sacred Wood*, p. 44.

[39] T. S. Eliot in *The English Review*, 53 (June, 1931), 118.

[40] *The Sacred Wood*, p. 43.

[41] *Ibid.*, p. 41.

[42] *Selected Essays, 1917–1932*, p. 386.

[43] *Ibid.*, p. 402.

[44] *The Sacred Wood*, p. viii.

[45] T. S. Eliot, *The Music of Poetry* (Glasgow, Jackson, Son & Co., 1942), p. 16.

[46] T. S. Eliot, *John Dryden* (New York, T. & Elsa Holliday, 1932), p. 24.

[47] *The Sacred Wood*, p. xiii.

[48] *Ibid.*, pp. 45–46.

[49] *Selected Essays, 1917–1932*, p. 18.

[50] "The Return of Matthew Arnold" (cited in n. 6, above), p. 162.

[51] "Criticism in England" (cited in n. 22, above), p. 457.

[52] T. S. Eliot, "A Brief Treatise on the Criticism of Poetry," *The Chapbook*, 2 (Mar., 1920), 3.

[53] *Ibid.*, p. 4.

[54] T. S. Eliot, "The Function of a Literary Review," *Criterion*, 1 (July, 1923), 421.

[55] T. S. Eliot, "The Idea of a Literary Review," the *New Criterion*, 4 (Jan., 1926), 5.

[56] *Ibid.*

[57] T. S. Eliot, "Literature, Science, and Dogma," *The Dial*, 82 (Mar., 1927), 243.

[58] *For Lancelot Andrewes*, p. 77.

[59] *Ibid.*, p. 81.

[60] *Ibid.*, p. ix.

[61] *The Sacred Wood*, p. viii.

[62] *Ibid.*

[63] *Ibid.*, p. ix.

[64] *Ibid.*, p. x.

[65] *John Dryden*, p. 62.

[66] *Ibid.*, p. 66.

[67] *Ibid.*, p. 67.

[68] *The Use of Poetry and the Use of Criticism*, p. 111.

[69] *Ibid.*, p. 96.

[70] *Ibid.*, p. 97.

[71] *Ibid.*, p. 73.

[72] *Ibid.*, p. 97.

[73] *Ibid.*, p. 106.

[74] *Ibid.*, p. 112.

[75] *Ibid.*

[76] *Ibid.*, p. 114.

[77] *Ibid.*, p. 6.

[78] *After Strange Gods*, p. 48.

[79] *Essays, Ancient and Modern*, p. 93.

[80] *The Idea of a Christian Society*, p. 80.
[81] *Notes Towards the Definition of Culture*, p. 22.
[82] *Ibid.*, p. 23.
[83] *Ibid.*, p. 28.
[84] T. S. Eliot, "The Aims of Education, I," *Measure*, 2 (Dec., 1950), 191.
[85] *The Use of Poetry and the Use of Criticism*, p. 15.
[86] *Ibid.*, p. 114.
[87] *Ibid.*, p. 120.
[88] Matthew Arnold, *The Works of* . . . (London, Macmillan & Co., Ltd., 1903–1904), XIII (*Letters,* I), 168.
[89] T. S. Eliot, *What Is a Classic?* (London, Faber & Faber, Ltd., 1945), p. 28.
[90] *Ibid.*, p. 27.
[91] *Ibid.*, pp. 28–29.
[92] *Ibid.*, p. 31.
[93] T. S. Eliot, *Milton* (Oxford Univ. Press, 1947, reprinted from *Proceedings of the British Academy*, Vol. 33), p. 3.
[94] Arnold, *Works*, II, 173.
[95] *The Idea of a Christian Society*, pp. 15–16.
[96] *Ibid.*, p. 17.
[97] *Ibid.*, p. 18.
[98] *Selected Essays, 1917–1932*, p. 16.
[99] *Essays, Ancient and Modern*, p. 107.
[100] *Ibid.*, p. 172.

NOTES TO CHAPTER VII

LIONEL TRILLING

[1] Lionel Trilling, "Elements That Are Wanted," *Partisan Review*, 7 (Sept.–Oct., 1940), 368.
[2] Lionel Trilling, *The Liberal Imagination* (Garden City, N.Y., Doubleday & Co., Inc., 1953), p. 270.
[3] *Ibid.*, p. 273.
[4] *Ibid.*, p. 261.
[5] *Ibid.*, p. 287.
[6] *Ibid.*, p. 126.
[7] "Elements That Are Wanted" (cited in n. 1, above), p. 372.
[8] Lionel Trilling, "Mr. Eliot's Kipling," *The Nation*, 157 (Oct. 16, 1943), 442.
[9] "Elements That Are Wanted," p. 373.
[10] *Ibid.*, p. 379.
[11] *The Liberal Imagination*, p. 250.
[12] *Ibid.*, p. 125.
[13] "Elements That Are Wanted," p. 373.
[14] *Ibid.*, pp. 367–368.
[15] Lionel Trilling, in "The Situation in American Writing," *Partisan Review*, 6 (Fall, 1939), 110.
[16] Lionel Trilling, "Willa Cather," *New Republic*, 90 (Feb. 10, 1937), 11.
[17] Lionel Trilling, "William Dean Howells and the Roots of Modern Taste," *Partisan Review*, 18 (Sept.–Oct., 1951), 526.
[18] Lionel Trilling, "Is Literature Possible?" *The Nation*, 131 (Oct. 15, 1930), 405.
[19] *The Liberal Imagination*, p. 35.

[20] *Ibid.*, p. 100.

[21] "William Dean Howells and the Roots of Modern Taste," p. 518.

[22] *The Liberal Imagination*, p. 99.

[23] *Ibid.*

[24] Lionel Trilling, "Shelley Plain," *New Republic*, 104 (May 5, 1941), 638.

[25] *The Liberal Imagination*, p. 240.

[26] Lionel Trilling, "Fitzgerald Plain," *The New Yorker*, Vol. 26, No. 50 (Feb. 3, 1951), p. 91.

[27] *Ibid.*, p. 92.

[28] "Elements That Are Wanted" (cited in n. 1, above), p. 374.

[29] *Ibid.*, p. 376.

[30] Lionel Trilling, "Determinist and Mystic," *Kenyon Review*, 2 (Winter, 1940), 96.

[31] Lionel Trilling, "Wordsworth and the Iron Time," *ibid.*, 12 (Summer, 1950), 491.

[32] "Shelley Plain" (cited in n. 24, above), pp. 637–638.

[33] *Ibid.*, p. 638.

[34] "Wordsworth and the Iron Time," p. 481.

[35] Lionel Trilling, "Literature and Power," *Kenyon Review*, 2 (Autumn, 1940), 434.

[36] Lionel Trilling, *Matthew Arnold* (New York, W. W. Norton & Co., 1939), p. 201.

[37] *The Liberal Imagination*, p. 190.

[38] *Ibid.*, p. 44.

[39] *Ibid.*, p. 45.

[40] *Matthew Arnold*, p. 358.

[41] *Ibid.*, p. 253.

[42] Introduction to Lionel Trilling, ed., *The Portable Matthew Arnold* (New York, Viking Press, 1949), p. 7.

[43] *Ibid.*, p. 3.

[44] "Literature and Power" (cited in n. 35, above), p. 434.

[45] *Ibid.*

[46] *Matthew Arnold*, p. 280.

[47] *Ibid.*, p. 180.

[48] *Ibid.*, p. xiii.

[49] *Ibid.*, p. 113.

[50] *Ibid.*, p. 159.

[51] *Ibid.*

[52] *Ibid.*, p. 164.

[53] *Ibid.*, p. 95.

[54] Lionel Trilling, "The Moral Tradition," *The New Yorker*, Vol. 25, No. 31 (Sept. 24, 1949), p. 98.

[55] "Elements That Are Wanted" (cited in n. 1, above), p. 368.

[56] *Matthew Arnold*, p. xii.

[57] *Ibid.*, p. xi.

[58] Lionel Trilling, "E. M. Forster," *Kenyon Review*, 4 (Spring, 1942), 173.

[59] *Ibid.*, p. 164.

[60] *Ibid.*

[61] *Ibid.*, p. 165.

[62] *Ibid.*, p. 168.

[63] *Ibid.*, p. 170.

[64] *The Liberal Imagination*, p. 5.

[65] *Ibid.*, p. 6.

[66] *Ibid.*, p. 7.

[67] *Ibid.*, p. 10.

[68] Lionel Trilling, "The America of John Dos Passos," *Partisan Review*, 4 (Apr., 1938), 32.

[69] Lionel Trilling, "Hemingway and His Critics," *ibid.*, 6 (Winter, 1939), 55.

[70] *Ibid.*, p. 56.

[71] Trilling, in "The Situation in American Writing" (cited in n. 15, above), p. 111.

[72] "Elements That Are Wanted" (cited in n. 1, above), p. 377.

[73] Lionel Trilling, "Greatness with One Fault in It," *Kenyon Review*, 4 (Winter, 1942), 102.

[74] Lionel Trilling, "Suffer All These Children," *New Republic*, 107 (Dec. 7, 1942), 750, 752.

[75] Lionel Trilling, "The Progressive Psyche," *The Nation*, 155 (Sept. 12, 1942), 217.

[76] Lionel Trilling, in "The State of American Writing, 1948: A Symposium," *Partisan Review*, 15 (Aug., 1948), 889.

[77] *Ibid.*

[78] *The Liberal Imagination*, p. 286.

[79] Lionel Trilling, *The Middle of the Journey* (New York, Viking Press, 1947), p. 305.

[80] *Ibid.*

[81] *Ibid.*

[82] *The Liberal Imagination*, p. 103.

[83] *Ibid.*, p. 287.

[84] Trilling, in "The State of American Writing, 1948: A Symposium" (cited in n. 76, above), p. 891.

[85] "Suffer All These Children" (cited in n. 74, above), p. 750.

[86] "The Moral Tradition" (cited in n. 54, above), p. 98.

[87] *Ibid.*

[88] "E. M. Forster" (cited in n. 58, above), p. 161.

[89] Lionel Trilling, " 'New Yorker' Fiction," *The Nation*, 154 (Apr. 11, 1942), 425.

[90] Trilling, in "The State of American Writing, 1948: A Symposium" (cited in n. 76, above), p. 891.

[91] *Ibid.*

[92] *The Liberal Imagination*, p. 189.

[93] *Ibid.*, p. 276.

[94] *Ibid.*

[95] "The Moral Tradition" (cited in n. 54, above), p. 101.

[96] "Literature and Power" (cited in n. 35, above), p. 442.

[97] "Suffer All These Children" (cited in n. 74, above), p. 750.

[98] Trilling, in "The State of American Writing, 1948: A Symposium" (cited in n. 76, above), p. 887.

[99] *The Liberal Imagination*, p. 243.

[100] "Elements That Are Wanted" (cited in n. 1, above), p. 374.

[101] "The America of John Dos Passos" (cited in n. 68, above), pp. 30–31.

[102] *The Liberal Imagination*, p. 214.

[103] *Ibid.*, p. 254.

[104] *Ibid.*, p. 257.

[105] *Ibid.*, p. 265.

[106] "Wordsworth and the Iron Time" (cited in n. 31, above), p. 496.

NOTES TO CHAPTER VIII

MATTHEW ARNOLD AND AMERICAN CULTURE

[1] Arthur Benson, "Leaves of the Tree," *North American Review,* 194 (July, 1911), 144.

[2] Northrop Frye, "The Function of Criticism at the Present Time," *University of Toronto Quarterly,* 19 (Oct., 1949), 12.

[3] Edward Mortimer Chapman, *English Literature in Account with Relgion, 1800-1900* (Boston and New York, Houghton Mifflin Co., 1910), p. 439.

[4] H. V. Routh, *Towards the Twentieth Century* (New York and Cambridge, England, Macmillan Co. and Cambridge University Press, 1937), p. 186.

[5] *The Citizen,* 2 (July, 1896), 173-175.

[6] A. B. Hyde, "Matthew Arnold," *The Chautauquan,* 4 (Feb., 1884), 271.

[7] William Dawson, *Matthew Arnold and His Relation to the Thought of Our Time* (New York and London, G. P. Putnam's Sons, 1904), p. 174.

[8] Samuel Parkes Cadman, *Charles Darwin and Other English Thinkers* (Boston, New York, and Chicago, Pilgrim Press, 1911), p. 233.

[9] Dickinson Miller, *International Journal of Ethics,* 16 (Apr., 1906), 353-354.

[10] George Santayana, *Scepticism and Animal Faith* (New York, C. Scribner's Sons, 1923), p. v.

[11] *Ibid.,* p. ix.

[12] Merton M. Sealts, Jr., "Melville's Reading," *Harvard Library Bulletin,* 1948-1950, p. 160.

[13] Quoted by Jay Leyda in *The Melville Log* (New York, Harcourt, Brace & Co., 1951), II, 795.

[14] *Ibid.*

[15] *Editorials, by Lafcadio Hearn,* ed. by Charles W. Hutson (Boston and New York, Houghton Mifflin Co., 1926), p. 212.

[16] *Ibid.,* p. 214.

[17] Lafcadio Hearn, *Appreciations of Poetry* (New York, Dodd, Mead & Co., 1916), p. 303.

[18] *Ibid.,* p. 310.

[19] Lafcadio Hearn, *Interpretations of Literature* (New York, Dodd, Mead & Co., 1915), I, 341.

[20] Eleanor Tilton, *The Amiable Autocrat* (New York, H. Schumann, 1947), pp. 381-382.

[21] Leonard Brown, "Arnold's Succession; 1850-1914," *Sewanee Review,* 42 (Apr.-June, 1944), 160.

[22] *Ibid.,* p. 179.

[23] Allen Tate, "Orthodoxy and the Standard of Literature," *New Republic,* 128 (Jan. 5, 1953), 24-25.

[24] Allen Tate, "The Self-made Angel," *ibid.,* 129 (Aug. 31, 1953), 17.

[25] Douglas Bush, "The Victorians, God Bless Them!" *The Bookman,* 74 (Mar., 1932), 589-597.

[26] Edmund Wilson, "Uncle Matthew," *New Republic,* 98 (Mar. 22, 1939), 199. This is a review of Trilling's *Matthew Arnold.*

[27] John Stuart Mill, *Autobiography* (London and New York, Oxford University Press, 1924), p. 109.

[28] Matthew Arnold, *The Works of* . . . (London, Macmillan & Co., Ltd., 1903–1904), X (*Mixed Essays*), 235.

[29] *Ibid.,* p. 245.

[30] John Henry Cardinal Newman, *The Idea of a University* (London, Longmans, Green & Co., 1929), p. 121.

[31] John Stuart Mill, *Dissertations and Discussions* (Boston, W. V. Spencer, 1864), II, 12–13.

[32] Edmund Wilson, *The Shores of Light* (New York, Farrar, Straus & Young, 1952), p. 715.

INDEX

INDEX

Agee, James, 238

American periodicals referred to: *The American*, 67, 68; *American Church Review*, 54; *American Presbyterian Review*, 50; *Andover Review*, 72, 74, 79, 81, 84; *Appleton's Journal*, 51–52, 71; *The Arena*, 138; *Atlantic Monthly*, 50, 54, 56, 57, 135, 138; *Baptist Quarterly*, 54; *The Bookbuyer*, 135; *The Bookman*, 86–87; *Boston Review*, 50; *Catholic World*, 81, 84, 141; *The Century*, 67, 68, 84, 131; *The Chautauquan*, 249; *Christian Union*, 54, 67, 68, 79, 133; *The Citizen*, 249; *Contemporary Review*, 138; *The Critic* (New York), 57, 59, 67, 68, 69, 70, 71, 74, 77, 79, 80, 86, 135, 138; *Current Literature*, 138; *The Dial* (Chicago), 4, 67, 77, 79, 80, 86, 87, 134, 137–138, 139; *The Dial* (Boston), 11; *The Forum*, 135; *The Galaxy*, 54; *Harper's Weekly*, 67, 68, 71; *Hours at Home*, 50, 53; *The Independent*, 54, 79; *International Review*, 56, 57; *The Lamp*, 136; *Lippincott's Magazine*, 52, 54, 76; *The Literary World* (Boston), 56, 67, 68, 79, 80; *Methodist Review*, 72, 76; *The Nation*, 19, 28, 50, 51, 52, 53, 54, 55, 56, 67, 68, 70, 79, 81, 89, 135, 137, 138, 139, 145, 163, 174, 179, 224, 260; *New England Magazine*, 131; *The New Englander*, 50, 51, 54; *New Princeton Review*, 81; *New Republic*, 83, 255; *New World*, 85; *The New Yorker*, 244; *North American Review*, 17, 19, 49, 50, 54, 56, 63, 77, 78; *Old and New*, 54; *Our Day*, 79; *The Outlook*, 133, 135, 138; *Overland Monthly*, 54; *Poet Lore*, 130–131; *The Review*, 164; *Scribner's Monthly*, 54, 56; *Sewanee Review*, 133, 193; *Unitariam Review*, 74

Anderson, Sherwood, 186, 242

Aristotle, 148, 166

Arnold, Edwin, 252

Arnold, Matthew: anticipations of Arnoldian doctrines in America, 7–13; initial reaction to and influence of in America, 48–57; American tour, 56–76; negative reactions of major American writers, 57–67; positive reactions of literary journals, 67–68; reactions to "Emerson lecture," 68–72; reactions to religious writings, 72–75; emergence of "Apostle of Culture," 76; reactions to *Civilization in the United States*, and obituaries, 76–80; early historical estimates of, 80–81; favorable estimates of younger critics and writers in late nineteenth century, 81–83; apotheosis, 83–87; hagiography and indifference in early twentieth century, 129–139; anti-Arnoldian forces, 140–145; influence on Impressionists, 145–147; influence on New Humanists, 147–149; influence on Liberals, 149–154; the problem of creation and criticism, 154–155; the problem of religion and literature, 155–157; the American middle class, 248–249; the American idea of change, 249; American practicality, 249–250; American philosophy, 250; the American idea of history, 250; American pessimism, 251–252; American optimism, 252; modern literary criticism, 253–254; American politics, 254–255; modern religion, 255–256; the New Humanists and T. S. Eliot, 256; Victorianism, 256–257; American relationship to Europe, 257–258; American relationship to France, 258; modern liberalism and conservatism, 258–261; the Arnoldian tradition in America, 261–262; literature and religion, 262–264; literature and society, 264–265

Civilization in the United States, 43, 66, 78, 79, 80, 115, 116, 145, 180

Culture and Anarchy, 10, 33, 48, 52, 102, 153, 154, 208, 209, 212, 213, 251

Essays in Criticism 19, 24, 26, 27, 31, 35, 48, 51, 56, 71, 83, 99, 136, 138, 165, 208, 251

Essays in Criticism, Second Series, 86

Essays in Criticism, Third Series, 48, 138, 139

"Friendship's Garland," 105, 153, 154, 209, 251

Arnold, Matthew (*Contin.*)
  "The Function of Criticism at the Present Time," 48, 106, 152
  God and the Bible, 75, 111
  Estimate of Grant's *Memoirs*, 65, 77
  Irish Essays, 251
  Last Essays on Church and Religion, 55
  Letters, 86–87, 95, 129–131, 179, 180
  Literature and Dogma, 53, 54, 75, 84, 85, 111, 208, 251
  Mixed Essays, 39, 55, 56, 136, 169, 251
  "Numbers," 114
  The Popular Education of France, 49, 112
  Saint Paul and Protestantism, 53, 111
  "The Study of Poetry," 86, 107, 133, 210
  "A Word About America," 26, 77
  "A Word More About America," 77
  "Wordsworth," 133

Babbitt, Irving, 117, 123, 160, 161, 162, 163, 165, 166, 168, 173, 202, 203, 204, 207, 210, 256, 259, 264; and Arnold, 147–149
Balzac, Honoré, 26
Baudelaire, Charles, 18, 29, 202
Beach, Joseph Warren, 181
Bellamy, Edward, 134
Benda, Julian, 206
Bennett, Arnold, 200
Benson, Arthur, 246
Bergson, Henri, 163
Billson, James, 251
Bourne, Randolph, 142, 151, 188; and Arnold, 150
Bowman, James, 154
Boyd, Ernest, 172
Bradley, F. H., 208, 231
Brooks, Van Wyck, 139, 203; and Arnold, 151–153
Brown, Leonard, 254
Brownell, Gertrude Hall, 92, 111
Brownell, W. C., 47, 56, 67, 135, 159, 160, 161, 166, 167, 168, 169, 170, 171, 172, 184, 187–188, 200, 204, 233, 260; life, 88–89; on Poe, 89–90; on Emerson, 90–91; on Lowell, 91–92; on James, 92–93; general estimate of Arnold, 94–99; Arnold's and Brownell's

analysis of France, 99–105; Arnold's theories of criticism, 105–110; Arnold and religion, 111; Arnold and modern culture, 112–115; Arnold and American culture, 115–125
  American Prose Masters, 92, 159, 167
  Criticism, 106, 167
  Democratic Distinction in America, 92, 115–125, 167
  French Traits, 89, 100–105, 115, 116, 121, 160
  The Genius of Style, 100
  Standards, 112, 114, 115, 141
  Victorian Prose Masters, 94, 135, 161
Browning, Robert, 132, 133, 157, 201
Buckley, Jerome, 30
Burroughs, John, 3, 60; and Arnold, 82, 131–132
Bush, Douglas, 257
Byron, Lord, 110, 113

Calverton, V. F., 143
Carlyle, Thomas, 8, 59, 61, 97, 131, 147, 209, 221
Carnegie, Andrew, 165
Cassirer, Ernst, 247
Chaucer, 211, 231
Clough, Arthur, 49, 132
Coates, Florence, 61, 75, 131
Cobbett, William, 163, 217
Coleridge, Samuel Taylor, 21, 131, 136, 144, 206, 210, 214, 223, 224, 235, 247, 261, 264
Cowley, Malcolm, 142
Croce, Benedetto, 107, 146

Dante, 91–92, 216, 221–222, 255–256
Daudet, Leon, 30
Dawson, William H., 137, 138, 249
De Quincey, Thomas, 227
Dewey, John, 161
Dixon, James, 138
Donne, John, 238
Dos Passos, John, 236
Dostoevsky, Fyodor, 239–240; "The Legend of the Grand Inquisitor," 241
Drake, William, 155
Dreiser, Theodore, 162, 166, 186, 226
Dryden, John, 136, 205, 207, 210, 211, 214

Eliot, George, 32, 141, 259, 271

Eliot, T. S., ix, 141, 144, 145, 151, 220, 221, 222, 223, 224, 225, 228, 231, 234, 243, 250, 253, 254, 255, 256, 257, 260, 262; reputation of, in early twentieth century, 193–195; obvious similarities to Arnold, 195–198; critique of Arnold, 199–200, 204–214; critique of American culture and literary criticism, 200–204; on Poe, 202; profound resemblances to Arnold, 214–218

After Strange Gods, 201, 211

The Cocktail Party, 222

Essays Ancient and Modern, 212

The Idea of a Christian Society, 201, 212, 223, 224, 225, 234

For Lancelot Andrewes, 197, 209

Notes Towards the Definition of Culture, 116, 201, 212

The Sacred Wood, 197, 204, 209

The Use of Poetry and the Use of Criticism, 194, 210, 214

The Waste Land, 254

Emerson, Ralph Waldo, 1, 2, 3, 6, 7, 17–18, 45, 58, 60, 61, 62, 63, 67, 81, 88, 89, 90, 92, 141, 159, 160, 175, 176, 179, 202, 246, 251, 252; and Arnold, 8–11, 68–72

Faverty, Frederic, 27

Feydeau, Ernest, 28–29

Fields, James T., 71

Fields, Mrs. James T., 71

Fiske, John, and Arnold, 85

Fitzgerald, F. Scott, 227–228

Flaubert, Gustave, 248–249

Foerster, Norman, 202, 203, 204; and Arnold, 149, 155

Forster, E. M., 234–235, 239, 242, 243

Frank, Waldo, 229

Franklin, Benjamin, 171

Freud, Sigmund, 143, 227, 231, 234, 239

Fry, James B., and Arnold, 77–79

Frye, Northrop, 246

Garfield, James A., 53

Gates, Lewis E., 147; and Arnold, 146

Gilder, R. W., 57

Goethe, 11, 32, 46, 64, 136, 137, 147, 215, 216

Goncourts, the, 30

Gourmont, Remy, 204, 209

Grant, Ulysses, 65, 77–78, 180

Guérin, Maurice and Eugénie, 21

Harper, George McLean, 73

Harrison, Frederic, 22

Harte, Bret, 54

Hawthorne, Julian, 287

Hawthorne, Nathaniel, 1, 168, 184, 202

Hearn, Lafcadio, and Arnold, 251–252

Heine, Heinrich, 151

Hemingway, Ernest, 237, 238, 243

Henry, O., 238

Higginson, T. W., and Arnold, 55–56

Holmes, Oliver Wendell, and Arnold, 252

Homer, 50, 51, 71

Horney, Karen, 238–239

Howells, William Dean, 30, 47, 58, 67, 226, 227; and Arnold, 65–66

Howgate, George, 156

Hugo, Victor, 59

Huneker, James, 139, 143, 144

Jackson, Andrew, 171

James, Henry, 1, 47, 67, 88, 89, 90, 92–93, 95, 99, 119, 120, 142, 150, 168, 172, 184, 187–188, 200, 202, 204, 215, 221, 225, 226, 250, 255, 257; general resemblances to Arnold, 46; analysis of Arnold's *Essays in Criticism,* 19–23; on Arnold's cosmopolitanism and analysis of French culture, 23–31; on Arnold's literary criticism, 31–38; on Arnold's views of England and America, 38–42; on Poe, 18; on Emerson, 18; on Lowell, 18–19; on American culture, 17, 42–45

The American Scene, 42, 43–45, 116

English Hours, 24, 41

French Poets and Novelists, 29, 31, 88, 92

Guy Domville, 25

Hawthorne, 17, 18, 92, 225

"The Lesson of the Master," 40–41

"Matthew Arnold," 35–38

The Middle Years, 22

Notes of a Son and Brother, 19

Portrait of a Lady, 33

A Small Boy and Others, 31–32, 33

William Wetmore Story and His Friends, 22

What Maisie Knew, 34, 41

Jefferson, Thomas, 259
Jewett, Sarah Orne, 83; and Arnold, 82
Johnson, Samuel, 136, 210, 211, 215, 263
Jones, Rufus M., 74
Joubert, 21, 182
Joyce, James, 186–187, 239, 242

Keats, John, 228
Kipling, Rudyard, 222–223, 224, 225
Kittredge, George, 174, 202
Knickerbocker, William A., 133

Lamb, Charles, 227
Langer, Suzanne, 247
Lazarus, Emma, 69–70
Leavis, F. R., 224, 233, 242
Lewis, Sinclair, 242
Lewisohn, Ludwig, 133, 145; and Arnold, 153–154
Lincoln, Abraham, 88, 119, 180
Littell, Philip, 182; and Arnold, 83
Lovett, Robert Morss, 93, 105; and Arnold, 47–48, 154
Lowell, James Russell, 2, 3, 5, 7, 17, 18–19, 46, 47, 58, 63, 65, 67, 70, 81, 89, 91, 92, 160, 169; and Arnold 11–13, 61–62

Mabie, Hamilton Wright, 68, 198; and Arnold, 129–130
Macaulay, Thomas, 8, 108
Macy, John, 142; and Arnold, 154–155
Mallarmé, Stephan, 202
Mather, Frank Jewett, 166
Matthews, Brander, and Arnold, 83
Matthiessen, F. O., and Arnold, 193
Melville, Herman, 1, 58, 252, 259, 264; and Arnold, 251
Mencken, H. L., 139, 141, 143, 144, 168, 171, 181, 182, 188, 203
Merrimée, Prosper, 26
Mill, John Stuart, 223, 224, 235, 259, 260, 261, 264
Miller, Joaquin, 165
Milton, John, 103, 108, 173, 253
Montaigne, 63
Moore, George, 163
More, Paul Elmer, 117, 160, 162, 163, 164, 165, 166, 167, 168, 176, 177, 178, 181, 203, 204, 256, 259, 264; and Arnold, 145–146, 147–149

Morley, Christopher, and Arnold, 140, 145
Morris, William, 151
Murry, John Middleton, 210, 212, 218

Newman, Francis, 182
Newman, John Henry, 27, 41, 207, 262
Nietzsche, Friedrich, 151
Norton, Charles Eliot, 25, 159, 160, 184; and Arnold, 80

Parrington, V. L., 142, 259
Pater, Walter, 145, 146, 160, 209, 211, 256
Patton, Francis, 73–74
Paul, Herbert, 135–136, 137
Perry, Bliss, 73
Perry, T.S., 54; and Arnold, 36
Plato, 119, 222
Poe, Edgar Allan, 5, 12, 17, 18, 89, 90, 159, 201, 202; and Arnold, 7–8
Porter, Noah, 54
Pound, Ezra, 205
Powers, Horatio N., 67, 76, 77, 79, 80, 82, 86
Proust, Marcel, 239

Renan, Ernst, 203
Richards, I. A., 193, 208, 210, 253, 255
Roosevelt, Franklin, 259
Rourke, Constance, 119
Rousseau, Jean Jacques, 163
Routh, H. V., 248
Ruskin, John, 136, 160, 209
Russell, G. W. E., 137, 138

Sainte-Beuve, Charles Augustin, 30, 32–33, 34–35, 82, 106, 107, 110, 133, 147, 160, 164, 187, 203, 204, 207, 246, 248
Saintsbury, George, 135, 136, 211
Sand, George, 26–27, 46, 55, 123
Santayana, George, 118, 184, 250, 259; and Arnold, 155–157
Scherer, Edmund, 30, 32, 36, 107
Schiller, Friedrich, 21
Scott, Walter, 227
Scudder, Vida, 134
Sedgwick, W. E., 172, 181; and Arnold, 140
Shafer, Robert, 149
Shakespeare, 5, 27, 62, 91, 101, 156, 221–222

Shaw, George Bernard, 243

Shelley, Percy, 26, 90, 143, 156, 201, 227, 230

Sherman, Stuart P., 110, 116, 123, 139, 157, 200, 221, 260; general influence of Arnold on, 158, 172–173; cultural influence, 173–175; ethical influence, 175–176; religious influence, 176; educational influence, 176–178; political influence, 178–181; stylistic influence, 181–182; personal influence, 182–183; course in Arnold, 158, 183–186; on Poe, 159; on Emerson, 159–160; on Lowell, 160; relationship to New Humanists, 160–162; break with New Humanism, 162–166; relationship to Brownell, 166–170; "Mission," 170–172; as demise of original Arnoldian tradition, 186–189

Americans, 165, 168

Critical Woodcuts, 181

Matthew Arnold: How To Know Him, 161, 173–174

On Contemporary Literature, 161, 164

Points of View, 167, 175

Shaping Men and Women, 184

Silone, Ignazio, 236

Smith, L. P., 140, 287

Spingarn, Joel, 107; and Arnold, 142, 146–147

Spinoza, 156, 215

Stanley, Carleton, 194

Stedman, Clarence, 58, 59, 60, 65, 67; and Arnold, 62–63

Steinbeck, John, 239

Stephen, Leslie, 2

Stevenson, Robert Louis, 41

Strachey, Lytton, 141

Symonds, John, 211

Synge, John, 163

Taine, Hippolyte, 96, 107, 108, 109, 155, 160, 203

Tate, Allen, 203; and Arnold, 255–256

Tennyson, Alfred, 59, 61, 132, 133

Thackeray, W. M., 94, 118

Thomson, James, 251

Thoreau, Henry David, 1, 46

Tolstoy, Leo, 81

Traubel, Horace, 59, 60

Trent, William P., 74, 75, 133, 135

Trilling, Lionel, ix, 1, 219, 257, 259, 260; and Arnold's heritage, 220–221; Arnold's weaknesses, 231–232; Arnold's strengths, 232–234; E. M. Forster's liberalism, 234–235; weaknesses of American liberalism, 235–239; what liberalism needs, 239–242; the concerns and methods of literary criticism, 242–244; the novel, 244–245; on Eliot, 221–225; on American criticism, 225–227; on the Romantics and the French Revolution, 227–231; on Freud, 231

The Liberal Imagination, 224, 235, 241

Matthew Arnold, 129, 231, 234, 257

The Middle of the Journey, 239–241

Trollope, Anthony, 32, 271

Turgenev, Ivan, 59

Twain, Mark, 1, 4, 6, 47, 58, 67, 122, 180, 257; and Arnold, 64–65

The American Claimant, 64–65

A Connecticut Yankee in King Arthur's Court, 65

Huckleberry Finn, 243

Valéry, Paul, 202

Viereck, Peter, 265

Virgil, 216

Wells, H. G., 151, 162

Wharton, Edith, 88, 120, 142; and Arnold, 136

Whipple, Edwin P., 65, 67; and Arnold, 63–64

White, Reverend Greenough, 132–133

Whitman, Walt, 1, 3, 4, 6, 47, 62, 63, 65, 67, 81, 82, 135, 157, 165, 170, 180, 186, 201, 202, 226, 232, 253, 257, 258; and Arnold, 58–61

Wilde, Oscar, 146

Wilson, Edmund, 144, 237; and Arnold, 257, 265

Wilson, Woodrow, 193, 237, 259

Woodberry, George, and Arnold, 81–82, 86–87

Woodbridge, Homer, 173, 182

Wordsworth, William, 11, 113, 133, 144, 205, 210, 222, 227, 228, 229, 233, 245, 264

Wright, Richard, 239

Zeitlin, Jacob, 182, 183, 184

Zola, Emile, 30, 36